Frederick Alexander Durham

The Lone-Star of Liberia

Being the Outcome of Reflections on our own People

Frederick Alexander Durham

The Lone-Star of Liberia
Being the Outcome of Reflections on our own People

ISBN/EAN: 9783337031381

Printed in Europe, USA, Canada, Australia, Japan

Cover: Foto ©Suzi / pixelio.de

More available books at **www.hansebooks.com**

THE LONE-STAR OF LIBERIA.

'All hail, Liberia! hail!
Arise and now prevail
　　O'er all thy foes.
In truth and righteousness,
In all the Arts of Peace,
Advance and still increase
　　Though hosts oppose!

'At the loud call we rise,
And press toward the prize
　　In glory's race.
All redolent of fame,
The land to which we came,
We breathe the inspiring flame,
　　And onward press.

'Here Liberty shall dwell,
Here Justice shall prevail,
　　Religion here;
To this, fair virtue's dome,
Meek innocence may come
And find a peaceful home,
　　And know no fear.'

　　　　　　　　　HILARY TEAGUE OF LIBERIA

THE

LONE-STAR OF LIBERIA;

Being the Outcome of Reflections on our Own People.

BY

FREDERICK ALEXANDER DURHAM,

AN AFRICAN,

OF LINCOLN'S INN (STUDENT-AT-LAW).

WITH AN INTRODUCTION

BY

MADAME LA COMTESSE C. HUGO.

LONDON:
ELLIOT STOCK, 62, PATERNOSTER ROW, E.C.
1892.

INTRODUCTION.

I WAS quite a child when I read 'Uncle Tom's Cabin,' by Mrs. Harriet Beecher Stowe, and became enthusiastic for the abolition of slavery. My heart was full of anxious thought on this subject. Later in life the tragedy of 'Toussaint L'Ouverture,' by Lamartine, opened my mind to fresh considerations. After reading it I apprehended that the sons of Ham have precisely the same human, as well as civil, rights as have the sons of Shem and of Japheth. The passionate interest which my uncle, Victor Hugo, took in the fate of the generous but unfortunate John Brown further fixed my attention on this question, which has humanitarian as well as social aspects. And when recently reading books and articles relating to the subject of the emancipation of Africa's sons, I have added indignation to compassion.

It is not right to reduce the ethics of that important question to the proportions of a mere work of mercy. It ought to be regarded as one of the gravest questions of our time—the final blow struck at an old tree, which mould has long invaded and rotted.

This great question of the emancipation of the African race has more than one interesting aspect. Perhaps its most striking feature is its connection with human progress and with advancing Christianity. The Gospel may be a creation or an imitation, but it is certainly full of social and moral principles which are useful and adaptable to the conditions of every period, because they are essentially wise and just. If religion or Christianity means the actual practice of Gospel principles, then even the most advanced man can make no reasonable objection to Christianity.

But things do not seem trending in the direction of the triumph of Gospel principles. Human Governments make their boast of their reverence for religion, and yet they commit all sorts of frauds and crimes against dependent populations, which are the antipodes of the requirements and recommendations of the New Testament.

Both Europeans and Americans may, with the help of Messrs. Froude, Laird Clowes, and H. M. Stanley, regard themselves as the natural and supernatural 'Magisterial Guardians' of the Ethiopian race, and they may proclaim, with mingled blasphemy and humour, that the Africans—or at least the mass of them—are half brutes and animals. But no right-minded, no fair-thinking man, will follow these writers in so savage and unworthy a conclusion.

The great 'pack-horse' of the Africophobists is a phrase which occurs in the Old Testament Scriptures: 'And Canaan will be their servant.' Mr. Jos. L. Janvier, a learned doctor and Haytian diplomatist, in one of his remarkable and witty books, has chosen these words for the epigraph: 'Hayti et ses Visiteurs.' We are exactly of his opinion. This Bible sentence is a very difficult one to apply in a universal way. The Bible is full of merely personal incidents and personal references, and we have no right to look in every part of it for such perfect and absolute directions as the Gospel alone can afford.*

* But apart from all this : had not Ham had three other sons besides Canaan ? Were not Cush, Mizraim and Phut

Mr. Durham's book, 'The Lone-Star of Liberia,' offers to our consideration a project which I regard as in every way a hopeful one both for the African and for the Caucasian. He pleads for the removal of the slave—enfranchised slave—populations to the republic of Liberia, where there is abundant space for them all, and where a certain population is already established which is doing its best to fashion for itself a civilized life and society and government. The climate of Liberia is good, and the soil is fertile; and it is an altogether legitimate and reasonable desire on the part of the sons of Ham that they should form a united and independent race on that very same continent from whence their fathers were arbitrarily, cruelly, and in ways involving untold misery and degradation, dragged away.

Mr. Laird Clowes himself, in his 'Black America,' wrote (see the last chapter, 'The Ideal Solution'): 'If America would do its duty by the Negroes, those civilized nations which have established themselves in Africa would, in pursuance of their own interests, aid her. Great Britain, France, and Germany would each and all welcome the immigration to their African possessions of large and leavening bodies of American blacks.' Why does not the government at Washington endeavour to carry out this plan, which would be so acceptable to the African, and which would relieve the States of one of their heaviest burdens? To accomplish the scheme only requires the formation of a vigorous financial executive. I need not say that I do not believe the Government at Washington is disposed to confirm the old Italian motto:

Canaan's elders? Did Noah also curse Cush, Mizraim and Phut? Are Africans, are Ethiopians, the descendants of Canaan? If they are—we presume, on the authority of the Bible, they are—the descendants also of Canaan's brothers, Cush, Mizraim and Phut, and were they cursed?

> 'Fra il dire e il fare
> C' è di mezzo il mare.'

('Between words and actions there is an ocean.')

Authorities in a country like America are not disposed to make promises only for that kind of people who can be contented with chaff. Why, then, when the question has been before it of helping to create a powerful black republic in Liberia, has it not brought the matter to an issue? Can it be that these excellent 'Magisterial Guardians' have such an amount of love to their black brethren that they are afraid of exposing them to the perils of a new-born independence? What a wonderful solicitude!

Mr. F. A. Durham, the author of this book, is animated by the eagerness of youth and the ardour of patriotic longings to secure the autonomy of his race. He mentions several distinguished men and women who belong to the race, and judging by the rapid yet great attainments and capabilities of these Ethiopians, we may reasonably hope soon to see all the progeny of Ham—all the descendants of Cush, Mizraim, Phut and Canaan—fairly civilized. But ought not the enterprise of securing that civilization to be placed in the hands of the Africans themselves; that is, in the hands of those who are already in the forward rank, and have shown talent for learning, ability to fill civil and governmental offices, and capacity for good citizenship?

Our own convictions are, in relation to the social movement, that the next stage of the world's progress will witness the triumph of Christian Socialism. But at the same time we admit that Africans, if they remain as they are now, cannot hope to march under the flag of the new social system. They must go through every phase of civil and national organization. Their aspirations towards *une patrie*, and their wish to gain autonomy, are, however, praiseworthy, and indicate awakening intelligence in them. Therefore we think that every man who values his own national liberties ought to sympathize with and support the Africans in their enterprise, which is in itself, and cannot fail to prove in its results, an advancement for the race in social and national life, in all that properly goes into the term 'civilization.' We shall never, of course, expect, request, or call in the sympathy and support of men like a messenger of the *Times*, or a great representative of Downing Street, and consequently our beliefs are not likely to be placed in either 'Black America' or 'Darkest Africa.' Let us hope that H. M. Stanley has learned a useful lesson by falling from general enthusiasm into general reprobation; but the lesson was a severe one for the public, as reminding them that sober mistrust of people who come with wonderful tales from far countries is no unnecessary precaution. There is in Stanley's story matter enough to arouse our indignation, and indignation is not always a vain sentiment. I might call slavery itself a prime mover in modern civilization, for the indignation which this long and grave infamy has generated has been the great stimulant in the struggle which has at last resulted in the African enfranchisement. Independence and autonomy will now follow, and when these come they will prove to benefit not only those directly interested, but also the whole civilized races.

The author of 'The Lone-Star of Liberia' in his third chapter gives a painful exhibition of the gross immoralities of well-known people who have not black skins. His story is not new—there is nothing new that is true—but the terrible record will call attention to the unreasonableness of Caucasian blame of African immorality. The Africans made their escape from the debasing conditions of slavery only very recently, and it is altogether unreasonable to expect from them a perfection which Caucasians, who have had ages of independence and civilization, have so demonstrably failed to reach—a perfection which, indeed, does not seem to be possible in this world. Rich and powerful men of the 'magisterial' race commit far worse iniquities than can be charged at the door of the Africans, but having at their disposal arsenals and constables, army and navy, judges and clerks and law, they can cover over their wrongdoings, and their tarnished honour and secret infamies can be hidden from view, and, if discovered, recriminations are prevented by shutting the mouth of the scandalized in a variety of ways.

Ham's son, on the contrary, is always vilified, and calumniated, and ill-treated, and the worst that can be said of him is paraded in view. Surely the time is now come when all prejudices should disappear! Are you not of my opinion? Then let us have more patience: Eroia's walls fell, the Bastille fell, the Vatican's doors fell, and prejudices against the African race will one day fall. At the end righteousness always wins the day.

COMTESSE C. HUGO.

LONDON,
March, 1892.

PREFACE.

1. THE aspersions and libels cast on the African Race by Mr. W. Laird Clowes in his 'Black America,' first issued in February of this year (1891) by Messrs. Cassell and Co., his publishers, impose on me the duty of repelling and refuting the same. Having dealt with Laird Clowes at length in the book to which this is meant to be the preface, I have little to say here so far as his (Laird Clowes) relations with the African are concerned. Yet I cannot forbear mentioning that while Homer, one of the greatest poets, and Herodotus, the 'Father of History'—mighty and illustrious Greeks of yore both of them—have eulogized and made immortal — Homer in song and Herodotus in history—the Ethiopian Race, Mr. W. Laird Clowes and Mr. James Anthony Froude, men who are not universally known even in Great Britain and Ireland, and men who are manifestly ignorant concerning African History, have thought fit to vilify it. They are surely men far inferior to Homer and Herodotus in intellectual attainments—they are but as pigmies before these intellectual giants; and nobleness of soul towards their African or Ethiopian fellow-men does not seem to be theirs.

Whatever may be the accomplishments of Clowes and Froude, the latter more particularly, as British literati, we cannot withhold the opinion that this great writer does not always prove the great man in his estimate of other races than his own. There is often an important distinction between the great *author* and the great *man*. Two of the greatest writers the white man's world produced in the eighteenth century were Voltaire and Jean Jacques Rousseau. But they were men whose nobility of character bore no comparison with the greatness of their intellectual or their literary power.

II. While this work is a criticism of these critics, it is also meant to be a summary of the history of the Ethiopian Race in Western Africa. No person can be properly termed educated who knows little or nothing of the history of his own race and of his own country. The African or other Ethiopian reader who reads Liberian Blyden's 'Christianity, Islam, and the Negro Race,' will have more than a fair knowledge of the History of his Race and Fatherland; and I venture to hope that this work will be found a not unsuitable appendix or supplement to that work.

How many Africans, both educated and uneducated, there are who foolishly believe that the Ethiopian Race has not produced even one truly eminent scholar, or philosopher, or soldier, simply because they do not happen to know of any! There are too many, unfortunately, who prefer to remain in ignorance; while there are many more who, although they do not know of one remarkable African, take no pains to find out for themselves what every intelligent African should find out and know concerning his own people. This work will, it is hoped, supply a long-felt deficiency. And at the same time it would be well for those who disparage my people—the African Race—to read these 'Reflections on Our Own People,' and also Dr. Edward Wilmot Blyden's 'Christianity, Islam, and the Negro Race,'* before rushing to any

* A larger and more exhaustive work than Dr. Blyden's is Africo-American Colonel the Honourable George W. William's

hasty conclusions, which are the untrustworthy consequence of incomplete and misguided researches, which have not duly revealed the achievements performed by the Africans through their eminent soldiers, governors, and literati. It is easy to argue that as Africa has never produced any great men, the Ethiopian Race must be inferior to the Caucasian.

After having fully exposed, refuted, and corrected the mistakes and misrepresentations of Mr. W. Laird Clowes, I have thought it advisable to point out to the African in the United States of North America, and to other non-Liberian Africans generally, what an important and advantageous thing it is for them to have a Free and Independent African Fatherland in Republican Liberia.

The African will and can learn the language of, and dress like, his white governor; but he cannot, and will never be, Caucasianized. It is impossible. History shows no precedent of a subject race becoming thoroughly like their rulers, when those rulers happen to belong to an essentially different race. The African will always be an African. His nature and racial instincts will always remain what they are to-day. On the other hand, the Caucasian will always be a Caucasian. His racial peculiarities or characteristics will remain the same. And it is better, in the interests of humanity as a whole, that the races should keep their distinctions. It is 'kismet.' We all know that the white man has been on the Gold Coast more than 400 years, but has not the Gold Coaster just the same peculiarities or

---

'History of the Ethiopian Race in America,' in two volumes, from 1619 to 1800, and from 1800 to 1880, published by G. P. Putnam's Sons. We would certainly recommend that, as well as the Honourable Liberian Blyden's work, to the self-respecting, and only to the *self-respecting* African, for close attention and study.

racial characteristics as his forefathers had before him? The European has failed to Europeanize him. Nor could the African Africanize the Caucasian were he to try to.

The African subject of the Caucasian has qualities which he cannot develop in the land of the white man and the stranger. He can only develop in a free and independent Fatherland of his own. Where can the African develop them so well as in Liberia?

Is Liberia improving? It has been shown that it is. But if that be not so, and the West African Republic is either stationary or retrograding, why does not the non-Liberian African hurry to the rescue of Liberia and make it progress?

As long as the African remains under white rule, so long will he be subjected to inconveniences and disadvantages. What the white man says, the average African, be he educated or uneducated, with charming simplicity implicitly believes in. The white man tells the black man that God is white and the Devil black, and the average African unreasoningly accepts that doctrine. The Liberian, the Haytian, and the Dominican, as a matter of course, know better. They have more sense. They reason for themselves, and do not allow the white man to lay down the law for them in this and other like matters.

There are Africans (I mean, of course, those living under and subject to the white man) who fervently wish they had never been born black, and who deem it the greatest privilege to have white associates. Vanity is a sin, they say, but I think it is better for a black man to be vain of his skin than wish he had never been born black. When a man wishes that he had never been born an African, he must, of course, be ashamed of a fellow-African whenever he sees him, particularly if he happens to be dwelling in a country where the whites are either in equal proportion to blacks, or in a large majority, and are the rulers.

Liberian Blyden, in his 'Christianity, Islam, and the Negro Race,' forcibly calls one's attention to the cringing and servile attitude of the subject black towards the ruling white; and I am of opinion that Blyden is justified in so writing. It is only too true. It is true not only of the uneducated, but even of the educated, African living beneath the sway of the European and the American.

There is another equally important matter which Mr. Blyden forcibly brings home to one's mind. He asserts that the Africans who were transported to the American Continent (the West Indies included) as slaves were not as a rule of the very best stamp or class. And I think he is certainly justified in making that assertion. I must be understood as interpreting his meaning in this way: The Africans as a whole are not satisfied with their position under the rule of the white. But does he not continue to remain under the rule of the white, while Liberia has been free and independent since 1847? The British African grumbles. He wants Home Rule and Representation. There are in Liberia Independence pure and simple, an elective Congress, and a full-fledged Government. The British, like the American African, is free to go where he lists. Still, Liberia has no charms for him. The American African sees his kinsmen and comrades daily lynched in the United States; does he make any vigorous and manly efforts to quit America, and be free and independent in Liberia? Neither the American nor the British Africans, nor any other non-Liberian Africans subject to white rule, do anything of the kind.

This is how, then, I think Dr. Blyden is justified in making that statement. For were the Africans living under Caucasian rule the descendants of *men*, Africans and Ethiopians, after the type of the Liberians and the Haytians and the Abyssinians and others, they would not continue to remain in their present position.

If the so-called leaders of the Africans in the United States of North America had any sense of shame, any spark of manliness, any touch of dignity, they would certainly have marshalled their hosts, after having brought pressure to bear on the Yankee Government for a subsidy, and left America, with her lynchings and other oppressions and persecutions, which is their land of bondage, far behind. Even now it is not too late to do so. The person who is admitted on all sides to be the leading African in the United States of North America is undoubtedly Mr. Frederick Douglass, the American Minister to the Haytian Republic; while it does not admit of a doubt but that Sir William Conrad Reeves, the Chief Justice of Barbadoes, is the leading British African. I propose to deal with these men, and to refer to their position. I shall take each separately. I take Mr. Frederick Douglass. He is the American Minister to Hayti at present; when his term is at an end, he will retire on a pension. He will retire into the obscurity from which he temporarily emerged. The reason for his representing the United States in Hayti is that no white American would accept the post of American Minister to Hayti were it offered to him. Frederick Douglass would not be in his right senses were he to indulge in the idea that some day he will be appointed to represent the United States of North America as American Minister in Europe. He would be in the same demented state were he to believe for a moment that the President of the United States of North America will send for him and charge him with the formation of a Cabinet, or believe for a moment that he will be made a Member of any American Cabinet. Were Mr. Frederick Douglass to come forward some day as a candidate, with the view to be elected to the Presidentship of the United States, and to sit in the Chair in which George Washington, John Adams, Thomas Jefferson, James Madison, James Monroe, and the seventeen other Presidents have sat, he would be promptly arrested by indignant Americans, and be lodged in bedlam as a dangerous lunatic, there to be detained during the President's pleasure.

But what can he not be in the Republic of Liberia, if he becomes a Liberian? In Liberia he can be President, an ordinary or even chief Member of the Liberian Government. As a Liberian he can also be the Liberian Minister at one of the European Courts, or in the United States of North America.

The Chief Justice of Barbadoes, Sir William Conrad Reeves, Knt. Bach., is himself placed in a predicament similar to that of Mr. Frederick Douglass. When his term as Chief Justice of Barbadoes expires, he will have to retire on a pension. He will not be promoted to the post of Chief Justice of one of the Australasian Colonies, nor will he be promoted to the Chief Justiceship of Newfoundland, or the Dominion of Canada. He would be termed demented were he to apply for the Lord Chief Justiceship of England and Wales, or the Chief Justiceship of Ireland, or the Lord Justice Clerkship of Scotland on the first vacancy; or were he to apply for the post of Lord High Chancellor of England and Wales, and to sit on the woolsack in the House of Lords, or that of Lord Chancellor of Ireland, or the post of Lord Justice General and President of Court of Session of Scotland on the first vacancy. A lunacy commission would be instituted to inquire into the state of his mind, and if he were to be found demented he would be locked up in bedlam 'during Her Britannic Majesty's pleasure' as a dangerous lunatic. Reeves cannot aspire to a higher post in the British Isles. But in Liberia he can be accommodated somehow in the public service. If Douglass and Reeves were to inform the Liberians that they would make use of their name and position, and try their level best to take with them as many Africans to Liberia as were willing to go, would the Liberian Government not compensate Douglass and Reeves for their trouble and time? If not, then I am much mistaken in the Liberian People and Government. But if Frederick Douglass and Reeves were to do so, they would earn immortal renown. Their names would live forever and evermore not only in Liberian, but in other histories and songs. Will they, like Moses and Aaron, do this, or even attempt now to do what they ought to have done long ago? or will they, from want of genuine ambition and through listless apathy, prefer to remain in obscurity until their Maker calls them unto Himself, when they will sink into the grave in Mother-Earth comparatively unwept, unhonoured and unsung? I fear that it will be the latter course that they will take. Douglass and Reeves have eyes, and *refuse* to see; they have ears, and *refuse* to hear.

There is a subject on which I should like to say a few words here. It is the use of the words *Negro* and *Coloured* by Africans, Europeans, and other non-Africans. Ham's descendants are Africans by Nation and Ethiopians by Race, just as the progeny of Japheth are Europeans by Nation and Caucasians by Race. We do not see where the *Negro* comes in at all. Again, Africans and other Ethiopians are black, as Europeans and other Caucasians are white. Here, also, we do not see where the *coloured* comes in at all. It seems a pity that Africans should blindly copy everything Europeans and other Caucasians set before them. Africans should be Men, form opinions worthy of Men, and act like Men. I am bound to say, with Reginald Scot, who flourished in the reign of James the First of England and Ireland, and Sixth of Scotland, '*truth must not be measured by time, for every old opinion is not sound. My great adversaries are young ignorance and old custom.*'

I anticipate that many of my readers will find fault with, and object to, many of my utterances in this work. I should like it to be understood that I am not asking for mercy or pardon, or writing in the 'Am I not a man and a Brother?' strain of the days of slavery, but I am defending and attacking vigorously, squarely and fairly. Not only do I defend my fortifications against the invader, but I assume the offensive and carry on the war in the enemy's territories. I have written, as a *freeman*, not only true facts and justifiable statements as known by me, but I have also given free and independent opinions compatible with the dignity of the *freeman* and the *free-born*. But, I ask, what man is there who can honestly and truly say that his writing or writings has or have met with undiluted favour or pleasure anywhere and amongst any people?

What I think the British or white reader may take objection to chiefly is my third chapter, which deals with Immorality. But what I have said in the book from beginning to end I stand by and am ready to repeat again. It is a fact that wherever the Africans have come into contact with Caucasian civilization, and lived under Caucasian domination, they (the descendants of Ham) have been contaminated, demoralized, and taught to wallow in the mire of immorality, at the instance of and under the direction of their white and unenviably apt preceptors—their Caucasian civilizers.

There are certain things W. Laird Clowes says in his 'Black America' which the author of this work has not thought fit to mention in the body of his 'Lone-Star of Liberia.'

He tells us, for instance, that the white, or rather he (Laird Clowes) is of opinion that the African 'more nearly approaches the quadrumana than does any other member of the human family; . . . (and that) his (the African's) arms are, on an average, two inches longer than his (Laird Clowes's).' This is the white man's, or, to be more correct, Laird Clowes's, opinion. It is an opinion as false as it is foolish. It is an opinion derived from the mere *ipse dixit*—the mere assertion of the erratic Charles Robert Darwin. At the same time Laird Clowes is forgetful of the fact that the African has an opinion of his own, and that he (the African) does not entertain and admit for one moment such an absurd and preposterous notion or opinion.

W. Laird Clowes proceeds to say that he, as a white man, is of opinion that the African's 'facial angle is about 70 degrees, while his is about 82 degrees'; that 'the average weight of his (the African's) brain is ten ounces less than that of people of his (Laird Clowes's) own family'; that the African has 'high and prominent cheek-bones'; that 'his (the African's) cranium is much thicker than Laird Clowes's'; that 'his (the African's) head is covered not with hair, but with wool of nearly flat section'; that the African's 'skin is thicker than W. Laird Clowes's, and that it is velvety and emits a characteristic odour,' unlike that of Laird Clowes, which is perfection; that 'his (the African's) frame, owing to structural peculiarities, is not as erect as W. Laird Clowes, the *Times* Commissioner's; that 'the cranial sutures of the Negro close up much earlier than those of W. Laird Clowes.'

The reader will have observed that these are all the peculiar and preposterous notions of W. Laird Clowes, who believes that he is perfection itself, and that the African 'is everything that is horrid.' How comes W. Laird Clowes to know that the African's facial angle is about

70 degrees, while his (Laird Clowes's) is about 82 degrees—that the average weight of the African's brain is ten ounces less than that of his (Laird Clowes's)—that the African's cranium and skin are much thicker than those of W. Laird Clowes—that the cranial sutures of the African close up much earlier than those of Laird Clowes? Whence did he derive these preposterous notions? Are these things so because W. Laird Clowes, big with importance and indulging in tall talk, would fain make them so?

The Caucasian must not try to lay down the law to the African, and force him to believe that he is this while he is that, or that he is that while he is this.

Caucasians know, or ought to know, what their own race is like; while we Africans know better than non-Africans what we are, and what we are not, like. Mr. W. Laird Clowes has an opinion, but the African has and can form another opinion.

And I add that it is preposterous and erroneous for the white man to suppose that the intelligent, self-reliant, and last, not least, *self-respecting* African will accept any doctrine as to his moral, mental and other peculiarities and capacities as he (the white man) lays it down and interprets, when it is to the disadvantage and detriment of the African.

F. A. D.

LINCOLN'S INN LIBRARY,
LONDON, W.C.

CONTENTS.

CHAPTER		PAGE
I.	THE AFRICO-AMERICAN	1
II.	IS THE ETHIOPIAN INFERIOR TO THE CAUCASIAN?	28
III.	IMMORALITY	76
IV.	SUPERSTITION IN THE NINETEENTH CENTURY	137
V.	UNDER CAUCASIAN RULE	180
VI.	AFRICA GOVERNED BY AFRICANS	222
VII.	REPATRIATION AND LIBERIA	240

THE LONE-STAR OF LIBERIA.

CHAPTER I.

THE AFRICO-AMERICAN.

COMMISSIONED by the *Times* of London, Mr. W. Laird Clowes (as he tells us in his introduction to 'Black America') betook himself, in the autumn of 1890, to the eight late Slave-holding States in the Southern portion of the United States of America, for the purpose of studying the condition of the 'ex-slave'—or, in other words, the 'Africo-American'—and his relations towards his white neighbours. And he further says that he gives 'an impartial review, not only of the present aspects, but also of the past history, of the complex problem which has thus been created.' We have given his work ('Black America') our careful attention, and we have set it down with that legitimate feeling of indignation which all good and true Africans, who have the welfare of their race at heart, must feel when they hear of the calumnies—base, false, and therefore unjustifiable—which are again and again heaped upon the devoted heads of the unfortunate, down-trodden, and long-suffering members of the African race in America, West Indies, and elsewhere, by prejudiced Caucasians such as Sir

Spencer St. John, James Anthony Froude, James Bryce, Manville Fenn, Henry M. Stanley (who slaughtered many of the Africans in Central and East Africa) and W. Laird Clowes.

As Mr. Clowes had been commissioned by the *Times*, it is not only possible, but also probable, that he threw himself into the arms of the Conservative Democrats of the Southern States, and asked *them* for particulars, and for *their* opinion of the Africo-Americans, the vast majority of whom are Liberal Republicans. Can we, then, expect to have an 'impartial review, not only of the present aspects but also of the past history, of the problem which has thus been created,' at the hands of the White Democrat-Conservatives, who are politically out of sympathy with their Ethiopian neighbours? All the world knows well how strong is the race hatred and prejudice that exists in the Southern portion of the United States.

Happily, however, only a very few of the British people are likely to endorse the malignant opinions and reports of Mr. Clowes, so far as they affect the African. It would seem that Laird Clowes has been following in the wake of James Anthony Froude and others of his school, and especially the traveller Stanley, who delights in seeing the Africans kept under as much as possible.

After going through some eighteen pages of more or less unimportant matter in 'Black America,' we come to the so-called 'Reconstruction' period in the eight old Slaveholding States in the Union. It would be superfluous for us, here or anywhere else, to dwell for a moment on the events and doings of that period, because Mr. Clowes has been both kind and imprudent in informing us that all the particulars concerning the doings of that time have been furnished him by Messrs. Hilary A. Herbert, Zebulon B. Vance, John H. Hemphill, Henry J. Turner, Samuel Pasco, Robert Stiles, Ethelbert Burksdale and B. J. Sage, all, presumably, Southern Democrat-Conservatives, imbued with prejudices and hatred of the African which border closely on childishness. When W. Laird Clowes gravely tells us that such White Conservative-Democrats as H. A. Herbert, Z. B. Vance, J. H. Hemphill and Co. (even supposing that they did not hate the African) have been his informants as to the alleged 'excesses' said to have been committed by the Liberal-Republican Africans of the South during the 'Reconstruction' period, are we not justified in asking whether we can ever hope to receive at the hands of the British Conservative Party any good testimonials and favourable reports respecting the Irish Parliamentary Party, even though the former may not entertain the slightest hatred and ill-will towards the latter?

As the American Africans are *black*, and *were slaves*, and as they are now freemen, and as they are, almost unanimously, Republican-Liberals, what man—what impartial man —is there who can ever hope that considerate and favourable reports can be received at the hands of political opponents, White Conservative-Democrats, such as Herbert, Vance, Hemphill, Turner, Pasco, Stiles, Burksdale and Sage? Is it at all probable that trustworthy reports of a party and a race like the Liberal-Republican African Party can ever be forthcoming from its opponents, when there is so much racial and party prejudice? But what is even more to be regretted is, that this blinding race-prejudice is not merely confined to the men. The fair sex, however, are often, we admit, as they ought to be always, gentle and pitiful. White women do, throughout America, intermarry with blacks, in spite of what Mr. Clowes may say to the contrary.

Apart from the fact that Mr. Clowes is probably himself a Conservative, it is on record, and a matter of history, that any 'irregularities,' not 'excesses,' which were committed during the 'Reconstruction' period were committed by the *White* Republican-Liberals; and the responsibility and blame consequently must lie, not at the doors of the *American Africans* of Liberal-Republican tendencies, but at the doors of the *White* Liberal-Republicans.

Mr. Clowes goes on to say, amongst other things, in chap. ii., p. 66, of 'Black America,' that 'there is or may be danger in the fact that the Negro as a citizen does not get all that to which he is legally entitled. How he is deprived of very much that the law affects to give him will be the subject of the next chapter.' And in the next chapter (iii.) Laird Clowes, on page 75, says, 'The attitude of the Southern white towards the Negro is, nevertheless, not exactly an unkind one. It is rather that of a magisterial guardian.'

The impartial will at once have noticed the inconsistencies which exist between the allegations on page 66, chap. ii., and those on page 75, chap. iii.

Why does not Laird Clowes say at once what he means, and what he would like us to understand? Why does he not frankly admit, without hesitation, and beating about the bush, that the American African is shamelessly and disgracefully cheated of the rights and privileges conferred upon him by Amendments xiii., xiv., and xv. to the Constitution of the United States of America?

Though the author of 'Black America' tells us that 'the attitude of the Southern white towards the Negro is that of a magisterial guardian,' he deliberately proceeds to contradict himself in substance by practically admitting, willingly or unwillingly, on pages 94, 95, 96, 97 and elsewhere, in effect, that 'the attitude of the Southern white towards the Negro' is *not* 'that of a magisterial guardian'; inasmuch as he quotes, and verbatim, the Washington correspondence of the *Pittsburg Dispatch* of January 11th, 1890, which runs as follows : ' It is impossible for the Negro to get any justice at the hands of Southern magistrates or juries. A man who resides in Augusta, Georgia—a Democrat and a hater of the Negro—admits that the whites' maltreatment of the blacks must one day recoil upon their own heads. "Why," said he to me to-day, "you can't convict a white man of the murder of a Negro, nor even of a white friend of the Negro. Just before I left home a Negro was found one morning in the street with his body riddled with bullets. I was pretty certain that his death was due to a certain gang of roughs, whose leader is under obligation to me for keeping him out of the penitentiary. Meeting him, I said, " Pat, who killed that nigger?"—" Oh, some of the boys," said Pat, with a grin.—" What did they do it for?" I asked.—" Oh, because he was a nigger," said Pat. "And," he continued, "he was the best nigger in town. Why, he would even take off his hat to me." I thought he must be a good Negro indeed who would take off his hat to that creature, and I walked away pondering upon what must be the outcome of it all. It is my opinion that several of the Southern States will have to be abandoned to the Negroes if we would avoid terrible consequences from the wrongs we are heaping on them.'

We ask Laird Clowes, or anyone else of his following, whether that attitude of the Southern white towards the African—as instanced in the murder recorded above—is that of a 'magisterial guardian' and 'not exactly an unkind one'?

Where is 'magisterial guardianship' of the African by the Southern white when 'it is impossible for the Negro to get any justice at the hands of Southern magistrates or juries;' when even 'a Democrat and a hater of the Negro,' avowedly admitted that one 'cannot convict a white man of the murder of a Negro, nor even of a white friend of the Negro'?

The following summary from a Barnwell letter of January 11th, 1890, in the *Charleston Budget* of that year and month, as given by Laird Clowes, shows that 'A Negro named William Black stole some trifling articles from the house of a white man, one Jim Bennett, near Robins, South Carolina. Bennett followed and caught the negro and, assisted by Dave Ready, Henry Sweat, and John Walker, tied the prisoner to a tree. Ready then placed a gun to the Negro's temple and blew out the man's brains. Bennett, Walker, and Sweat were arrested as accessories in the first degree, but were discharged by Justice Dunbar. Ready apparently escaped.' Now, is that a fair specimen of Anglo-Saxon civilization and humanity, as well as a fair specimen of the 'magisterial guardianship' of the African by the Southern white of the United States? Because the African, William Black, 'stole some trifling articles from the house of a white man,' he was set upon by four men and murdered in cold blood. In any truly civilized and Christian country the murderers would not have escaped. William Black, it is true, committed an offence by stealing 'some trifling articles,' it would seem, 'from the house of a white man.' Then he ought to have been tried by the laws of the land; but a man's valuable life ought not to have been taken away in this lawless manner. Such barbarities can only be met with in uncivilized countries, and are equalled only by the excesses committed by Henry M. Stanley in Central Africa. Black's offence was what lawyers call simple 'larceny,' and had he been properly tried and found guilty, he would only have been given a term of imprisonment, which might have exercised a beneficial influence on him and brought about his reform; but his murder by four scoundrels, who succeeded in evading justice, put an end to everything, and substituted injustice for justice—injustice aggravated when these murderers succeeded in evading punishment.

Laird Clowes furnishes us with more arguments, or, rather, evidences, which are like so many scourges to his own back, because they prove that 'the attitude of the Southern white towards the Negro' is *not* 'that of a magisterial guardian.' He gives a summary of a despatch from Augusta, Georgia, dated October 24th, 1890 (see Charleston *News and Courier*), in which it is said : 'Two boys—Williams, a Negro, and Robertson, a white—were playing together near Waynesborough with a gun, which, being accidentally discharged, killed Robertson. The Negro boy was arrested, but was taken from custody by a mob of white men, who tied him up and shot him to death.' Is that felonious act a specimen of the 'magisterial guardianship' of the African by the Southern white? The poor African boy was brutally murdered for an act which was the result of accident. In any civilized and Christian country the unhappy and unfortunate boy, after a trial, would have been acquitted ; but in America things are done differently. And yet Laird Clowes tells us that 'the attitude of the Southern white towards the Negro' is 'that of a magisterial guardian.' Perhaps those brutal outrages are, in Laird Clowes's sight, acts of 'magisterial guardianship.' We referred to the boy Williams as 'poor,' 'unhappy,' and 'unfortunate'; but he is neither now : he is in a better land, where no difference is made between the dark skin and the pale face.

Is the following account which Laird Clowes has culled from the *Boston Advertiser* of June 2nd, 1889, also a specimen of white man's magisterial guardianship?—' The report comes from South Carolina that a coloured man, unarmed and defenceless, fell into an altercation with a white man of that State named Gallman. Gallman slit the coloured man's throat from ear to ear, and drove to a neighbour's house, where he procured a shot-gun, and emptied the contents of one barrel into the wounded man. At a late hour that night Gallman's friends, hearing that the victim had not died, although he was at death's door, rode to where he lay, and carried him to the nearest churchyard, where they riddled his body with bullets.' In this case the victim was unarmed and defenceless. We reproduce another quotation from ' Black America.' Clowes takes it from the *Greenville News* of September 10th, 1889 : ' In Fulton County, Georgia, a black boy, of eighteen years, was taken from gaol and hanged for " assaulting " a white girl, the assault consisting of catching the child by the arms and running away, when she and her companions screamed. Then a pack of white ruffians, heavily armed, went from one cabin to another in an alleged search for the criminal, and barbarously whipped and maltreated inoffensive Negroes, who were powerless to defend themselves against shot-guns and revolvers presented at their heads.'

These are murders and other outrages committed on unarmed and defenceless Africans. They are the evidences of ' magisterial guardianship ' towards the Ethiopian only too truly. Britishers hold Guildhall meetings to protest against inhuman treatment of Jews by the Russian Government, but they sit apathetic, listless and unmoved, though they hear the groans of Christians (who happen to be black) like themselves, who have innumerable claims on their sympathy by reason of their having been torn away from their Fatherland, and held for generations in dehumanizing bondage. Has the Lord Mayor of London sent a memorial to the President of the United States to protest against the ' American-African Horrors ' daily perpetrated in America?

The Anglo-Saxons—who to-day pride themselves on the fact that their ancestors handed down to them that great bulwark of liberty, 'Magna Charta,' the grant of which was wrenched from the hands of tyrannical and unwilling John at Runnymede—now deny to the members of an unfortunate and downtrodden race the privileges and blessings of that Great Charter. What laws, we ask, protect the personal liberty and property of the Africans in America? Laird Clowes will answer that question. For he quotes an extract from the 'Augusta (Georgia) *Chronicle*' of January 5th, 1890, which says: 'Laws are powerless either to prevent the commission of crime or to punish the criminals, unless public sentiment forbids the one and commands the other. Where there is little regard for human life—and we fear this is the case in many portions of our country—the courts are often to blame for not hanging those who slay their fellow-men. Is it not a fact that it is almost impossible to convict a man of the crime of murder who has any social position or means to defend himself? If a Negro kills a white man he is pretty sure either to be lynched or hung. But if a white man slays a Negro he is in no danger of being lynched, and as to his being hung for the crime, there is not much probability.' And this frank confession comes from a journal of the South, which is edited by a white Conservative-Democrat!

The British people stand aghast at the tales of the Siberian horrors, which are from time to time drifted to their shores, and demonstrative meetings are held to devise the best possible means for bearding the Russian bear. But those blood-curdling horrors of daily occurrence in America, and which are always directed against the Ethiopians, are thought nothing of. Africans are constantly murdered by bloodthirsty mobs. Does the British Press ever say anything about these things? The Jews and the Poles are undoubtedly more fortunate than the African race. The African is forgotten. But will he always be forgotten?

We think not. It is on record that out of 108 persons lynched in the United States of America during the year 1890, fully 90 were Africans, and—oh, horror!—one was an Ethiopian woman. And yet Mr. Clowes tells us that the attitude of the Southern white towards the African is nevertheless 'not an unkind one.' It is rather that of a 'magisterial guardian.' Perhaps we do not quite understand what 'magisterial guardianship' is. We certainly do not if the blood-curdling murders committed by ruffianly White Americans on their Black compatriots, and their equals *de jure*, in the United States, form one of the component parts of 'magisterial guardianship'!

Mr. Clowes, on page 11 (and we ask the reader to take a glance at page 11 of 'Black America'), says that the Black Americans 'have at present no strong ambitions and very few wants'; but yet, with characteristic inconsistency, on page 90, in 'Black America,' he admits that 'on the side of the Negro there is a desire to be what the white man is, and to do what the white man does—to elevate himself to the same level of privileges.' If this be so, then the African evidently *has* 'strong ambitions and very great wants,' and Mr. Clowes is inconsistent with himself.

Speaking of the fair sex of the Sunny South, Laird Clowes gives it as his opinion, that the Southern white women entertain a general aversion towards intermarriage with the American Africans. We are not going to deny that there may be some who do. But only a few are found who can be so narrow-minded. It is safe to say that the great majority of the fair sex among the Southern whites are not averse towards intermarriage with the Africans. This is the truth even concerning the prejudiced Sunny South!

As Laird Clowes seems to know so much about Mr. Frederick Douglass, he ought to be aware that the American Minister to Hayti, and the acknowledged leader of all

Africans living under European and American flags, is joined in the bonds of wedlock with a Southern white woman, a 'belle' of the Sunny South.

We, as much as anyone else, deprecate all so-called assaults alleged to be committed on the Southern white women from time to time by Africans of too amorous and affectionate a temperament. The 'assaults' committed by the American Africans on the Southern white women are as a rule petty, and can hardly be called assaults. Whilst we do not approve of the conduct of the few among our kinsmen and countrymen in America who now and again commit so-called 'assaults' on women, by allowing their too affectionate dispositions to get the better of them, we offer our firm and unqualified protest against the daily murders, euphemistically termed lynchings, of the Africans by the whites which follow these 'assaults' by the Ethiopians on the white women. It is our opinion that if our kinsmen and countrymen do commit real and serious assaults on the white women in the United States, those assaults are the offspring of powerful reasoning, and we think they reason in this way : 'Whereas we American Africans cannot get justice, and have no voice in the South, and cannot get our grievances redressed at the hands of the white magistrates and juries against our oppressors, be it resolved that those of us American Africans who can do and dare, and have sufficient courage to perform achievements of " derring do," retaliate on those on whom we can retaliate, and so attract notice and get our grievances righted.' It is the privilege of the weak—the grim resolve of despair.

We certainly discountenance all such thoughts; yet, at the same time, we cannot but think how many Americans of colour, both women and children, have been barbarously outraged and murdered, and even burnt alive, by the whites; and these things have been done with little or no cause. But if the Africans do afford sufficient occasion for the resentment of the Whites by violating the social laws, then by all means let the law take its ordinary course with them. But *mob*-law is the rule in America; the law of the land is the exception when the Africans are concerned.

Here are two of many instances of Africo-Americans being burnt alive: 'Louisville, Kentucky, September 2nd, 1889.—The *Courier Journal* has a special from Somerset, Kentucky, which states that news has reached there of a brutal outrage committed upon the twelve-year-old daughter of William Oates, a prominent and wealthy farmer residing a few miles from Montecello. Mr. Oates has two daughters, aged respectively twelve and fourteen years. Mr. and Mrs. Oates left home on business, and left the two young girls in charge of the house. Mr. Oates had in his employ a Negro boy about grown. Knowing that the old folks were away, he entered the house, and, after locking the door upon the two girls, assaulted the younger. The elder girl escaped from the room, and, going to a neighbour's house, gave the alarm. A posse was organized and started in pursuit. The Negro was caught in the woods and tied to a stake. A rail-pen was then built around him, coal oil was poured over him and upon the rails, matches were applied, and the Negro was burnt to death.' The above appears on pages 132 and 133 in 'Black America.' The murder of an Africo-American boy by burning, because he happened to have been too passionately inclined towards the young girl Oates, was, to say the least, brutal, outrageous and unjustifiable. Where was the law of the land? Why did it not intervene if the unfortunate African boy was guilty? When that murder was committed in the United States, did we read of 'American Persecution' or 'Persecution of the Africans,' as we are now reading 'Russian Persecution' or 'Persecution of the Jews,' in the British daily press? Oh no! we never do. Says the Caucasian, We must keep the Ethiopian down. If that be not so, where was the influential and largely attended Guildhall meeting on behalf of the Africans? Did the Lord Mayor and the Earl of Meath send a petition to the President of the United States to protest against the 'American African Horrors' perpetrated by the White Americans? Did the Right Honourable W. E. Gladstone write a pamphlet entitled 'American African Horrors,' as well as his 'Bulgarian Horrors'?

When the 'Commander of the Faithful'—the Turkish Sovereign—and his Government some years ago barbarously butchered a number of Christians, all Europe from one end to the other raised a loud cry, and intervened between the Porte and her Christian subjects. But where are those who intervene on behalf of the dark-skinned American? You British people who snatched us from our native land and from our fathers' homes, and carried us to America and to the West India Islands against our will, we ask you to take us back—to give us money to return to the land of our fathers, where we can be free and independent, and where we can govern ourselves. One day (who knows?) you may find that you have to reap the whirlwind of the wind which you are now sowing! We are justified in saying this, because it is admitted on all sides that we Africans are a prolific race, and many times more prolific than the Caucasian race; and consequently one day we may be in a position to avenge the shameful wrongs that are being inflicted upon us now. It ought to be remembered that we are but mortals, and even good old Job himself, with all his patience, were he alive to-day and subjected, together with his people, to the outrages which the African is to-day receiving at the hands of his White compatriots, would lose his world-wide reputation for patience, and would surely resent the wrongs inflicted on him and his.

Here is another instance of an African being burnt to death; it is a man this time who suffers. Dalziel's Agency, dated New Orleans, May 31st, 1891, telegraphing to the London *Daily Telegraph*, of Monday, June 1st, 1891, says: 'The details of a sensational lynching case have just transpired, an official report of the matter having been forwarded to the Governor by the authorities of the Claiborne parish. The victim was a Negro tramp named Hampton. He was suspected of stealing pigs from the parish, and a warrant was issued for his arrest. In the attempt to take him Hampton shot a farmer dead. He was, however, arrested, but on being tried for murder was acquitted; he was then put on his trial for stealing, and being convicted, was sentenced to a year's imprisonment. The friends of the farmer whom he had killed took an oath that they would revenge his death upon the Negro as soon as his time expired. Hampton was released from prison on May 20th, and as soon as he walked out of gaol was seized by a number of men and handcuffed. He was then taken to a forest in the vicinity of the town, tied to a stake, and burned to death. The authorities have found no traces of the man except his ashes and the manacles by which he was secured.'

Comment, we think, is unnecessary. Such a brutal murder is simply a crying shame. There is no white woman at the bottom of it this time.

But why is it that to-day, in the prejudiced Sunny South, Africans are murdered more for 'assaulting' white women than for other sorts of offences? We answer with one of the numbers of the Montgomery *Herald*, for August, 1887: 'Why is it that white women attract Africans more than in former days? There was a time when such a thing was unheard of. There is a secret to this thing, and we greatly suspect it is the growing appreciation of the white Juliet for the Ethiopian Romeo as he becomes more and more intelligent and refined. If something is not done to break up these lynchings it will be so that after awhile they will lynch every African that looks at a white woman with a twinkle in his eye.' Just so. Laird Clowes, however, sees the situation with different eyes, and calls that article 'brutal.' But we think otherwise, and see no 'brutality' in the article of the Montgomery *Herald*. On the contrary, we think that it reflects the opinions of all good and true Africans all the world over.

There is one panacea, however, for all these lynching evils which exist in the United States wherever there are Africans, and that panacea is the universal cure of *wholesale Emigration*, which must carry with it as its almost inevitable consequences (1) Repatriation and (2) Independence in Africa, our Fatherland. We do not propose, however, to dwell at length on that panacea here.

Laird Clowes commits a great blunder when he asserts, on page 176, that: 'Mulattoes intermarry, and, in some cases, have intermarried for generations. In more than one place in the South they, with occasional admixtures of Quadroons, constitute a small, distinct community of highly respectable people, living to themselves for the most part, and having as little in common with their black as with their white neighbours; for white blood, even in small quantities, " tells," and the pride of the Mulatto or Quadroon, as a rule, rebels as much at the idea of alliance with the Negro, as does the pride of the white at the idea of alliance with coloured or black.' And, says this Commissioner of the *Times*, in another page (178): 'In the coloured man, again, we find the natural leader of the Negro in all movements, political, religious, and social.' We begin with, ' Mulattoes intermarry, and, in some cases, have intermarried for generations;' we then read, 'having as little in common with their black as with their white neighbours; for white blood, even in small quantities, "tells," and the pride of the Mulatto or Quadroon, as a rule, rebels as much at the idea of alliance with the Negro as does the pride of the white at the idea of alliance with coloured or black.' But Laird Clowes takes care to tell us that only 'in some cases' Mulattoes 'have intermarried for generations,' for these 'some cases' may mean in 'very few instances' they (the Mulattoes) have intermarried for generations amongst themselves, to the exclusion of their full-blooded kinsmen; but, on the other hand, there are the 'other cases,' the greater number of cases, in which they have *not* intermarried for generations exclusively amongst themselves. Whom do those who compose the 'other cases,' the greater number of cases, then marry, if they have 'as little in common with their black as with their white neighbours'? Do these marry their pure-blooded kinsmen and countrymen, or do they marry their white neighbours, whose pride rebels 'at the idea of alliance with coloured or black'? If these do neither, what do they do? Do they stand aloof from their black as from their white neighbours, and consequently wither and perish? Our ideas of human nature and our common-sense tell us that the Mulattoes and other Africans of mixed blood, when they do not intermarry amongst themselves, do not wither and become extinct, but intermarry, not only with their full-blooded African kinsmen, but also in many instances intermarry with the whites, just as the full blacks intermarry with the whites all the world over. Mr. Frederick Douglass (who is a Mulatto) had for his first wife a Black American lady of full, unmixed blood. That one example will suffice for many.

It is also an absurdity to say that white blood 'tells'

when blacks intermarry with whites nowadays. Mr. Frederick Douglass's present wife, it is well known, is a white 'belle' of the Sunny South. That the late General Solomon, the distinguished President of Hayti, was married to a Parisian lady of 'la belle France,' and by her had a daughter, who is a lady doctor of great eminence, who graduated in one of the very best of Parisian medical institutions, and is now practising in her Hayti home, in her Fatherland, is common knowledge. General ex-President Légitime, of Hayti, is also wedded to a fair Parisian. And that hero of duty, the late gallant, brave, honest and patriotic French soldier, General Faidherbe, Senator and Chancellor of the Legion of Honour, who in 1870-71, as commander-in-chief of the Army of the North, distinguished himself against the Germans, particularly at Pont de Noyelle and Bapaume, and who, from 1854 to 1865, was Governor of Senegal, was married to an African—a Senegalese who was as black as she was beautiful. The chief magistrate of the Gambia, John Renner Maxwell, Esq., an African, has a British wife. If Mr. Clowes tells us that the white blood of the Romans who did not intermarry with Britishers 'told,' we shall believe him. It is on record, indeed, that the Latin blood of the Romans really rebelled at the idea of matrimonial alliance with degenerated Britishers. If Laird Clowes is ignorant of the fact and doubts us, there are several histories of England, and it would be well to look these up.

Africans, however, as we have had occasion to mention, do intermarry with whites, though sixty years of freedom have not yet gone over the heads of those of us Africans who live under European and American flags; and our forefathers, and the immediate fathers of many of us, were slaves. The Liberians, Haytians, and Dominicans do also intermarry with Caucasians.

Let us suppose that the Mulattoes, and other Africans of mixed blood, have 'little in common with their full-blooded kith and kin,' and that their white blood 'tells;' if so, we are at a loss to understand how the African of mixed blood can be 'the natural leader' of the other branch of Africans—that is, the full-blooded blacks; and we should like the uninformed reader to be reminded that there are two chief branches of Africans, viz., (1) the Full-blooded African, whose blood has never been mixed, and (2) those whose veins may contain an admixture of Caucasian, Asiatic, or American Indian blood, coupled with that of the Black; who nevertheless belong to the same African-Ethiopian family, and are therefore kinsmen, and descendants of Ham—'in all movements, political, religious, and social,' when they have 'little in common' with the Full-blooded African. Can it be that the Mixed-blooded Africans have only to show themselves amongst the Full-blooded Africans, and are instantly made leaders, or do they simply elect themselves leaders? But the Mixed-blooded is *not* the 'natural leader' of the Full-blooded African in movements political, religious, or social. He may be the leader when he is the most capable man, but he is not the 'natural leader.' It is true that Frederick Douglass, a Mulatto, is the recognised leader of the Africans in the United States to-day, but that fact does not prove the Mixed-blooded to be universally and always the 'natural leader' of the Full-blooded African. The choice of leadership lies always with the *Full-blooded African.* If he is the most distinguished man, he leads; if he is not, he may follow the leadership of one of Mixed blood. The Full-blooded and Mixed-blooded Africans have fought shoulder to shoulder and side by side in bygone days, and will fight again shoulder to shoulder and side by side in the future. We Africans—both Full and Mixed-blooded—are proud of Frederick Douglass, and recognise in him the capable and distinguished generalissimo of all Africans living under European and American flags throughout the world. On the other hand, we ask Laird Clowes this question—when the Haytians rose in insurrection in 1791, who were their leaders? Were their leaders of full or mixed blood? History tells us that Jean François and Biassou were Africans of full blood, and they were the leaders of the Haytian insurrection of 1791.

When the Haytians were bravely battling for Independence (after the leadership of Jean François and Biassou terminated by their deaths), who was their 'natural leader,' a Mixed or Full-blooded African? History tells us that Toussaint the Great—Toussaint L'Ouverture, the Liberator of his fellow-countrymen, who gave Hayti practical Independence—was a Full-blooded African. He was the Creator and Regenerator of the Haytians, and their first President. He was the most distinguished African statesman and soldier of modern times—one of the most distinguished statesmen and soldiers of all times. He takes rank among all distinguished soldiers and statesmen of European parentage, both ancient and modern. After the treacherous seizure of Toussaint the Great, and his conveyance as a prisoner to France, where he was confined in a dungeon and died, under the refined cruelties perpetrated at the instance of the First Napoleon, round whom did the Haytians rally? Did they rally under a Mixed-blooded African? We say not. Jacques Dessalines (afterwards Jacques I., Emperor of the Haytians) was their commander-in-chief, was *the leader*, and he was a Full-blooded Ethiopian, and coal-black; he was African born; he came from the Gold Coast, and ably did he fill up the place of Toussaint the Great, a nd lead to victory his Haytian people.

When the Jamaican Maroons rose in rebellion in 1750 and 1795, whom had they to lead them? Were their leaders of mixed or full blood? It is on record that their leaders and advisers were Africans of full blood.

Sebituane, chief of the Makololo, in South Africa—who was the contemporary of Livingstone, and whom Livingstone praises and alleges to have been 'unquestionably the greatest man in all that country' (*i.e.*, South Africa), and who fought so bravely and successfully to regain the possession of his native land—was an African of full blood.

We repeat that the Mixed-blooded African leads when his abilities qualify him, and George William Gordon, the Jamaican African, the hero-martyr of 1865, and Leader of the Opposition to Colonel Eyre's Jamaican Government, was, we believe, a Mulatto. He it was who raised the standard of Africo-Jamaican Rebellion in 1865, and had he been actively supported by the great majority of his countrymen, who sedulously kept aloof, Jamaica would ere this have come to occupy a place amongst the independent nations of the earth. We referred to Africo-Jamaican rebellion; it was not a rebellion : if anything, it could only have been a mere revolt—a rising. The rising was suppressed, and George William Gordon, the leader of the rising, was seized, underwent a mock trial for high treason, and was lynched, not hanged—murdered, not executed. For the so-called execution by hanging was the result of a mock trial. That it was so can be evidenced by the protest raised by the British people after Gordon's judicial murder, against Colonel Eyre, on whose head lie the blood and responsibility of the death of the martyred Gordon. It makes no difference to us whether the Mixed or the Full-blooded African leads. Let the man who is capable lead, whoever he may be.

Theodore, the greatest King or Emperor of the Abyssinians, was an African of full blood. And he was a distinguished ruler, though unfortunate. He was also a capable soldier, and thoroughly civilized. Osai Tutu Quamina, who was King of the Ashantees from 1800 to 1824, was a Full-blooded African. He it was who inflicted the demoralizing defeat on Britishers under Sir Charles McCarthy in 1824, on the banks of the Adoomansoo. King Tshaka, or Chaka, who lived at the beginning of this (nineteenth) century, and who was the founder of the great Zulu Empire, which stretched from the confines of Cape Colony to the lands watered by the Limpopo and Makoma, was a Full-blooded African Quamina.

Langalibalele, Chief of the Amazulu Caffirs, in Natal, who led the well-known movement in 1873, was a Full-blooded African. Placido, the Cuban patriot and poet, who fell a victim to the resentment of the Spaniards, at whose hands he suffered death, was a Full-blooded African. Zulu King Cetewayo, who inflicted the disastrous defeat on Britishers at Isandhlwana, Inyezane, Intombi, and Hloblane, not long ago, was a Full-blooded African. His unfortunate son, Prince Dinizulu—who a few years ago led the well-known movement to regain his fatherland and the throne of his ancestors, and is now an exile in St. Helena—is an African of full blood. His Lordship the Right Rev. Dr. Crowther, who was made Bishop of the Niger by the Archbishop of Canterbury, under the auspices of Lord Palmerston's Government, in 1864, was formerly a slave. He was an African of full blood, and is the first black Bishop the British ever consecrated. The Right Rev. Bishop Burns, of the American Methodist Episcopal Church, was a full-blooded African, and he was a very learned man. An eminent American-African scholar was the late Right Rev. Bishop Payne, Principal of the Wilberforce University for the Freedmen in America, but he was not of mixed blood.

To say, then, that the Mixed-blooded is 'the natural leader' of the Full-blooded African is absurd in the extreme, and shows that Mr. Clowes knows very little about Africans. To say, also, that the mixed-blooded has 'little in common' with the Full-blooded African is equally absurd. The full-blooded and mixed-blooded Africans fought shoulder to shoulder under the leadership of Toussaint the Great, and then under that of Dessalines. In the days of slavery they (the Africans) suffered together and perished together. The full-blooded and the mixed-blooded Ethiopians have one common destiny because they are one African people.

Laird Clowes has certainly made a clumsy attempt to sow discord and dissension amongst us Africans. There are to-day, in Liberia, in Hayti, and everywhere else where the descendants of Ham are to be found, both full and mixed blooded Africans. They are one people, and must live and die together. The greatest ruler Hayti has ever had—next to Toussaint the Great, Jacques I. (Dessalines), Henry I. (Christophe) and Boyer—was undoubtedly *Pétion*, and he was a Mulatto, and an administrator of more than ordinary talent.

Says Laird Clowes, on pages 172 and 173 of 'Black America': 'In our West Indian colonies there are about 10,000 coolies, of whom Mr. Froude says: "They are proud, and will not intermarry with the Africans. If there is no jealousy, there is no friendship. The two races are more absolutely apart than the white and the black."' First of all, in the British West Indies there are, at the very least, 100,000, and not 'about 10,000,' Coolies. Consequently Clowes blunders from the very beginning, and so on to the end, as we shall prove in due time. Mr. Froude, when he says, in his 'English in the West Indies,' 'there are about 10,000' Coolies, is undoubtedly wrong. And Mr. Clowes slavishly fell into the same error by taking Froude's statement as law on the subject. Mr. Froude speaks of the Trinidadian Coolies, and he knows very little about them (just as little as he knows of the Africans), for there are in Trinidad at present 70,000 Coolies at the very least. And we make bold to say that when Froude took his short trip to Trinidad there were over 60,000 Coolies in the aforesaid island. Now for other blunders.

Laird Clowes cannot in any way be congratulated on his prudence or foresight, which we would have been only too happy to have seen in him, our opponent though he be; for had Mr. Clowes, before quoting James Anthony Froude, who says on page 73, chapter vi., in 'The English in the West Indies,' that 'They' (meaning the coolies) 'are proud, however, and will not intermarry with the Africans,' looked on page 68, and higher up on the same page (73) in the same chapter (vi.) in 'The English in the West Indies,' he would have observed that Mr. Froude says on page 68, that 'My friend' (*i.e.*, Bertie Gatty, who was a briefless barrister before he was given a Civil Service appointment in the West Indies through backstairs influence) 'drove me round the town in his buggy the next morning' after his arrival in Trinidad; and who (the same Froude) further on in the same chapter (vi.), on page 73, moreover adds, 'In Trinidad, as everywhere else, my own chief desire was to see the human inhabitants, to learn what they were doing, how they were living, and what they were thinking; and this could best be done by drives about the town and neighbourhood.' Now, could Mr. Froude, whilst driving in his buggy round the town of Port-of-Spain, the city and capital which contains 35,000 inhabitants, have seen between 60,000 and 70,000 Coolies, have learnt what the human inhabitants were doing, and how they were living, all in one morning's drive? If there ever were grave statements made that were, in fact, ridiculous and childish, those statements quoted above are. Mr. Froude could not have seen all the human inhabitants, 35,000 souls, in one morning. Since there are few Coolies in the capital—the greater part being in the country—it was impossible for him to have seen all the Coolies, or

the greater part of them, in one morning, and found out that
'They are proud, and will not intermarry with the Africans.'
Froude no doubt saw *some* of the Coolies of the capital 'by
drives about the town and neighbourhood' in one morning!
The Coolies, as we have said, are few in numbers in the
capital, but there are two divisions of Coolies, at least, in
religion : there are Hindoo Coolies, and there are Mahommedan Coolies ; these, however, in no way represent the
voice of their countrymen in the country districts, who are
in a preponderating majority. We venture to say that Mr.
Froude did not see all, or even the majority, of the few
Coolies resident in Port-of-Spain, in County St. George. To
that fact let us add the fact, that he did not see the vast
majority of Coolies scattered throughout the Counties of
St. David, Caroni, St. Andrew, Victoria, Nariva, St. Patrick,
Mayaro. As his 'drives about the town' did not enable
him to see these latter, how came he to know that 'they
are proud, and will not intermarry with the Africans'?
The vast majority of the Trinidadian Coolies are illiterate.
Because they are illiterate they do not correspond with
each other; we mean, that those in the country do not
write to those in the capital, and *vice versâ*, because they
are almost all illiterate. As they are illiterate, they neither
write books nor read books; they neither read the newspapers
nor have they newspapers ; nor do they write to the newspapers to express their thoughts and make the world
know that 'they are proud, and will not intermarry with
the Africans.' Those in the capital do not see those in the
country, and they do not write and exchange confidences
with each other, and say that 'they will not intermarry
with the Africans,' because they are illiterate. There is
not one barrister, solicitor, or doctor to be met with
throughout the length and breadth of Trinidad who is of
Asiatic, Indian, or Coolie parentage. They are an illiterate
class. If so, what can they have to be proud of? Mr.

Froude could not have seen, we say, all the Coolies—even all of those resident in the capital—even though the horse which drew him in his friend's buggy was the winged horse Pegasus himself, and its driver and master, Bertie Gatty, or James Anthony Froude, was himself a Bellerophon.

Here is an entire absence of evidence to bear out Froude's statement, that the Coolies are proud and will not intermarry with the Africans. No man has yet ventured to express similar sentiments, and no representative Coolies have yet come forward to bear out the statements; we therefore say that Froude's mere assertion that the Coolies 'are proud,' and because of their pride 'will not intermarry Africans,' does not hold water. Moreover, he did not know the Coolies in the provinces. We do not know whether he formed his own independent opinion, or whether his host Gatty put him *au courant* by giving his own opinion with regard to so-called Coolie pride, and their alleged aversion to intermarriage with the Africans. It is, however, of no great consequence to us whether Froude formed his own opinion or Gatty told Froude what he thought. Gatty knows as little about the Coolies as he knows about the general affairs of the colony. Gatty, a Member of both the Executive and Legislative Councils, and the Crown's chief law officer in the island, ought to have known, at least from official sources, and as an official, if not as a private individual, that there were in Trinidad, during Froude's visit, at least 60,000 Coolies in the Island, and ought not to have allowed Froude to fall into such an error. But Bertie is a bird of passage and migratory—is not really interested in the affairs of the colony.

The same remarks apply also to the other portion of Clowes's quotation from Froude, viz., 'if there is no jealousy, there is no friendship. The two races are more absolutely apart than the white and the black.' We must add, however, a few words, and say that the Africans are the people who will not intermarry with the Coolies, because they (the Africans) are too proud; and the Coolies render matters worse by their general behaviour. Let the Coolies give up the heathenish and barbarous custom of blackening* their teeth; let them stop mangling their ears and noses and the reddening of their tongues, by giving up their customs and ceasing to partake of nauseous, unsavoury, and unpalatable articles of food, because such things are distasteful and abhorrent to us Africans, who despise all things that have a tendency to degrade us, or which savour of the uncivilized. When the Coolies see the propriety of dressing in a manner which would make the casual observer believe that they are a civilized people, if only in an outward sense, and when they cease to go abroad in a state of semi-nudity; when the Coolies give up boiling and eating their repulsive food or diet; when the Coolies put a stop to oiling their bodies, an act which gives their shiny bodies the appearance of gliding snakes, especially in the dry season; when they cease bathing their heads with oleaginous liquid, the smell of which is the reverse of odoriferous; and, lastly, when they see the propriety of changing their Hindoo or Mohammedan faith, with the superstitious rites accompanying it, and embrace the truths of Christianity—when they do all these, we say, and when they have undergone a complete transformation, then, and only then, shall we progressive Africans join in wedlock with them (the Asiatic Indians), but not before. It is we Africans who will have nothing to do with the Indian Coolies as far as intermarriage is concerned. And we say, in conclusion, that 'the two races'—that is, the African and the Asiatic Coolie—are only too truly 'more absolutely apart than the white and

* One may use either 'blacking' or 'blackening,' for which see Webster's International Dictionary, Johnson's English Dictionary, or Chamber's English Dictionary.

the black' in Trinidad. Whatever the attitude of the African towards the Asiatic, and the Asiatic towards the African, may be in Trinidad, in the British West Indies it is not a hostile one. Let us leave the African and the Asiatic in Trinidad, and view them elsewhere. Let us for a moment consider the condition of the Asiatic and the African in Asia.

Are Mr. Clowes and Mr. Froude aware that there are thousands of Africans in Asia, particularly in Arabia and India? Are they aware that, when the Indian Mutiny broke out, and throughout the year it lasted, the Nizam of Hyderabad, with a splendid force of 100,000 soldiers, of whom the best and the most efficient and bravest were Africans, held, with the greatest facility, the southern portion of India for the British; and that if the Nizam, the most powerful prince of the most powerful native State in India, had but joined the Sepoys, the British Empire would have crumbled to pieces? Is Mr. Clowes and is Mr. Froude aware that the best officers and the best soldiers in the present Nizam of Hyderabad's Army are African Mahommedans?

Are they aware that an African, in the ninth century, reigned and ruled as Khalif at Bagdad?* Are they aware that the Great Asiatic, Mahommed, had as Crier or Herald an African?† Are they aware that more than three-fourths of the Africans of Africa are Mahommedans, and were converted by Asiatics?

* 'Ibn Khallikan's Biographical Dictionary,' translated from the Arabic by Baron Mac Guckin de Slane, vol. i., pp. 16, 17, 18 and 19.

† Muir's ' Life of Mahomet,' vol. iii., p. 54.

CHAPTER II.

IS UNCLE REMUS INFERIOR TO THE CAUCASIAN?

WHEN given the same advantages, the African can always hold his own with the Caucasian, and is in no way inferior to him. We have shown our strength in the past, and have produced our scholars, as we are doing at the present time. We have ourselves witnessed the proud and glorious spectacle of black scholars snatching away prizes which their white *confrères* thought were within their easy grasp. There are those who do not think thus, however, but regard us as mentally inferior. Those who do are, as a rule, very ignorant concerning the achievements of the Africans in all the various branches of knowledge—of both arts and sciences. Indeed, Laird Clowes throughout his book displays the greatest ignorance respecting the past and present history of Africans. He applies the term 'childish' to the African; but that term only reveals the ignorance of the man who uses it. Even Froude has not displayed so much ignorance as Laird Clowes, though Froude's knowledge is within very narrow limitations.

This is what Laird Clowes says on page 76 of his 'Black America': 'No one who has associated much with the Negro race can have failed to have remarked that in the natural time of childhood the Negro is apparently as vivacious and as intelligent as the white. With the approach of puberty, however, the two races begin to betray marked intellectual divergence. The white steadily progresses in intelligence, the black stops short; so that in a few years the latter is by comparison dull, stupid, and indolent, though still frivolous, affectionate, good-natured, and mischievous. I speak, of course, of the average Negro, and more especially of the full-blooded one. There are exceptions, but they are few. As a rule, the grown Negro, even if he have received a better education than the majority of his fellows, is in mind always a child.' In brief, Mr. Clowes is of opinion that the Ethiopian is in nature inferior to the Caucasian.

We Africans, who claim the extinct Carthaginians as our countrymen, cannot be inferior. Does Mr. Clowes know the part that Carthage played in the world's history? Her part was a most distinguished one. Carthage was the greatest State that ever existed in Africa. We all know that the Romans never encountered a mightier nation in arms than the Carthaginian. They disputed the empire of the world with the Romans. But some people say that the Carthaginians were not of the Ethiopian, but of the Semitic stock. Now, we all know that the Carthaginians were of Phœnician origin, and we are also aware that the Phœnicians were the descendants of the Canaanites, and often styled themselves Canaanites ; as we also know that the Canaanites were the descendants of Canaan, who was a son of Ham, who was the founder of the African Ethiopian Race. Then, by their being the descendants of Ham, the Carthaginians must have belonged to the Ethiopian stock. The Carthaginians were inferior to none of the nations of the ancient world in ability.

By the way, those who say that the Carthaginians were of Semitic origin allege that the Bible is wrong in classing Canaan amongst the sons of Ham ; and that Sidon, the Hethite, the founder of the Phœnicians, and Canaan's firstborn son, was not a descendant of Ham. We say that if objections be taken to that part of the Bible in which the statement is made concerning Canaan, that he was a son of Ham, what objections may not be taken to other parts of the book when it treats of other historical facts? If we believe in one part, we ought to believe in another part, or discard the Bible altogether. We believe the Bible to be quite correct in giving Canaan as a son of Ham. Besides, it is not given to the white man to lay down the law to the African in the matter of Ethnography. The African can see and reason for himself.

To resume. The Carthaginian navy was the best the ancient world ever saw. Carthage produced men like Hamilcar Barca, who, as a statesman and soldier, was second only to his son Hannibal the Great, amongst the great men of Carthage. Carthage also produced Hasdrubal, the son-in-law of Hamilcar Barca, and he (Hasdrubal) was a capable soldier, but a more distinguished statesman. Carthage gave birth also to the brothers Barcidæ, Hannibal, Hasdrubal, and Mago, the 'lion's broods' of Hamilcar Barca. The three sons of Hamilcar whom we have just mentioned were distinguished for soldiership and statesmanship, but the eldest of them, Hannibal, was the greatest man that Carthage ever produced. The Romans, it is a matter of history, never had a more formidable foe to contend with. He it was who maintained himself for sixteen years in Italy, in the enemy's country, with a mixed army of Africans, Gauls, Spaniards, Ligurians, etc., unaided and unsupported by his country, because of party strife at home. Hannibal the Great is entitled to rank with Alexander, Cæsar, and Napoleon, both as a soldier and as a statesman. Alexander was in some respects inferior to Hannibal; and it is a moot point with historians whether Julius Cæsar and Napoleon were really greater than the Carthaginian Hannibal.

If the Carthaginians had belonged to an inferior race, they would never have played such a prominent part as they have done in the world's history.

The mother-country and parent of Carthage, Phœnicia (which consisted of Sidon, Tyre, Aradus, etc.), was not very inferior to Carthage, and it also occupies a distinguished place in ancient history. The Phœnicians were the descendants of Sidon the Hethite, who was the first-born of Canaan, who was the youngest son of Ham. The Empire of the Phœnicians was a mighty one, and their navy was formidable. If the Phœnicians had been an inferior race, they would never have attained such greatness in the olden times as they did. Does not the Bible give the country and city of Nineveh, the country of the Philistines, and the colossal Babylon as belonging also to the children of Ham? And Nineveh and the Philistines were renowned, while the Babylonian Empire, at least, equalled that of Carthage.

The Moors of Morocco are the descendants of Asiatics and Africans, and they are the persons whose ancestors introduced the manufacture of cotton, wool, sugar, silk, and other things into Spain and Portugal,* when those countries fell before their conquering arms in the years 710 and 711 A.D. Nor did the ancestors of these same Moors quit Spain and Portugal until the year 1609 of our era. Those who disparage the African forget that the great and illustrious geometrician, Euclid, was an African and an Ethiopian; that P. Terentius Afer, commonly called Terence, the friend and associate of P. Cornelius Scipio, the African (Africanus), and Lælius, who from being a slave became an eminent Latin Author, was not only an African, but an Ethiopian.† Victor I., who succeeded Eleutherius as Pope of Rome about 185 A.D., and died about 197 A.D.,

* 'Encyclopædia Britannica.'
† Grégoire's 'Enquiry on Africans,' p. 45.

could hardly have been of any other race than the African-Ethiopian. At any rate, it is certain that he was a native of Africa. He could not have been childish, nor could his talents have been in any way of an inferior order, or the European — the Italian — ecclesiastical dignitaries, the College of Cardinals, would not have made him Pope.

Aurelius Augustinus, better known as St. Augustine, who was born at Tagaste, now called Tajelt, in Northern Africa, and who was afterwards Bishop of Hippo, could not have been of European origin, or a descendant of Shem; at all events, there are no records extant to show that he was of European or Asiatic parentage; and we must, *primâ facie*, as he was born in Africa, take for granted that he was an Ethiopian. He was one of the most illustrious Fathers of the Catholic Church, and was even more distinguished than Ambrose, Jerome, or Gregory the Great, his great European colleagues. He wrote some forty theological works, some of them of permanent value. St. Augustine lived from 354 to 430 A.D., and is held in high honour by all good and true Catholics, and by other Christians. Such a man could not have had talents of an inferior order. The Catholic Order of Augustinians derives its name from this illustrious St. Augustine.

The next greatest African theologian was undoubtedly Tertullian, who was a priest of Carthage, and lived in the third century, and was an eminent author, the best known of his works being the 'Apology' and the 'Prescriptions.' Cyprian, Bishop of Carthage, who lived in the third century, who perished as a martyr under Valerian, was of African origin, and takes his place next to Augustine and Tertullian among the eminent uninspired writers and saintly men who are of African birth.

Origen of Alexandria was a very prolific and distinguished author, who wrote many more books than even

Augustine. Indeed, we do not believe that there ever existed a more prolific author in ancient or modern times than Origen.

Clemens Alexandrinus, who was born about the middle of the second century, and wrote thirty books; Cyril of Alexandria; Monica, the mother of St. Augustine; Leonidas, the father of Origen; Perpetua and Felicitas, who suffered martyrdom under Septimius Severus; Theophilus of Alexandria: were all Africans, and their careers were distinguished ones.

Were all these men and women, then, 'dull, stupid and indolent,' or did they 'stop short' after attaining puberty? Was every one, or any one, of those just mentioned 'in mind always a child'?

Would the grateful and impulsive French general Laveaux, after he was (as the result of a conspiracy) arrested at Cape Town, in Hayti, and then released by Toussaint L'Ouverture, full of enthusiasm and admiration for his black deliverer, have proclaimed him the protector of Frenchmen and the avenger of the constituted authorities, and created him first a general of brigade, next a general of division, and subsequently commander-in-chief of the French forces of San Domingo, if Toussaint the Great had been 'dull, stupid and indolent'?

Surely the Frenchmen who drove the English from France (A.D. 1451) in the reign of Henry VI., and finally wrested Calais from the grasp of the First Mary; and who recaptured Toulon in 1793 from the Britishers; and who, in 1794, chased the allied British and Austrians, under York, out of Flanders and Holland; and who inflicted the humiliating and disastrous defeat on the British and Austrians at Fontenoy, in 1745, must be supposed to know how to choose their commanders. And these same Frenchmen made Toussaint the Great, an African, commander-in-chief of San Domingo and of the French army therein. Yes; Toussaint

L'Ouverture, who gave freedom and practical independence to his Haytian nation, and under whom agriculture and commerce flourished, and the arts of peace and good government were encouraged, could not have been 'dull, stupid and indolent,' nor could he have been 'in mind a child.'

Was Dessalines (who afterwards ascended the Haytian throne as Jacques I., Emperor of the Haytians), who, after he had seen Toussaint L'Ouverture treacherously seized and conveyed as a prisoner to France by the perfidious French, organized a Haytian National Army to regain the Independence which Toussaint had practically given them, to punish the French, if possible, for their perfidy and treachery, 'in mind a child,' or was he 'dull, stupid and indolent'?

Was that same eminent Dessalines, who, when he saw that fortune was doubtful, and that there was an uncertainty of his successfully coping with the French with his thin lines of Haytians, sent ambassadors to his native Africa to the courts of its princes, to ask for a reinforcement of Africans, 'stern and wild'? He knew how to fight in the cause of freedom and independence, and he succeeded in driving away the French from San Domingo, and regaining the Independence for his Fatherland; and was he 'dull, stupid and indolent'?

Was Christophe (afterwards Henri I., second Emperor of the Haytians), who, when he perceived that the scheming Frenchmen were taking advantage of dissensions in Hayti, and were trying to regain San Domingo, had the good sense, patriotism and statesmanship to make overtures for a truce, and sink his differences with his rival Pétion, and unite his forces with those of the latter to defend his Fatherland against the encroachments of the Gaul, 'dull, stupid and indolent,' or was he 'in mind a child'? Was Pétion 'dull, stupid and indolent,' and 'in mind a child,' for accepting Christophe's overtures? Geoffrey L'Islet, who was an artillery officer in the French army, who founded a scientific society in Mauritius, when that island belonged to France, who, it is on record, although he had very few facilities for acquiring knowledge, and never set his foot in Europe, was an accomplished astronomer, was a skilful botanist, and excelled in natural philosophy and geometry; and who, in 1786, was appointed correspondent in Mauritius by that illustrious body, the French Academy of Sciences; who was also a hydrographer of the first class, and a skilful meteorologist; and whose works on astronomy received official recognition by the French Government in 1791, could not have been 'dull, stupid and indolent.' And he was an African.

Antony William Amo, an African, born in African Guinea, about the year 1703; who in 1729 published his 'De Jure Maurorum,' and in 1734 published another physiological dissertation; who in the latter year (1734) graduated as Doctor in Philosophy at the University of Wittemburg, in Germany; who spoke Hebrew, Greek, Latin, German, French, and Dutch; who was an accomplished astronomer; who was afterwards made Councillor of State by the Court of Berlin, could not have been 'dull, stupid, and indolent.' And he was a full-blooded African.

Johann Friedrich Blumenbach, the eminent German, who was a Member of the Academy of Sciences of Paris, and physician to the Third Hanoverian George of Great Britain and Ireland, it is said, recognised the great abilities of the African, and eulogized the West African, Antony William Amo.

Another African, and full-blooded Ethiopian, was Benjamin Banneker, of Ellicott's Mills, in County Baltimore, in the State of Maryland, in the United States. He takes rank as an astronomer with other great astronomers the world has produced, and could not have been 'dull, stupid, and indolent.'

But what men of letters and arts has Africa not produced? Toussaint L'Ouverture was himself an author, for he wrote a Memoir of his Life.

Phillis Wheatley, the African Poetess of Boston, Massachusetts, was born in Africa about 1754; she was a full-blooded African, and, like Toussaint the Great, Dessalines, Christophe, Amo, Banneker, and others, she was a slave. She wrote several poems before she was seventeen, which attracted and received the approbation of eminent scholars, and became bard to Selina, Countess of Huntingdon, who founded the branch of the Church now known by the name of the 'Countess of Huntingdon's Connexion.' Phillis Wheatley published several poems, and wrote a monody on George Whitefield's death. She was a full-blooded African, and very patriotic, and she died in 1784. Wheatley is not the only poet that Africa has produced, but she is perhaps the best. At any rate, her name is in the front rank of African poets. We now ask the reader, Was Phillis Wheatley, the contemporary of Benjamin Franklin, who received the patronage of Selina, Countess of Huntingdon, and the admiration of John Wesley, 'dull, stupid, and indolent,' or was she 'in mind a child'? Supposing she were 'in mind a child,' then she could have been 'in mind' only the 'poetic child,' to use the language of Sir Walter Scott. Africa, 'stern and wild,' was her 'meet nurse.' Was that Africo-Frenchman, General of Division Alexandre Dumas, who was surnamed by the first Napoleon the 'Horatius Cocles of the Tyrol,' and who died in 1807, 'dull, stupid, and indolent,' or was he 'in mind a child'? Was that distinguished novelist, dramatist, and romancer, his son, Alexandre Davy Dumas *père*, who flourished from 1802 to 1870, and who wrote 'Monte Cristo,' 'The Three Musketeers,' and a vast number of novels, dramas, and romances too numerous to mention, 'dull, stupid, and indolent,' or was he 'in mind a child'? And are the children of the last-named (Alexandre Davy Dumas *père*), and grandchildren of the first-named (Alexandre Dumas, General of Division), Madame Petel, the romancer, and Alexandre Davy Dumas *fils*, novelist, romancer, and dramatist, who wrote 'La Dame aux Camélias,' and sundry other able works, 'dull, stupid, and indolent,' or are they 'in mind children'?

The same comments and remarks will apply to the African poet, Ignatius Sancho, who was, it is said, the correspondent and contemporary of Laurence Sterne, of 'Tristram Shandy' and 'Sentimental Journey through France and Italy' celebrity, as well as to the Cuban Placido, the African Poet-Patriot; to the Africo-American poet Cæsar, who was born in North Carolina; to Capitien, who wrote Latin in both prose and verse, and was, like Phillis Wheatley, noted for his saintly life; to the African poet, Francis Williams, who was, it was said, a protégé of one of the Dukes of Montague; to the poets Mrs. Harper, Miss Watkins, and James Whitbread; and also to the Kafir Poet-Chief Suana.

These are not the only celebrities the African race has produced. The good people of Glasgow, we do not doubt, retain the memory of Dr. James McClure or McCune. Smith, an African, who, when he graduated in medicine in the Scottish commercial metropolis, earned the distinction of bearing away the first prize from five hundred University of Glasgow alumni. He was not 'dull, stupid, and indolent,' nor was he 'in mind a child,' but was enabled to defeat the Scotchmen on their own soil and in their own University.

Give Africans the same chances as Caucasians, and the descendants of Ham will more than hold their own against Japheth's descendants; they will not 'stop short.'

But, we ask, has Laird Clowes, and other disparagers of

the African, ever heard of such men as Thomas Fuller the great Arithmetician; James Derham, a very distinguished Physician of New Orleans; Samuel Ringgold Ward of Toronto, Ontario, Can., the brilliant Abolitionist, Orator, and Clergyman, who was for two and a half years (from April, 1841) the *black* Pastor of the *white* Congregational Church of South Butler, Wayne Co., N.Y.; Thomas Jenkins; James William Charles Pennington, D.D.; Henry Highland Garnett; Alexander Crummell; Thomas Sipkins Sidney; Amos G. Beman; Madison M. Clarke; Charles Lewis Reason; Patrick Henry Reason; James Forten; Theodore Sedgewick Wright; Samuel Todd; William Hamilton; Richard Allen; John Gloucester; Peter Williams; George Hogarth; Samuel E. Cornish; Jehiel C. Beeman; Stephen Smith; Timothy Este; William Whipper; Pory-Papy, who was the Deputy for the Colony of Martinique in the French National Assembly in 1872; William Wells Brown; Henry Bibb; Roper; Christopher Rush; Robert Morris; Macon Bolden Allen; John V. Degrasse; Thomas Joiner White; William G. Allen; George B. Vashon; William Douglass; William Paul Quinn; Daniel A. Poyne; William H. Bishop; William Howard Day; John J. Gains; Charles Mercer Longston; William J. Watkins; C. E. Taylor; Ralph Taylor; Tanner; C. H. Thompson, D.D., of Newark, New Jersey; John M. Brown; James Johnson; George T. Downing—all eminent scholars and philosophers and *optimates* of our (African) Race and the world?

Blyden, on whose authority these names are given (see 'Christianity, Islam, and the Negro Race,' by Dr. E. W. Blyden), also notices, on the authority of Muir, that Mahommed's first Muezzin, or Crier, was an African, Billâl by name. He mentions, too, a celebrated African Khalif, who reigned at Bagdad in the ninth century; and on the authority of Ibn Khallikan, one Abu'l-Aswad is said to have been the first to reduce to system the Arabic language.

Another distinguished Ethiopian, whose name might have been previously given, is the Africo-American, George W. Williams, who is perhaps the only African who has attained high military rank in the American army. He played a distinguished part in the late American Civil War, as an officer of the Federal Army of the North; was a member of the Ohio Legislature, and Judge-Advocate of the Grand Army of the Republic of Ohio, and is an eminent author.

The thirteen rulers of the Haytians were not 'dull, stupid, and indolent,' nor is the present President of Hayti, General L. M. F. Hippolyte, who is a man of distinguished parts, and has many admirers amongst Caucasians. Likewise the Presidents of Liberia were men of distinguished ability. The present President of Liberia is Mr. J. H. R. W. Johnson, who was repeatedly elected to the office, the people thereby showing the confidence they placed in him. He is also a distinguished and able man. It would be absurd to apply the term 'dull, stupid and indolent' to him; it would be an insult. Joseph Jenkins Roberts, the first President of Liberia, who was more than twice re-elected to the office by his fellow-citizens, was a man of the greatest ability: we doubt whether Liberia has ever had a more distinguished man as her President; and he was—like Toussaint, the first President of Hayti—born a slave; but he could not have been 'dull, stupid, and indolent,' nor could he have been 'in mind a child.' We dare say Messrs. Hyde, Hodge, and Co., of London, contractors with Her Britannic Majesty's Aberdeen Government, underrated the powers and capacities of the great Roberts, and thought him 'dull, stupid, and indolent,' and 'in mind a child,' for the aforesaid gentlemen, who held a contract with Lord Aberdeen's Government for furnishing African labourers to the West Indies, sent, in 1853, some of their ships to the coast of the Liberian Republic in quest of labourers, at the same time offering an advance of ten dollars to anyone who might be induced to emigrate. President Roberts was sufficiently astute to perceive that Messrs. Hyde, Hodge, and Co., the contractors, were trying to revive slavery and the slave-trade; and by Proclamation the great Roberts put a veto on all emigration from the Liberian Republic, and warned the agents of Messrs. Hyde, Hodge, and Co. off his shores.* Joseph Jenkins Roberts, one of the fathers of Liberia, and one of the authors of its Independence, died on February 25, 1874.

George William Gordon, the Leader of the Opposition to Colonel Eyre's Government in Jamaica; Richard Hill, Edward Jordan, Peter Moncrieff, were all of Jamaica, and were eminent statesmen, but they were Africans; these were not 'dull, stupid and indolent,' nor were they 'in mind children.'

Would Mitchell Maxwell Phillip have been appointed Solicitor-General of Trinidad had he been 'dull, stupid and indolent'? Or if he were 'in mind a child'? Small credit would be given to the British Government if it appointed an African to a Government post who was 'dull, stupid and indolent,' or who was 'in mind a child.' Maxwell Phillip was not only a law officer of the Crown, but he was a legislator, and figured as an author, but he was an African. The late Mr. John Jacob Thomas, whom we knew personally, was a grammarian and author. It was his pen that supplied a long-felt want of those who were ignorant of the French Creole *patois*. The 'Creole Grammar,' by John Jacob Thomas, was published not many years ago.

When we referred to the statesmen of Liberia, we might have mentioned the illustrious, the immortal Hilary Tange,

* See Proclamation of February 26, 1853.

late Secretary of State of the Liberian Republic. He was one of the founders of Liberian Independence, and takes rank with Joseph Jenkins Roberts, James Spriggs Payne, A. W. Gardner (who was dubbed Knight of the Grand Cross of the Royal Order of Isabel the Catholic by the late King Alfonso XII. of Spain), and the present President or Liberia, J. Hilary R. W. Johnson. Another great Liberian is Professor Edward W. Blyden, M.A., D.D., LL.D., who figured as a Member of more than one Liberian Government. He is certainly not 'dull, stupid and indolent.' And he is a full-blooded African.

Though thirty years have not elapsed since the Africo-Americans were given their freedom, they have produced such men as E. D. Bassett, J. U. Langston, J. E. W. Thompson, who were formerly United States Ministers to Hayti. Would such men, were they 'dull, stupid and indolent,' or 'in mind children,' have been appointed Ministers to Hayti, to represent a great Republic like that of the United States? Would the United States Government have appointed Frederick Douglass, the present Minister of Hayti. to that post were he 'dull, stupid and indolent'? The American Government appointed these four men to the American Ministership of Hayti because they believed they were capable men. But these are not the only men who have come forward with Africo-American Emancipation. Pinchback, Lieutenant-Governor of Louisiana ; B. K. Bruce, of Mississippi ; and R. B. Elliott, formerly Members of Congress ; the Right Reverend H. M. Turner, D.D., LL.D., of Atlanta, Georgia, Bishop of the Africo-American Methodist Church, who was in 1876 appointed Vice-President of the American Colonization Society ; the Right Reverend Petre, Bishop of the Africo-American Methodist Episcopal Church, are all prominent men who have come to the front since the Emancipation. These ornaments of the African-

Ethiopian Race are not 'dull, stupid, and indolent,' nor 'in mind children.' They are 'affectionate,' but not 'frivolous and mischievous,' nor are those whom we have previously enumerated 'frivolous and mischievous.' Because he could not bear the hardships of slavery, and because his brethren in Canada were enjoying the boon of freedom under the Union Jack, young Hawkins fled from the slaveholding South, and marched to Canada. The Right Reverend gentleman, Bishop Walter Hawkins, of the Africo-British Methodist Episcopal Church in Canada, who escaped from slavery, is a full-blooded African. He has now reached the age of the psalmist—the hearty and hale old age of fourscore. There are twenty thousand Africans in Canada belonging to his diocese. He is a genial old man, and pleasant-faced.

The race which can produce the Honourable Sir William Conrad Reeves, Knt., Chief Justice of the Colony of Barbadoes; His Worship Hendrik Vroom, District Commissioner of Secondee, in the Gold Coast; His Worship Augustus William Thompson, District Commissioner of the Gold Coast; and His Worship D. B. Yorke, also District Commissioner in the same Colony; the Honourable J. R. Maxwell, M.A., B.C.L., Chief Magistrate of the Gambia; His Worship L. P. Pierre, Magistrate of Arima and Blanchisseuse, in the Colony of Trinidad; with but fifty-three years of British African Emancipation, argues well in favour of the progress the African has made and is making.*

* Mention may also be made of His Honour Francis Smith, Puisne Judge of the Colony of Gold Coast; the Honourable Charles Pike, C.M.G., Colonial Treasurer of the Colony of Gold Coast; J. H. Spayne, Colonial Postmaster-General of Sierra Leone; Roland Cole, Colonial Postmaster-General of Gold Coast; J. C. Parkes, Minister for Native Affairs in the Colony of Sierra Leone; James A. McCarthy, LL.B., Queen's Advocate of the Colony of Sierra Leone; Archdeacon Robbin, the right-hand man and able lieutenant of the white Bishop of

This shows that the African is not 'dull, stupid, and indolent,' nor is he 'in mind a child,' as Laird Clowes would like to make out. If these men were 'dull, stupid, and indolent,' 'in mind children,' 'frivolous and mischievous,' it is not likely that the British Government would have honoured them with their suffrages and patronage; and even if we could suppose that they had degenerated into those weaknesses since they received their respective appointments, we may be sure that they would have been sent about their business by the British Government long since.

Nor have we Africans 'stopped short,' producing as we do still similar men of distinction. That the African is often a property-holder, a clergyman, a lawyer, a dentist, a doctor; that he is often a merchant, an engineer, has medical schools and colleges, law schools and colleges, theological schools and colleges, public and normal schools, colleges of arts and sciences, schools for secondary education, and commercial schools; that he is often a mechanic, and has Reformed, Episcopal, Presbyterian, Methodist, Baptist, and Roman Catholic churches and chapels—all testify that the African is not 'dull, stupid, and indolent,' but is progressive, and, moreover, marching

---

Sierra Leone, the Right Rev. Ernest Graham Ingham, D.D.; Archdeacon Crowther; Dr. Esmon, Senior Assistant-Surgeon of the Colony of Gold Coast; Drs. J. S. Smith and Papafio, Assistant-Surgeons of the Gold Coast Colony; Dr. Wm. Renner, Senior Assistant-Surgeon of Sierra Leone Colony; Dr. Garrett, Assistant Colonial Surgeon of Sierra Leone; Drs. J. Rendell and O. Johnson, Assistant Colonial Surgeons of Lagos; Charles Barnes, Colonial Engineer and Assistant Surveyor of the Gold Coast; O. Morre, a Professor, and the Principal of the Colonial Grammar School of Sierra Leone; the Honourable Samuel Lewis, Syble Boyle and T. J. Sawyer, Members of the Legislative Council of Sierra Leone, and others.

on to claim equality with other races. These are recognised and admitted facts.

But what says Laird Clowes? On page 76 are these words: 'The black stops short, and is dull, stupid, and indolent, as well as frivolous and mischievous, and in mind a child.' This we have sufficiently refuted; but, on page 116 of his 'Black America,' does he contradict himself or confirm his previous statement? He says: 'Educationally the Coloured man' (*i.e.*, the African) 'has undoubtedly made great progress since his Emancipation. In the slavery days ignorance was imposed by law upon the slave.' We take it that as the 'African has undoubtedly made great progress since his Emancipation,' he cannot have 'stopped short,' nor is he 'dull, stupid, and indolent,' especially when we know that 'in the slavery days ignorance was imposed by law upon the slave.' Why should Laird Clowes confuse his readers? why does he not say what he means? Why does he say one thing on one page (76), and, apparently, another thing on another page (116)?

Again, there is another way of showing that we Africans have not 'stopped short,' and are not 'dull, stupid, and indolent.' We argue from the fact that, though the sun of sixty years of Emancipation has not yet set over our heads, we are already permitted to marry our rulers; surely that speaks volumes. Such a thing could not have happened in the slavery days; but it does happen to-day. 'There was a time when such a thing was not heard of. There is a secret behind this fact; we suspect it is the growing appreciation which the white Juliet has for the African Romeo, as he becomes more and more intelligent and educated and refined.' The Romans entertained the greatest antipathy to intermarriage with their British subjects, on account of their inferiority, and their tendency to retrogradation; but Caucasians, and more particularly the leading Caucasian races, *i.e.*, the Saxon and the Gallic, intermarry with Africans who are black—yes, black, it is true, but 'black and comely.' And if proof were required to show that black is as good a colour for humanity as the white, surely the fact that the whites, who are the ruling race, marry their black subjects, proves it, and speaks volumes for the African. The British, moreover, did not produce one single learned man when they were under the Roman rule, from the time of the landing of Julius Cæsar, in the year 55 B.C., up to the year, say, 650 A.D., when England was under the rule of the third Bretwalda, King Ethelbert of Kent—that is, a period covering 705 years. The earliest writer was Gildas of Dumbarton, a Scotchman, but the earliest English writer, Cædmon of Whitby, did not write until several years after Gildas of Dumbarton.

But Africans have been far quicker in taking advantage of civilization than the British were, yet we do not call the British 'dull, stupid, and indolent.'

Speaking under the heading of his so-called 'Ideal Solution,' Laird Clowes (page 199) says : 'One of the most conspicuous characteristics of the Negro is, as I have already had to point out, his childishness. Referring to the Negroes of Africa, Mr. H. M. Stanley, writing in December last (1890) to the *Times*, said : "If one regards these natives as mere brutes, then the same annoyances that their follies and vices inflict are, indeed, intolerable. In order to rule them, and to keep one's life amongst them, it is needful resolutely to regard them as children, who require, indeed, different methods of rule from English or American citizens, but who must be ruled in precisely the same spirit, with the same absence of caprice and anger, the same essential respect to our fellow-men."

'Another recent writer has said of them (the Negroes) : "They are children—children naughty or children good;

pleased or angry; children to be ruled firmly, treated kindly—but always at bottom children."'

With regard to the latter part of Mr. Clowes's quotation, *i.e.*, his quotation of 'Another recent writer' on the childishness of the African, the author of 'Black America' is prudent enough to conceal the identity of this 'Another recent writer,' and consequently we are quite in the dark as to his status, and as to his qualification thus to give an opinion of the Africans. We therefore, as a matter of course, ignore the opinion of this 'Another recent writer,' which is valueless until we can measure the extent of his knowledge and authority. But have we not in the preceding pages sufficiently shown to Laird Clowes, or anyone else, that the African is not childish, if this word refers to the mental ability of the race?

With H. M. Stanley, however, we must deal; and we shall endeavour to show that Stanley's opinion of the Africans counts for very little, and is not to be trusted, because he has a bad record, and is therefore disqualified from speaking authoritatively on the qualities of the race which he has thought fit thus to libel. And we shall show that he has a bad record, as far as the Africans are concerned, in two ways. In the first place, Stanley ill-treated the Africans in Africa : it is the very Africans who were his victims whom he has thought fit maliciously to libel. In the next place, Stanley, with the Emin Pasha Relief Expedition, plunged into the heart of the forest and the desert of Africa with such alacrity and perseverance, not from zealous philanthropy or for scientific purposes, but for political purposes. Stanley was only too evidently actuated by desire for fame, and perhaps for wealth.

The disgraceful dispute about the Rear-guard horrors, which began immediately after Stanley's triumphal entry into Britain, after his being dined and fêted on an extensive scale; after he had received the patronage of Oxford and Cambridge, and the freedom and degrees of their respective Universities; and, in brief, after he had been made much of—fairly took the world by surprise, and certainly scandalized it. When the cannibal stories, and Stanley's other misdeeds, were first bruited about, a loud howl of indignation was raised, not only throughout the length and breadth of the United Kingdom, but also throughout France. Germany echoed it. Russia echoed it; as did Austria, Hungary, and Italy. The greater part of the United States of America were not a whit behindhand, but they also echoed it. The public, and the newspaper press of Britain, loudly denounced Stanley in his capacity of chief of the 'Emin Pasha Relief Expedition,' and said that he was responsible, as such, for, first, the cruelties perpetrated by the commanding officer (Major Barttelot) of his Rear-guard at Yambuya Camp; and, secondly, for neglecting to leave medicine, and sufficient and proper provisions, for the Africans who composed Stanley's Guard.

Mr. Stanley, though he well knew Major Barttelot's character, his nervous irritability and great want of self-control, and his unconquerable hate for the Africans; and though he knew well that he was about to plunge further into the interior of the African Continent with his advance-guard, and expected to be away for five months, did not hesitate to leave the Africans of his rear-guard just as if they were so many brutes, under the care of a man with an ungovernable temper, whose irreconcilable hatred for the natives under his command was notorious. Major Barttelot was left at Yambuya with unlimited powers by Stanley, while the latter plunged into the interior and absented himself for ten months. We may well imagine how terrible must have been the sufferings of the Africans for those ten long months under the tyrannical and despotic Major

Barttelot. It is, however, best to let the European speak of his fellow-Europeans; the Britisher, of his British fellow-countrymen; the officer, of his brother officers. And no man is better qualified to speak of Major Barttelot and his atrocities, or of Stanley's 'Emin Pasha Relief Expedition,' and its doings, than Lieutenant Troup, one of the chief officers of that Expedition. And this is what he says of Barttelot as well as of Stanley: 'I admit that certain things were done which I would not have done; but it must be remembered that Major Barttelot was quick-tempered and nervous, and had no control over himself. He was unquestionably the wrong man to place in control of the natives, no matter how large a force there might be. The Major hated the natives, and made no effort to conceal his dislike for them. He had never had any experience in the jungle, and really did not know how to manage the natives even if he had had the will. Mr. Stanley knew intimately just what kind of a man Major Barttelot was; and if there was a blunder, Stanley was entirely responsible for having placed such a man in control of the Rear-guard.' This is what every sensible man recognises. On another occasion, Lieutenant Troup, speaking to an interviewer at Boston, Massachusetts, U. S. America, thus expressed himself: 'I admit Major Barttelot's cruelty. I am returning to England to-morrow. If Mr. Stanley is going to bring an action against Major Barttelot's brother, and against the surviving officers of the expedition, I suppose I will be included. That will suit me immensely; for then I will have a chance to cross-examine. I am not afraid to have my record laid bare by the most searching investigation, and Mr. Stanley must understand that he is the accuser, not I. I said nothing about the disasters to the rear-column until he drove me to the wall, and forced me to defend my reputation from the false and unjust accusations he made; but if Mr. Stanley thought he could intimidate me he made a great mistake. I did not say a word against Mr. Stanley or Major Barttelot until somebody first made charges; and I say again that I believe Mr. Stanley was primarily responsible for the fate of the poor fellows (*i.e.*, the poor Africans) at Yambuya Camp: first, on account of his (Stanley's) poor judgment in the selection of a commanding officer; and, second, by his neglecting to provide sufficient food and supplies in case of emergency. This emergency was Mr. Stanley's delay in returning to Yambuya Camp. He promised to return in five months, and made provision for only five months. This was almost criminal negligence.' We think it was 'criminal negligence' when Stanley neglected 'to leave proper provision for the Black men.' It was also 'criminal negligence,' on the part of Stanley to fail in providing medicines, so that ' when,' to quote Lieutenant Troup, 'the Blacks were ill there was no medicine, thanks to Stanley,' as well as when 'no medicine was sent from the camp' of the advance-guard to the Africans. To use again the language of Lieutenant Troup, 'when ten months had passed, and Stanley had not returned, the people (*i.e.*, the Africans), whom he had left behind with barely food enough for five months, were in a starving condition.'

Britishers were not alone in their denunciation of Stanley for his direct and indirect ill-treatment of the Africans. The French *Journal des Débats* of November 12, 1890, commenting upon the Rear-guard scandals, says: 'It is necessary in the dilemma to decide whether Major Barttelot and Mr. Jameson were guilty of the cruelties imputed to them—and everyone is free to excuse the sorry courage of Mr. Stanley in saying so—or whether they were not guilty. In the latter case, there is no possible allowance to be made for Mr. Stanley, and his charges constitute a calumny, the responsibility of which he bears, and which becomes an act more perverse than man has ever committed.' Indeed, it is a matter of common knowledge, that such was the indignation felt in France, as in Russia, against Stanley, because of his ill-treatment of the Africans, that Frenchmen and Russians of all shades of opinion unanimously said that they, from the moment it was first bruited about that Stanley was on the point of plunging into the heart of that Land of Mystery—Africa— for exploring and philanthropic purposes, and in quest and relief of Emin Pasha (who wished neither to be sought after nor relieved, for he was safe and sound), suspected that he (Stanley) was bent on a politico-filibustering and trading mission. Stanley's philanthropy in the cause of humanity was scouted to the winds and derided, so much so that, when an influential and largely attended meeting was held at the Mansion House, about December, 1890, to protest against the persecution of the Jews in Russia, and to send a memorial to the Russian Emperor, respectfully and humbly requesting him to repeal, or otherwise use his influence to repeal, the new and severe laws operating against the Czar's Hebrew subjects, whereby the observers of the Law of Moses were plunged into the greatest distress, the Russians indignantly, but justly, declared that Britishers would be more profitably occupied if they gave their due attention to removing the stain cast upon their reputation by the scandals originating from the doings, or rather the misdoings, of Stanley and his piratical Rearguard column in Central Africa. And the semi-official journal, the *Novoye Vremya*, it is on record, furiously but truly said: 'This concern for the Jews on the part of the English, who have impoverished fertile Hindostan and Egypt, who are poisoning the population of China with opium, who have annihilated the native population of

Australia (*i.e.*, the Australian Africans) just as if they were vermin, and who now, under the pretext of putting an end to the slave-trade, are exterminating in the most savage manner numerous tribes of Africa, is extremely touching. Who is not aware of the value of English philanthropy!'

This is how Stanley in the first place ill-treated the Africans. But it is for us to show that, in the next place, Stanley had otherwise a bad record when he marched into Africa for political and mercenary ends, though giving out that he was bent on African exploration in the interests of humanity. Let his own countryman, and one of Stanley's right-hand men in the Stanley politico-filibustering expedition into Africa, speak. Lieutenant Troup thus disburdens himself: 'Mr. Stanley is a great explorer, but he went into this Emin Pasha Relief Expedition for fame, and what he could get out of it. He has no more philanthropy than my boot. I will go further, and say that the expedition was in the nature of a speculation, and not a philanthropic relief movement. The capitalists backing it were after the ivory which Emin Pasha was supposed to have collected. The officers (including Lieutenant Troup) of the Expedition were promised certain shares in the expected big supply of ivory as a reward for their services. The release of Emin Pasha was a secondary consideration entirely. Emin Pasha did not wish to be released. He had been up there ten or twelve years, and held his own to, at any rate, his own satisfaction.

'These facts explain the entire situation; and the Expedition must necessarily lose some of the glamour which surrounds it, when it is known that greed for fame and riches, instead of humanity, prompted the movement.'

This statement, coming as it does from one of Stanley's chief officers, cannot fail to carry the greatest weight, and helps to show up the sort of man that Henry M. Stanley is. Many of the individual States composing the American Union positively refused to see and hear Stanley when that gentleman proposed journeying on a lecturing tour in those States. Texas especially was loud and active in its denunciation of him, refused to hear his lectures, and challenged Mr. Stanley to cleanse his reputation of its stain.

Germany not only condemned Stanley for his misdeeds in Africa, and gave out that he went on a politico-filibustering and mercenary mission, but took care to add that Emin Pasha did not wish to be rescued, because he had been for years safe and secure in his Province of Equatoria.

Dr. Carl Peters, a German, and one of the Pasha's right-hand men in Equatoria, writing in the *Contemporary Review* for November, 1890, says : 'What I am about to publish now was told me at Upwapwa by Emin Pasha himself, with the understanding that I should be permitted to publish it. According to what Emin told me, the first time Stanley arrived at the Mwata Nzige he was in an almost ruined condition. When Stanley arrived at the Mwata Nzige for the second time, he at once announced to the Pasha that he had with him orders from the Khedive to evacuate the Equatorial province. The Khedive, he said, wished to give up the whole Soudan, and could not allow any longer that one of his Governors should maintain himself on the Upper Nile. This communication, made by Stanley, cannot fail to appear strange—the more so that it was in direct opposition to the interests of civilization and European politics, the only motives which had ostensibly led to Stanley's expedition. Stanley, by making himself the carrier of a message, doing away with all the work of civilization on the Upper Nile, was working for barbarism in general, and for Mahdism in particular. If it was intended to open up Central Africa to European civilization, the first thing to do was to strengthen Emin's position in Equatoria, not to abolish it. What interest could Europe, and especially England, have in removing this last stronghold of a higher civilization? The Emin Pasha Relief Expedition had been organized in Europe, not so much in order to save the person of Emin as in order to strengthen the bearer of European civilization and culture and political influence on the Upper Nile. I must say that in this proposition as made to Emin there is something quite unintelligible; nor can I help thinking that it was made for the purpose only of rendering Emin Pasha more willing to accept the propositions to be made afterwards.'

Continuing, Carl Peters says the Pasha told him that: 'After several days, while I was considering Stanley's first proposition, he surprised me with a second one. It was just the reverse of the first one, but that did not prevent Stanley from bringing along both of them in his pocket.'

'In the name of the King of the Belgians Stanley requested Emin not to obey the Khedive's orders, not to evacuate Equatoria, but to hoist there the flag of the Congo Free State. If he would do so, the King would make him his Governor-General for that district, and would grant him £1,000 per month for the expenses of the administration of the district. As to Emin's personal interest, he was asked to name his figure, and was told in advance that it would be granted. But Stanley, said Emin, very soon afterwards told him that he did not advise him to accept that proposition. The Congo Free State, he said, was in a bad state of confusion, and Emin could plainly see how he (Stanley) had been treated by the King of the Belgians. It was only several days later that Stanley came out with his real plan, the third proposition, which again stood in direct opposition to the two former ones. In the name of the British East African Company he proposed to Emin to go round the Victoria Nyanza to its north-east corner, to Kavirondo. There Emin was to be established on an island, and left to fortify his position. Stanley would then hurry for the coast, and go to Mombasa to raise ammunition and troops for Emin. The British East African Company was to take the whole army of Emin into its service, every man with the rank and pay he possessed while under Egyptian rule. Emin Pasha was to be Governor under the Company of all lands in the Upper Nile. As for his salary, that was to be settled by him with the Company. Stanley brought forward a contract with that Company, stamped and sealed in London, and only needing Emin's signature to make it perfect. Finally £3,000 was agreed upon as the salary. The troops which Stanley was to bring back from Mombasa were to restore the Christians to Uganda under the leadership of Emin, fight Unyoro, and then reoccupy Emin's old province, all this to be achieved in the name of the British East African Company. Stanley, after having brought up these auxiliary troops for Emin, was then to withdraw and go off to England. Of course, the pliability of Stanley, who was himself the bearer of three messages or propositions whereof any one, by its nature, excluded the possibility of even considering the other two, was somewhat confusing; but however that might be, Emin Pasha, with a heavy heart and under the force of circumstances, made up his mind to accept the third offer. Then a part of his people, who would not quit their homes on the Nile, which had become dear to them, mutinied, and refused to proceed. Stanley and Emin Pasha, however, left the district and advanced on the west side of the lake. When camping at Busagala, west-south-west of Uganda, they received the messengers of the Christian King Mwanga, imploring their help against the Arab party. The chief of this Uganda mission was a certain Marco, who, later, spent two months in my camp and in my immediate neighbourhood, and to whom I owe several details regarding Stanley's departure. Stanley refused to help the Christians, remarking "that he was too weak for such an undertaking." It was then,' the learned Doctor proceeded, 'that Emin Pasha offered to go to Uganda alone with his own people, if Stanley would permit it. But Stanley had Emin Pasha put under watch, and threatened to proceed against him by force should he attempt to carry out that idea.

'As for Stanley, having reached the south end of the Victoria Nyanza, at Usumbiro, he could not make up his mind to carry out the promise held out to Emin, viz., to bring him around the east coast of the lake to Kavirondo, and establish him there as agreed. He (Stanley) suddenly declared himself unable to do so without an express order of the Queen of England. Emin understood then that he had been taken out of his own country under pretences or promises not to be realized afterwards. He had lost what he possessed, and now was forced, against his inclination, to accompany Stanley to the coast. As a matter of course, cordial relations could not exist between the two parties under such circumstances.

'I shall not personally take part against Stanley, but in the interest of truth I must add, that what I heard about Stanley's personal behaviour, not from Emin, but from the missionaries on the Nyanza, could not diminish the naturally bad feeling between the two parties. One day two Catholic missionaries came from Ukumbi to Usumbiro to pay their respects to Emin. They found the whole party at dinner, Stanley at the head of the table, *with a half-bottle of wine, and served in European fashion*, but *all others at the same table without wine, and living on " Negro" fare.* Such a glimpse of the social intercourse among the members of the expedition speaks volumes, and it would be perfectly useless for me to add a single word. I am not at all surprised that

Stanley should speak contemptuously of Emin Pasha. The two men were too different to understand one another. I believe Stanley lacks the organ necessary to appreciate a delicate and sensitive character like that of Emin Pasha, just as a man with a bad cold is unable to enjoy the beauty of a field of roses, but the beauty exists nevertheless. To me (Carl Peters) Emin Pasha appears as a model in the faithful performance of duty, and in the seriousness of his scientific labours and his moral tact.

'The fact of his not caring to go to Europe,' concludes the worthy Doctor, 'to be feasted and honoured like others, is proof enough of genuine modesty and candour of principle, as is also the fact that he refrained from taking £3,000 to enter the British service, not, however, mainly from national feelings, for he had been willing to take service with the British, but because his innermost feelings had been hurt by Stanley's behaviour towards him.'

Now, the man who has cruelly ill-treated the Africans, both indirectly and directly, not only by his appointment of Major Barttelot in command over them at Yambuya Camp, with extraordinary and unlimited powers for ten months, well knowing the Major's brutality and bad temper, and his unconquerable hate for the Africans; but also by leaving the blacks without a sufficiency of provisions for five months, and without any at all for another five months, and still more by leaving no medicine for the Africans in case of sickness for ten months, and even by cruelly and shamefully ill-treating the Africans, shooting them down (for he did do that) wholesale, for little or no fault whatever, just as if they were 'mere brutes'—this man ventures to come forward with daring defamatory statements on his lips, and to say that the Africans are 'mere brutes,' and that 'it is needful resolutely to regard them as children.' Because Stanley regarded these African natives as 'mere brutes' and as 'children,' he ill-treated them, permitted Major Barttelot to shoot them as well as flog them without mercy; because Stanley regarded the Africans as 'mere brutes' and as 'children,' he left them with an insufficiency of provisions for five months, and without any at all for another five months; because Stanley regarded these same Africans as 'mere brutes' and as 'children,' he left them to perish of disease for ten months without medicine; because Stanley regarded the blacks as 'mere brutes' and as 'children,' he massacred them by reason of the 'annoyances' they brought on him through 'their follies and vices.'

We have already said that Stanley was unanimously denounced by British, French, Russian, and German public opinion, and by the newspaper press, and to a great extent also by the voice of the American people, and we have, moreover, given the opinions of Troup and Peters, as well as those of Emin Pasha. Stanley has not yet thought fit to demand a trial of his conduct when in 'Darkest Africa,' as every honourable man in his position would have done. We therefore say—and the reader, we are sanguine, will bear us out—that it does not lie with Stanley to express any opinion of the Natives whom he ill-treated, and even massacred, and towards whom he was guilty of criminal negligence. We should think a second time, if we were Mr. Clowes, before we borrowed Stanley's expressed opinion of the Africans, after we had heard the scandals associated with Stanley's name and with the doings of his Rear-guard in Central Africa. We should hesitate the more seeing that the man, after being repeatedly challenged and invited to institute what Stanley, as plaintiff, would call libel proceedings against eminent and philanthropic Britishers and the British press, has not thought fit to redeem his sullied reputation from the foul stigma cast upon it. If Stanley wants to speak with authority on the qualities of the Africans in Africa, he must come with clean hands, and not with a bad record, such as we have described, and add his insults to the Africans whom he has injured.

What a striking contrast Stanley presents to Chinese Gordon, the British hero who died at Khartoum! Stanley went to Africa, as Troup says, for fame, riches, and the acquisition of ivory. The simple and gentle-minded Gordon went to Africa, not for fame, because he was very modest and indifferent to praise or reward, but in the interest of humanity; not for riches and ivory, for it is a matter of ommon knowledge that Chinese Gordon had the greatest contempt for money and wealth, but to give freedom to his African fellow-men, and to check slavery and the slave trade. Stanley destroyed as many Africans as possible, and robbed the African chieftains and their clansmen; but the sympathetic Chinese Gordon protected as many Africans as he possibly could, and spared as many lives as circumstances permitted, and did not rob the Soudanese. Stanley returned to Europe and to Britain a very wealthy man, and was received at first in triumph and with open arms, though afterwards he was shown the cold shoulder by many; but Chinese Gordon remained in Africa and the Soudan, and when the Mahommedan soldiers carried the capital of the Egyptian Soudan by assault at the point of the spear, Chinese Gordon, the hero, earned the martyr's crown by perishing among the people whom his philanthrophy had freed in Khartoum; and there he, the white man, the European and the Britisher, found a common grave with the black man, the African and the Soudanese, revered by all men in his death. Institutions and memorials were raised, and statues erected in his honour. Chinese Gordon is kindly remembered by his nation, but that same nation looks suspiciously on Stanley, whose reputation is, for many of his fellow-Britishers, under a cloud.

Having sufficiently confronted Stanley, and shown up what the man and his opinion are worth, we now pass on to foes worthier of our steel.

We must refer the reader to page 168 of 'Black America,' in which Laird Clowes summarizes an article Mr. Cone contributed to *Belford's Magazine* for September, 1889, a part of which summary runs thus: 'The cases of Hayti and Jamaica are cited to prove that the black man, when raised by a higher race to a level of life which he was unable of himself to attain, has never shown any ability to maintain himself there; he lacks the brain fibre, the brain power, which is necessary to do so, and left to himself he retrogrades, reverts.' We are of opinion that greater nonsense could not have been uttered than these statements that we have reproduced. What authority has either Mr. Cone or Mr. Clowes for speaking on the condition of the Haytians and Jamaicans? Has either Cone or Clowes lived in Hayti or Jamaica, or do they study the Haytians and Jamaicans? The fact that Frenchmen once ruled the Haytians and held them in ignominous bondage does not prove that the French belong to a 'higher race' than our Haytian cousins. And the fact that the British rule the Jamaican Africans, and once held them in servile thraldom, does not prove that the British belong to a 'higher race' than the Africans in Jamaica. If anyone can feel himself justified in saying these things, then we ask him this: Since the Romans ruled the Britons, and sold them as slaves in the markets of Rome, did these Romans belong to a 'higher race' than the Britons? And since the Angles, Jutes, and Sovereign tribes of Saxons ruled the Britons, did these former belong to a 'higher race' than the latter? And since the Northmen and Normans ruled the Anglo-Saxons, did the former belong to a 'higher race' than the latter? And since the German Franks subdued the Gauls, did the former belong to a 'higher race' than the latter? And since the Visigoths, or West Goths, subdued and ruled the Iberians, did the former on that account belong to a 'higher race' than the latter? And since the Moors (*i.e.* the descendants of Asiatics and Africans) subjugated and ruled Spain for several centuries, did the former belong to a 'higher race' than the Spaniards? And since the Moors subdued the Lusitanians and ruled them, did the former on that account belong to a 'higher race' than the latter? And since the Visigoths ruled Portugal, did the former on that account belong to a 'higher race' than the Lusitanians?

No man is justified in saying that the white man belongs to a 'higher race' than the black because accident or fortune makes him the temporary ruler of the latter. The Jamaican African has made wonderful progress in the arts of civilization since Emancipation, all things being duly considered. We have to bear in mind that a master, during the period of slavery, was forbidden by law, by custom and by public opinion, to educate his slave. And we should also remember that the sun of two-thirds of a century of freedom has not yet set over the heads of the Jamaican Africans.

But Sir Henry Arthur Blake, the British Governor of Jamaica, shall deal with this question, and tell us whether the Jamaican African 'has never shown any ability to maintain himself' in a high level of life, and whether the lacks the brain-fibre, the brain-power.

The Jamaican Governor surely ought to know the character of the people over whom he is sent to rule. And we undoubtedly prefer to accept his opinion of the Jamaican Africans rather than that of Mr. Cone or that of Mr. Clowes. Writing in the *North American Review* for February, 1891, on the condition and characteristics of the Jamaican Africans, amongst other interesting facts he says : ' A thoughtless estimate of these people (*i.e.*, the Jamaican

Africans) has been generally accepted. It may be summed up in the statement that they are densely ignorant, unspeakably lazy, and incapable of improvement. My experience for the past twelve months has shown me that this estimate is not true. During that time I have visited every portion of Jamaica, and spoken to large numbers of the people. I have met the peasant proprietors in the mountain valleys, where, with the exception of the clergyman and the doctor, the face of a white man is not often seen. I have met them in the lowland plains of the seaboard, and I am bound to say that I have met among them men equal in intelligence, shrewdness, and dignity of mind to men of their class in the United Kingdom. Nor is the estimate of laziness a true one. Both men and women work with the full average of diligence.

'The people who in times gone by had worked as slaves on the estates were gradually extending into the higher grounds of the interior, acquiring property, reclaiming and planting, with all the diligence that is the offspring of ownership.' To add words to what Sir Henry Blake has thus stated is unnecessary. We therefore pass on to the Haytians.

The Haytians were not taught by the French, for ignorance was imposed by French law upon the slave; and every master was forbidden by law, custom, and public opinion to educate his slave. The Haytians received their lessons in the arts of government from Toussaint the Great, who was their king in everything—and in every way but in name he was what is called an 'uncrowned king.' Toussaint the Great was a born Governor as he was a born Commander; his genius and governing qualities were innate: he taught his able lieutenants, Dessalines and Christophe, and others, how to govern, and encouraged literature and the fine arts. When Toussaint the Great, thanks to the perfidious French, disappeared from his

Fatherland, Dessalines, and then Christophe, followed in the wake of the Liberator of San Domingo.

It cannot be correctly said that the Haytian, because he has been left to himself, has 'retrograded' or 'reverted,' as we shall endeavour to show. We are of opinion that, if a State be misgoverned, it necessarily yields a decreasing revenue, and its commerce remains stagnant, if it does not decline. If a State does not yield a reasonable yearly income, then it may be fairly taken for granted that the Government which pilots the destinies of that State is an incapable one. The British Empire is the first in the world to-day because its great wealth, derived from its commerce and exports, is unsurpassed. The richness of the British Empire, then, is a sure sign that it is well governed. If the British Empire were misgoverned, where would its commerce be? But the reverse is the case with it, as may be seen in the fact that its commerce is the first in the world, and more capital can be found put into it than is the case in any other Empire.

As the commerce of the British Empire, then, testifies that the Empire is being properly governed, and is progressing, we shall argue fairly if we show that Hayti is, as evidenced by her commerce, also being properly governed, and shows signs of progress. But that Hayti's progress may be seen to greater advantage, we shall compare the monetary value of her commercial transactions, and her revenue, with those of other States which have an equal or a larger population than that of Hayti. Hayti, with a population of 550,000 Africans, had in 1887-88 a revenue, *customs only*, of the value of £1,342,604. Its imports were returned at £964,382, and its exports were valued at £1,485,023. The Republic of Bolivia, with 2,300,000 inhabitants, had its public revenue valued at £753,285 in 1887-88; that is, an amount nearly twice less than that of the revenue of Hayti. Hayti's exports and imports were greater than those of the Transvaal Republic, which contains 800,000 inhabitants. The Republic of Guatemala, with 1,427,116 inhabitants, had in 1889 a revenue valued at £769,919, with £1,113,842 as total exports, and £839,934 as value of total imports for 1888; that is, less than the revenue, imports, and exports of the Haytians.

The Republic of Costa Rica had not a greater revenue in 1889-90 than £612,526, that is, an amount more than twice less than that of the Haytians, while her total imports in 1889-90, amounting to £900,915, and her total exports in 1889-90, which did not exceed £995,051, were also both less than the proceeds of Hayti's imports and exports. The Republic of Honduras in 1888-89 had her revenue valued at only £431,000; that is, more than three times less than that of the Haytian Republic.

The Haytian Republic's revenue exceeded that of the Republic of Nicaragua, which had but £635,690 in 1887-88 as public revenue, while her imports in 1886-87 amounted to £587,146, and her exports were valued at £578,315 in 1886-87, but they were considerably less than those of Hayti in the corresponding period. San Salvador, with a population of 651,130, that is, a Republic having over 100,000 inhabitants more than the Republic of Hayti contains, had her exports for 1889 valued at £840,561, and her imports at £427,563, both considerably less than those of Hayti, while the public revenue yielded but £608,885; that is, more than twice less than that of Hayti. The Republic of Ecuador, with 1,000,000 inhabitants, received only £607,152 as her public revenue for 1890. The imports and exports of Madagascar, which is under a French protectorate, with an estimated population of 4,000,000, did not realize more than £162,071 and £164,771 respectively in 1888; that is, they were considerably less than those of Hayti, with only 550,000 inhabitants. The French possessions of Annam and Tongking, with 15,000,000 inhabitants, had their joint revenue estimated at only £692,400 in 1888, while the imports in 1889 were valued at £872,400 and the exports at £674,400; that is to say, that they were considerably less than those of the Haytians. Hayti's revenue exports and imports exceeded and exceed those of French Cochin-China, she having a population of 1,700,000, while they also exceed those of French Cambodia, with 1,500,000 people. Palestine, under Turkish rule and pilotage, with 620,000 inhabitants, had her imports valued at £232,000, and her exports at £271,461, in 1889, the Holy Land consequently being left far behind by Hayti in the race of progress and wealth and commerce. Nepaul, with 2,000,000 Nepaulese, follows the leadership of the Haytians, for her revenue did not amount to more than £1,000,000 in 1885.

The Sultanate of Oman, with 1,600,000 demoralized Asiatics, had her imports in 1889-90 valued at £305,000 only, while the value of her exports did not reach a higher figure than £243,000; her annual revenue not exceeding £37,500, the Asiatic thus yielding the palm in business capabilities to the Haytian.

Under native rule, Hayti amasses a greater revenue than does the Colony of the Straits Settlements, with a population of over 600,000 under the British rule.

The imports and exports of Tripoli, under the Sultan of Turkey, with a population of 1,010,000, did not yield more than £282,100 and £323,000 respectively in 1889.

The Asiatic Kingdom of Corea, with 10,518,937 inhabitants, who own allegiance to his Corean Majesty, Li Ying Kum, did not export more than £217,149, and imported only £597,005 worth of goods in 1888.*

Europeans have been four centuries in the Gold Coast,

---

* For confirmation of these statistics, if necessary, 'Whitaker's Almanac' for 1891 should be consulted.

four centuries in the Gambia, one century in Sierra Leone, and more than half a century in Lagos, yet Gold Coast, Lagos, Sierra Leone, and Gambia, with a grand total of 1,616,000 inhabitants, under British rule, altogether yield less revenue and exports than Hayti does under native rule; and the imports of Hayti also exceed those of the Gold Coast, Lagos, and Gambia put together. The amount of Hayti's yearly imports and revenue is far in excess of the amount of the revenue, exports, and imports realized by Montenegro, Luxemburg, Monaco, Liechtenstein, San Marino, and Andorra together. Hayti's exports, revenue and imports are not far behind those of the Venezuelan Republic in extent, while they are nearly equal to those of the Kingdom of Servia.

Haytian imports and exports for the year 1889 were returned at £1,250,000 and £2,500,000, and those for 1890 amounted to £4,062,500 and £3,125,000 respectively, while the customs-revenue received during the year (1890) amounted to £1,791,666.*

Hayti, then, has undoubtedly made great progress, as her exports, revenue, and imports—the two former more so—greatly exceed those of twenty different States with about an equal number, or, to speak more correctly, with a greater number, of inhabitants than Hayti has, some of these States being under the government of men who glory and rejoice in the fact that they are of European descent. Hayti has *not* retrograded nor reverted. When the Haytian people were beginning to undertake the government of their State, they had to engage to pay over to the French the handsome sum of 90,000,000 francs by way of compensation for

* See page 5, Annex A, and page 1, No. 902, of the Report for the year 1890 on the Trade and Commerce of Hayti, by Acting British Consul-General Arthur Tweedy to the Marquis of Salisbury, May, 1891.

the losses supposed to have been incurred by the French colonists during the great Haytian struggles for Independence; and this, of course, had the effect of crippling the progress of Hayti. But, nothing daunted, Hayti emerged from her fetters in a few years, and is now free, and occupies no mean place in the ranks of civilized and independent nations in the way of wealth and general progress.

There are Faculties of Law and Medicine, Colleges, a Military Academy, 600 Schools,* and what not in Hayti. Of the long line of poets and historians Toussaint-L'Ouverture le Grand and J. Jacques Dessalines's Fatherland boasts, the following are a few: Demesvor Delorme, Fénélon Duplesis, Paul Lochard, Alfred Williams, Ducas-Hippolyte, Tertulian Guilband, Battier, Emmanuel Edouard, Jules Auguste, Arthur Bowler, Thomas Madion, B. Ardouin, Saint-Rémy, J. J. Chaney, Thalès Manigat, Emile Deslandes, Chenet *père*, Oswald Durand, Arnold Laroche, while Joseph Arelim, Louis Joseph Jauvier, Cauvin *père*, François and Guillaume Manigat, A. Firmin, Dalbewar Jean Joseph, Nemours Pierre Louis, Apollon, Stewart, Montasse, Saladin Lamour, Nelson Desroches, Léger and Luxembourg Cauvin, Jacques Nicolas Léyer, E. and A. Desert, and others, too numerous to mention, distinguished in the arts and sciences, literature and social matters, are the pride of Hayti and the Ethiopian race. The minerals gold, silver, tin, iron, copper, with timber, are found in abundance. The Haytian grows sugar, cocoa, coffee, cotton, tobacco,

* Free or Assisted Education has existed in Hayti, a country not a hundred years old, from the year 1860, during General Geffrard's residency; and yet Britain, a country as old as the flood, is not able to boast of *free education*, in the strict sense of the word. Education in Liberia, as in Hayti, is compulsory.

and he has honey, wax, gums, hides, logwood, and mahogany—all testifying that Hayti is not 'retrograding' nor 'reverting.' Manifestly, then, the Haytian is not childish, nor inferior to the Caucasian in any way.

Mr. Laird Clowes, not believing what he has said on the score of African childishness, perorates with the following sentences, 'And everyone who knows thoroughly the African, either in Africa or in America, can have no other estimate of his character.'

We say that the Island of Jamaica belongs to the American Continent, and Sir Henry Arthur Blake, who knows the Jamaican African 'thoroughly,' eulogizes the Africans, as we had occasion in preceding pages to show. We should like it, however, to be understood that in quoting Sir Henry Blake we quote him merely as a private individual, for we do not look up to Sir Henry with any admiration as an administrator. But we prefer Sir Henry A. Blake's opinion of the Africans to those of Stanley, Clowes, Cone, or any other of their following. The British Governor of Jamaica, however, does not stand alone in his praiseworthy and appropriate eulogy of the Africans. Mr. Charles Foster Smith, of Vanderbilt University, who, unlike Clowes, *lives* in America, and therefore can speak with unqualified authority of the qualities of the Africo-Americans, contributes a letter, on the 'Negro in Nashville,' to the *Century* illustrated monthly magazine for May, 1891, in which he says: 'I have long believed that of all places in the South the Negro has had in Nashville, Tennessee, the fullest opportunity to show what he could make of himself, has there been more nearly than elsewhere accorded all that the law accords him. For some time, therefore, I have watched pretty closely his progress, and now offer some of the results of my observation, so far as I can, without advancing any theory or pleading any cause.

'It has doubtless been very fortunate for the Negroes in Nashville that they have been in a decided minority, so that they have given less attention to politics than they might otherwise have done. Nashville is a city of schools and colleges and churches, of considerable culture, decided liberality of thought, a thriving place where honest men can make a living and more, where the people like to own their homes, and make themselves comfortable in them. It is a good place, therefore, for the Negro to learn by contact.

'The city superintendent of public schools says that the Negroes show even more eagerness to get an education than the whites, and he claims that no discrimination is made against them in the appointments of their schools, which are now taught exclusively by Negro teachers, thirty-six in number. To the credit of these teachers, he mentions that, at the last examination for teachers, the highest marks were made by two Negro applicants. Besides their public schools, there are three Negro colleges in Nashville—Fisk, Central Tennessee, and Roger Williams. Two decades ago the two older of these institutions were little more than primary schools, most of the pupils just beginning to read, some in the Fifth Reader, none beyond cube root in arithmetic. In 1888 the college department of Fisk numbered 42, the normal 46 ; in Central Tennessee college 16, normal (in classes corresponding to Fisk) about 61 ; in Roger Williams college 7, normal (in classes corresponding to those at Fisk) 21 ; total in Fisk (in all departments) 475, in Central Tennessee 541, in Roger Williams 192. All these students were, perhaps, as far advanced as were the furthest twenty years ago. At Central Tennessee there are also regular departments of medicine, dentistry, and law. Though the charge is just that the Negro, at his present stage, needs Latin, Greek, and the so-called liberal studies less than anything else, surely 42 A.B. students out of 475 is not an excessive proportion. The ministry and other professions need already a larger ratio. The greater part of the remainder are simply getting the plain elements that are necessary to any man's or woman's well-being. Besides, these institutions pay considerable attention to industrial training. All boarding pupils are required to devote an hour a day to such forms of labour as may be required of them, and the cleanest school-building I ever saw is Livingstone Hall, of Fisk University, which is kept clean by the pupils. A certain number of young men at Fisk learn printing every year, and others will henceforth learn carpentry and other useful handicrafts; while the young women are taught nursing the sick, and the rules of hygiene, cooking, dressmaking, and plain sewing. The course of industrial training in Central Tennessee College and Roger Williams University is about the same.

'The catalogue of Fisk University informs us where its graduates are, and what they are doing. Of 62 college graduates, 38 (or 61 per cent.) are teachers; 18 (or 13 per cent.) are preachers; of 48 normal graduates, 32 (or 66 per cent.) are teachers; eight of the remainder are wives, leaving only eight (or 17 per cent.) for other occupations. Doubtless the great majority of all that study in any department become teachers at present. Does this education lift up the Negroes as it usually does the rest of humanity? I visited lately, with the city superintendent, a Negro school, the average attendance of which is nearly eight hundred, in "Black Bottom," the very heart of the worst quarter of the city, and I saw there hundreds of Negro children—very many of whom came from environments hostile to all that is good and elevating—with clean faces, for the most part neatly dressed, orderly in behaviour, studious and attentive —in conduct equal to any school I ever saw. A college president, who has an exceedingly frank way of talking of the dark as well as the bright side of the situation, says that of more than four thousand pupils in twenty years he has never heard of one in the penitentiary; and there had never been, so far as known, a case of unchastity among the pupils boarding at the college. Other evidences will be given indirectly below.

'Just here I wish to say that Nashville has been blessed in the character of the Northern men and women who have come to teach in these Negro colleges. They have come in the truest missionary spirit; have patiently submitted to a kind of social ostracism; have endeavoured to cultivate in the Negro only such qualities as make for peace, patience, honesty, and good citizenship. They have "respect unto the recompense of the reward," but do not expect it here. They possess their souls in patience. The good men and women estimate their own trials and sacrifices as less than those of foreign missionaries, while those of their (white) Southern neighbours who appreciate them know how much easier it is to go to China and Japan and Africa, and be considered heroes and heroines, than to do this home-mission work. They are the best friends of the Southern whites, as well as of the Southern Negroes, but only the next generation of us will fully know it.

'But the country knows more about the Negro's education than about his efforts in business and how he lives at home. I have visited the places of business of a large number; *e.g.*, a tailor's shop where from five to eight hands are employed; a shoe shop employing from eight to fifteen men, two of them white; a poultry and egg store, having two branch houses in other towns, and a trade extending into several States, the business amounting to 100,000 dozen eggs per month, and a shipment of five car-loads of poultry per week, requiring seven clerks, two of them white book-keepers; a feed store with a business worth over $1,000 per month; three furniture stores, new and secondhand; a coal and wood yard requiring four waggons; two undertakers' shops; the offices of three doctors, one of whom requires two horses, and though two-thirds of his practice is charity, collected last year $2,600, another a graduate of the Harvard Medical School, and already after three months making a living; grocery stores and butchers' shops; a livery stable; several offices of lawyers and real-estate dealers, to say nothing of hack-drivers, owning from one to several carriages; barbers, and the like. I have heard white business men commend the character of some of them in a manner of which any man might be proud. The trade of most of them is mainly, or very largely, with the whites. They are only a few of the most thriving of the well-to-do Negroes of Nashville; but of course the great majority are still only day labourers. A number of Negroes told me with pardonable pride of their investments in real estate. One had made his first purchase with money saved while in a Government clerkship, and now his income from city property is $100 per month. Most buy, I am told, with the view to building a home. The Negroes realize already that nothing so elevates them in the eyes of the world as property, and the "business" fever among the young is so strong that one of the colleges has found it necessary to have sermons preached against excessive eagerness to make money.

'The Negroes of Nashville have also made a promising beginning in the way of combining for church or benevolent enterprises.

'The only Negro-church publishing house in the world is located here, the building, five stories high, being situated on the public square. It was purchased with the contributions of the children of the African Methodist Episcopal Church. A home for aged and indigent Negroes is the latest enterprise, while a shop for teaching mechanical trades was opened a year or so ago. The number of benevolent church societies is, of course, legion.

'More interesting still were the discoveries I made in the homes of the Negroes. Through the courtesy of a well-educated Negro who works ardently for the welfare of his race, I had the opportunity, in company with a friend, to inspect in one day more than twenty of the better class of homes. The list of representative homes we were to see included more than fifty; but the time was too short. Most were taken by surprise, but willingly showed their houses from cellar to garret. The result may be summed up as follows: The occupant was the owner in every case but one. In most parlours there were pianos, and handsome carpets on the floor, with other furniture to match; indeed, the houses were generally carpeted throughout, while bedrooms, dining-rooms and kitchens were remarkably clean. I noted with pleasure several bath-rooms, and remarked how one thrifty pair had so arranged their handsome base-burner stove that it heated comfortably the whole house of four or five rooms at a cost of only a few cents a day. It was interesting to learn that in most cases where the heads of families were young, they had been educated at one of the Negro colleges in the city; where old, that the children had attended these. Let one example stand for all. A—— is the janitor of one of the banks of the city. By working hard at the bank, while his wife worked and saved at home, he has graduated one son and two daughters at Fisk University, the fourth and last child being now there. His son, at first a teacher, is now in the service of the Pullman Company; one daughter is married, the other is a teacher. His house is comfortably furnished, and his lot extends one hundred feet in a very respectable street in the heart of the city.

'Just two or three remarks at the close. First, I am quite sure that more comfortable and well-kept homes could not be found anywhere among the same number of whites of the same income, and the owners of these homes have the same interest in good government, peace, good morals, the well-being of society, as the better class of whites have. These well-kept homes are not only the best proof of the progress in civilization of the Negro race, but they are also the best security for the welfare of the whites in property and in morals ; and I have never had so much hope for the future of this region as since I learned these things. Granted that these may be the picked few, it is most hopeful that there is a picked few, whose example will inspire others to lift themselves up. Finally, an interesting fact which I have not found place for elsewhere—one of the daily papers of Nashville reports a circulation among the Negroes of more than eighteen hundred copies.'

Even Mr. James Bryce, M.P. for Aberdeen, who is not by any means the African's friend, is compelled to admit that the American Africans 'have not relapsed into sloth and barbarism ;' and he further says: 'The proximity of trading and manufacturing towns draws a number of the Africans into closer relations with the whites, and gives an impulse towards progress to the whole mass.'*

With all these testimonies before us, dispelling the theory that the African is inferior to the Caucasian, and is 'childish,' the statement as made by Laird Clowes, that ' Everyone who knows thoroughly the African Negro, either in Africa or in America, can have no other estimate of his character ;' that is, that he is childish, and therefore inferior to the Caucasian, is but a sorry joke, if it may not be more strongly characterized.

Mr. Bryce's testimony as to the Africans speaks volumes for our people, inasmuch as the Honourable Member for Aberdeen is in the ranks of the opposition to the Africans.

* Bryce's 'American Commonwealth,' Vol. III., Part VI., chap. cxvi., p. 671.

We do not know whether we have said enough in disproof of the saying, that the intellectual capacity of the African is of an inferior order to that of the Caucasian, and we are not sure, therefore, whether we ought to carry on the discussion a little further. We have cited the testimonies of men, white men, competent to judge of the relative position of the black and the white man on the score of intellectuality. We have done more. We have mentioned by name many distinguished Africans. But how many eminent men there have been of our people whose names we, unfortunately, do not even know, because they have been 'unhonoured and unsung' in public print!

We are, however, greatly indebted to Liberian Blyden for telling us, in his 'Christianity, Islam, and the Negro Race,' p. 46, on the authority of Ticknor, who wrote on p. 582, in his 'History of Spanish Literature,' that an African, the 'el Negro Juan Latino' of Cervantes, who was born in Africa, and early in his youth transferred to Spain, rose by his learning to be Professor of Latin and Greek in the school attached to the Catholic Cathedral of Granada, and was the distinguished author of a Latin poem in two books, in the sixteenth century.

Liberian Blyden also tells us that Henry Diaz, the distinguished and celebrated Brazilian African General, is held in the highest estimation by Brazilian Historians.

It is not only the Ancient and Pagan, and the Modern and Christian, worlds which have produced African optimates in camp, cabinet, and church. The Modern Mahommedan world has produced just as many (if not more in point of numbers) Africans of distinction. But there is a difference between the Mahommedan African and the Pagan or Christian African.

The Mahommedan African differs from the Christian and the Pagan African in this much, that whilst the virtues and other great qualities of the Mahommedan African have been not only 'honoured and sung,' but written eulogies have been handed down to posterity, those of the Christian African have been 'unhonoured and unsung' as a general rule; while those of the Pagan African, if they have been 'honoured and sung,' have not been handed down, as a general rule, in written eulogies to posterity.

For the same eminent man and brilliant author, Liberian Blyden, teaches us that 'it is well known that numerous characters have arisen in Africa—Negro Muslims—who have exerted no little influence in the military, political, and ecclesiastical affairs of Islam, not only in Africa but in the lands of their teachers. In the biographies of Ibn Khallikan are frequent notices of distinguished African Mahommedans. Koelle, in his "Polyglotta Africana," gives a graphic account of the proceedings of the great Fodie, whose zeal, enthusiasm, and bravery spread Islam over a large portion of Nigritia.'

He (Dr. Blyden) makes mention of the celebrated Sheikh Omaru Al-Hajj, a native of Futah Toro, who subjugated several mighty chiefs of powerful Pagan tribes lying to the east and south-east of Futah Toro. One of his sons, Ahmadu by name, is now, says Blyden, King of Sego in Bambarra, while another rules over Hamd-Allahi, two of the largest cities in Central Africa.

'Al-Hajj Omaru,' Liberian Blyden again informs us, 'wrote many Arabic works in prose and poetry. His poems are recited and sung in every Mahommedan town and village, from Futlah-town, in Sierra Leone, to Kano. His memory is held in the greatest respect by all native students, and they attribute to him many extraordinary deeds, and see in his successful enterprises, literary and military, proofs of divine genius.'

CHAPTER III.

IMMORALITY.

IN this chapter we propose to treat of 'Immorality.' But if there is a subject less pleasant, and more uninviting to discuss, it surely is the subject of Immorality. The unpleasant duty is not self-imposed, nor does the subject derive its origin from us; and yet we cheerfully and unhesitatingly take up the task which has been forced upon us by the unrivalled libellers of that African race to which we have the honour and pleasure to belong.

We shall, then, deal with Immorality as it exists in the world to-day, and have also a look at the past, and see what are the mischievous effects of which immorality can be traced as the direct or indirect cause.

Immorality prevails everywhere—in Asia and Australasia, as well as among the Africans; and it is just as rampant in America and in Europe. We must, however, in the first place, look at Immorality as it affects the African Race.

Those who are responsible for whatever immorality there is amongst the Africans are the Europeans and Americans, all those Caucasians who engaged in the infamous traffic of slavery and the slave-trade, and who owned slaves. We admit that Immorality exists amongst the Africans; yet we must not be misunderstood as saying that it exists to a greater extent than among Caucasians. Immorality was always in the world, and always will be while men are swayed by sensual passions; and that will probably be as long as there are men upon the earth.

But to return to immorality as it affects the African. That kind of Immorality which we propose to deal with, and which is often laid at the African's door by his enemies, is none other, though it may not be thus designated, than 'Lust.' Of other kinds of immorality, Africans seldom stand accused before the reading public. That kind of immorality, lust, the African is often accused of, and we shall deal with it under the general term 'Immorality,' leaving out the word 'lust' altogether, which, however, the reader will understand as meant, whenever the word 'immorality' is used. We take that step because Immorality is, in our opinion, a less repulsive and a more refined term.

The responsibility, then, for the Immorality which may lurk among the Africans lies at the door of those who once enslaved them and put them into a degrading thraldom.

When the dissipated, giddy, and licentious young, and their seniors, the sensual old men, with the flickering fires of wanton senility, owned the Africans as slaves, full swing was given to their passions, and the female Africans, whom the whites had in their power as bondswomen, dare not raise a word of protest against the ill-usage and the brutal conduct of their masters without courting severe punishment at their hands. Many an African woman was ruined, her life blighted, and her modesty sapped in those days. The African females never were willing victims; but they had to submit to their fate and their shame. That was the baneful example set the slaves by their masters. When the masters were compelled to manumit their slaves, and slavery received its deathblow, the example of shame, the pernicious example of Immorality set them by their late masters, did not in any strength survive with the African freedmen. There were a few, certainly, who allowed themselves to be influenced by the example set them by those who had been their masters. Yet when the facts are carefully considered and noted, by the unbiased mind, that two-thirds of a century have not yet elapsed since freedom was given to the African, it will have to be admitted that the African has contrived to raise his standard of morality to a much higher level than it was at in the old days of slavery.

Whatever individual cases of immorality there may be amongst the Africans, it is certain that the standard of African immorality will compare favourably when brought into comparison with the standard of Caucasian immorality. Indeed, we assert that, with the Caucasian, immorality is the rule and morality is the exception.

Mr. Clowes is not of our opinion, however, and thinks it is the other way; and he quotes the Rev. Dr. Tucker, an American citizen, who thus expresses his views on African immorality: 'In all the country districts the removal of the restraints of slavery, such as they were, has resulted in an open abandonment of every semblance of morality, and the loss almost of the idea of marriage. Why, in one county of Mississippi, there were, during twelve months, 300 marriage licences taken out in the county clerk's office for white people. According to the proportion of population, there should have been, in the same time, 1,200 or more for Negroes. There can be no legal marriage of any sort in Mississippi without a licence. There were actually taken out by coloured people just three! . . . Soon after the war the Legislature passed an Act legalizing the union of all who were then living together—marrying them whether they wished it or not; and for years afterwards the courts were crowded with applications for divorce from coloured people, which mostly had to be granted, since there was ample cause for divorce under either the Divine or the statute law. I know of whole neighbourhoods, including hundreds of Negro families, where there is not one single legally married couple, or couple not married, who stay faithful to each other beyond a few months, or a few years at most—often but a few weeks. And if out of every five hundred Negro families one excepts a few dozen who are legally married, this statement will hold true for millions of coloured people. And these things I tell you to-night are but hints. I cannot, I dare not, tell the full truth before a mixed audience.'

That is what Dr. Tucker says. Of course we do not accept his statement, but if there be any truth in it there is undoubtedly much exaggeration. And his statement would have been still more one-sided and exaggerated if he had not been 'before a mixed audience.' Let us take it for granted that, in the country districts, and in those country districts only, as Mr. Tucker tells us (whom Laird Clowes blindly follows in an unquestioning and unreasoning manner), there are Africo-Americans who are averse to marriage, and prefer leading the lives of single blessedness, and yet lead immoral lives, then we must respect their reasons for avoiding marriage ; for they have the same reasons for not marrying, or wishing to marry, as a great many of their white American countrymen, their European and other Caucasian fellow-creatures. The Africo-American, like the Caucasian, may have aged feeble and infirm relatives to provide for ; he may have some young brothers or sisters, or both, in addition to the authors of his being to care for ; and he may be earning just barely enough to keep his body and soul together. In either of these cases, why should a man marry when he cannot afford to keep a wife ?

Just recently—it was only in the latter part of the past

year (1890)—an eminent French legislator proposed, in the French Chamber of Deputies, that a tax, a heavy tax, should be levied on all Frenchmen—bachelors of a certain age—who either did not promptly marry, or who were resolved to remain bachelors; that Bill was calculated to have the effect of not only increasing the number of the French population and adding to the defenders of *La Grande Nation*, but was also calculated to raise the French standard of morality, which is at a low ebb; as it was thought that the severity of the bachelor-tax would drive many inveterate French bachelors, there and then, into the arms of matrimony. The Bill, however, fell through.

There are those, again, of the sexes who, though not married, yet cohabit, and with regard to these a few words must be said. A woman may be thought good enough, in the estimation of her paramour, to live in concubinage with him, yet a Caucasian may not think her sufficiently deserving to be his recognised wife. This remark, as it holds good for the white man, in whatever part of the world he resides, must also hold good for the Africo-American. If there were American Africans in the country districts who detested marriage, and consequently avoided it for a few years after the Act of Emancipation was passed in the glorious and immortal year 1863 (and year 1838 for the British Africans), they were few who disliked and avoided marriage. The great majority knew better; they did not follow the example set them by their late but licentious masters. To-day the Africo-American's standard of morality is higher than it was before 1863, for when the American Africans received emancipation they immediately began to reorganize their hitherto demoralized ranks, which had been shattered in the days of slavery, and unfurled the standard of virtue and raised their moral condition to its present high level. They buried rampant immorality in a common grave with slavery.

IMMORALITY.

To continue. If matrimony before 1882 (for Dr. Tucker made his statements before the Episcopal Congress sitting at Richmond, Virginia, in 1882) had no charms for those Africans (and these were very few) who, although they lived in adulterous concubinage, avoided marriage, why, as we said before, they had their reasons, and their scruples must be respected, just as are those of Caucasians.

The Red King, the second Norman William of England, lived in adulterous concubinage with sundry and divers women, but he would not have married one of them, or any other woman, for a consideration. And he died as he had lived, an unmarried man.*

But we are told that when the Mississippi Legislature, immediately on the conclusion of the American Civil War, ' passed an Act legalizing the union of all who were then living together, marrying them whether they wished it or not,' that ' for years afterwards the courts were crowded with applications for divorce from coloured people, which mostly had to be granted, since there was ample cause for divorce under either the Divine or the statute law.' If such a state of things did exist in Mississippi, in or before 1882, to the extent depicted by the Rev. Dr. Tucker, we deeply deplore it ; but, unfortunately for himself, Dr. Tucker was only too prudent not to attempt to substantiate his statements by adducing proofs, since the fact is that he had none to bring forward : consequently we see no reason at all why we should believe his word in the absence of all satisfactory proofs.

Even though immorality existed, and may exist to-day in ever so small an extent, among the American Africans, it is

* Lingard's ' History of England,' vol. ii., chap. ii., pp. 136, 137, and 147, second edition ; ' The English Cyclopædia of Biography,' vol. vi., p. 717; Freeman's ' History of the Norman Conquest of England,' vol. v., chap. xxiii., p. 72, A.D. 1876.

a matter to be deplored; but it is consoling to think that there are those—and they are the large majority—who are not immoral, whose commendable example will serve to influence others to lift themselves up from the mire of immorality.

In every country and in every city, among all peoples and in every community, Immorality must yet be a force and a power as long as men are liable to carnal sin in this world of ours; and as they will always be liable to this sin, immorality must perforce be found everywhere in our world.

Let us take the British peoples by way of illustration. They are as immoral as other peoples are; they are as immoral now as their ancestors have been in the buried past; and we have every reason to believe that they will be so in the future. We may have occasion, later on in this chapter, to refer again to the past history of immorality in Britain, but we shall for the present confine ourselves to dealing with immorality as it exists to-day in England.

We say that immorality prevails in England to-day even as it does in every other country; and as the outcome of immorality there were, up to the year 1890, according to the best-known computation, at least 16,220 petitions for divorce filed in England alone (Ireland and Scotland being excluded), reckoning from the time of the establishment of the Divorce Court in 1858.

Of those filed there is an average of 800 petitions annually, to say the least; and it may not be inaccurate to say that more than five-sixths of those petitions presented at the Divorce Court are granted, and their decrees made absolute. It can be safely said that the great majority of those parties who figure as respondents in the divorce causes must admit, that the presence of their names on the Divorce Court list is the outcome of their failing to remain faithful to their petitioning husbands or wives, even for a few weeks ; and it may not be out of place to mention that there must be many married parties who, though they have grievances on the score of immorality against their husbands or their wives that sorely need redressing, yet refrain from publishing them to the world, and consequently avoid the Divorce Court.

Very often—and it is a fact well known ; a matter, indeed, of common knowledge—as many as five co-respondents figure in *one* divorce case ; while it is a deplorable thing to contemplate, that the present year's (1891) Divorce Statistics bid fair to throw those of previous years into the shade completely.

But do not brothels and houses of ill-fame fall under the heading of immorality—are they not the temples of immorality ? And their frequenters and worshippers are, as a matter of course, all immoral men and women ; such temples of ill-fame are to be met with in Britain as in France. And we venture to say it is a matter of common knowledge, that in Paris many a shrine of ill-fame exists which is known to the Minister of the Interior and to the Prefect of Police ; but these establishments are in no way interfered with. To be brief, French immorality is notorious. We presume, then, that we are justified when we say that, if immorality exists to any great extent in Britain and in France (and it unfortunately does exist to a very great extent indeed both in Britain and in France), it is likely to exist to an even greater extent among the white American people of the United States of America than it does even among Britishers and Frenchmen.

Britain and France are in the front rank of nations, and may be termed the pioneers and leaders of civilization and Christianity. If immorality, then, exists to a great extent in either or both of these countries (and it only too truly exists to an enormous extent in both of them), we do not see why we should hesitate to say that it exists to a greater extent among the white Americans of the United States, seeing that American liberty is greater than the liberty which a Britisher or a Frenchman enjoys. White American liberty is unenvied by all good people, because it almost always is synonymous with license—with unbridled license. What a white American citizen dares do in his own country would not for a moment be tolerated in Britain or in France. The Britisher or the Frenchman would not even give it a thought; he would certainly shrink from doing it. Do we ever hear of lynchings in Britain and France as we constantly do of lynchings in the United States of North America? Do we hear of British New Orleans lynching-tragedies? Do we hear of French New Orleans lynching-tragedies? Do we hear of British or French mobs overpowering sheriffs' guards, taking hold of the Africans they are conveying to gaol and lynching them? Or do we hear of British or French breaking into the gaols of North Carolina, Virginia, or Florida, in bloodthirsty quest of Africans or other unfortunate victims, that they may lynch them? We say, then, that white American liberty is greater than that enjoyed by either the Britisher or the Frenchman; and that American liberty is virtually license. Those who read the daily papers, especially the American papers, the *New York Herald*, the *New York World*, and the *New York Police Gazette*, will certainly bear us out in our assertions, and agree with us that American liberty is virtually license. Then, in a country where there is the greatest license, we may expect to find the greatest immorality. And we may say that gross immorality is the offspring of gross license. These are, then, our reasons for saying and believing that greater immorality exists among the white American people than among Britishers and Frenchmen.

That unbounded license which the white American has,

his black countryman, the American African, does not share. Yet we must mention by the way that the American Republic contains more inhabitants within its territory than either the French Republic or the United Kingdom. And the fact must be borne in mind, that immorality will very often, we do not say always, be more rife and prolific in a country which contains a very large number of people than it will be in a country which contains a very small number of inhabitants.

We now return to Laird Clowes, who, commenting on the statement made by the Rev. Dr. Tucker, writes on page 111 of 'Black America' in this wise: 'These words were originally spoken before the Episcopal Congress at Richmond, Virginia, in 1882; they were subsequently published in a pamphlet, and I am generally assured, and implicitly believe, that they were true then and are true now.' And Laird Clowes proceeds to add that, 'Even the Negroes themselves dare not deny them. One Negro preacher published a pamphlet in which he admitted that "This speech reveals humiliating facts, so truthful yet so hard to acknowledge. Not one of our social circles, if we can be said to have any, is clean morally. They are full of base, downright hypocrisy and falsehood, and fully two-thirds of the whole are members of the churches. Moral character is not the standard. Crimes that should cause a blush on fair cheeks assume a front of brass, and defy you to speak of or talk about them. . . . A coloured man only a few days ago contended with me that the Negroes were right in certain of their practices, because the Lord Jesus Himself said that "Seven women should lay hold of one man."' 'Such was the confession,' proceeds the *Times*' Commissioner, 'of the Rev. Isaac Williams, with whom four other Negro preachers fully concurred, adding, "Our acquaintance extends over seven to ten thousand coloured people, concerning whose lives we know the truth, and that truth is set forth in Dr. Tucker's speech without exaggeration. There are exceptions; but the general truth is stated exactly as it is. We agree, also, that he has only given hints as regards many things of such a nature that only hints are possible."'

Mr. Laird Clowes tells us that he 'implicitly believes' that the Rev. Dr. Tucker's words 'were true then, and are true now,' but what unfavourable report respecting the African will Mr. Clowes not believe in? Fortunately for us Africans, Laird Clowes' belief is of no moving force, and in no way affects us, and we can afford to ignore him and his belief. But does not the Commissioner of the *Times* candidly tell us, on page 91 in 'Black America,' to which reference should be made by the reader, that the author of 'The Silent South'—which has the praiseworthy 'desire to do all that lies in the writer's power to abate the prevalent race friction'—has 'unwise love for the Negro'? When a man like Mr. Clowes takes Mr. George W. Cable to task for having what he (Mr. Clowes) calls '*unwise* love for the Negro,' what statement prejudicial to the African is he not capable of 'implicitly believing'? Because Mr. George W. Cable has 'a desire to do all that lies in his power to abate the prevalent race friction' in the Sunny South, that commendable 'desire' is dubbed 'unwise' love for the African by Mr. Laird Clowes. Would Mr. Clowes like to see the 'prevalent race friction' continue as long as possible? We are sure that it is no fault of Mr. Cable's if he happens to think differently from Mr. Clowes, and entertains brotherly affection for the African.

Mr. Cable is an honourable man, and the talented author of many works, mostly novels: he, like a true Christian and like the good Mussulman Abou ben Adhem, is a philanthropist and 'loves his fellow-men.'

Mr. Clowes tells us that, 'Even the Negroes themselves dare not deny' Mr. Tucker's statements; but we ask Mr. Clowes, Who are those Africans who 'dare not deny them'? It is true that the Rev. Isaac Williams, 'with whom four other Negro preachers fully concurred,' to all intents and purposes, *primâ facie*, admitted them; yet it is also true that their admission carries little or no weight. In an age when oppression and tyranny are rife; in an age when the members of an unhappy people are looked down upon as belonging to an inferior and degrading race; in an age when a subject-race reckons amongst its ranks the whimpering and the fawning, there will not be wanting those who are ashamed of their fellow-men; nay, more, there will be found base and unmanly dastards who, in order to court the smiles, and win the good graces, of those of their rulers who spurn them, are only too ready, like so many Judases, to denounce their fellow-countrymen. Such things have happened in the days of old; history furnishes us with many instances, and we are satisfied that they are happening also in our own time. They have happened among the pale-faced Caucasians in times immemorial, why may not they unfortunately happen to-day amongst the subject and dark-skinned Africans? When the Scottish Presbyterians were sore-constrained, and matters fared ill with them, in the days when the second Charles was King, they sent one James Sharp as their ambassador, with full powers to plead their cause before the third Stuart; but when that astute ambassador perceived that the Merry Monarch and his ungodly court entertained the most deeply-rooted and unyielding aversion towards all Presbyterians and their creeds, Sharp—when he might have pleaded the cause and urged the suit of his hard-pressed and corner-driven Scottish compatriots and co-religionists, who implicitly confided in him, and made him their commissioner—betrayed them, by neglecting the duty involved in his commission, and, with a view to currying favour, and as a stepping-stone to power, embraced the faith of the Merry Monarch and his depraved court, which the majority of the British people professed — and that faith was Episcopacy. He was rewarded for his breach of faith with the Archbishopric of St. Andrews; but when, early in 1679, he closed his inglorious career, meeting with his death from the knives wielded by the hands of indignant assassins— leaving his character as one of the basest to be found in Scottish History — few Scotsmen pitied him; fewer still lamented him. Irish history also furnishes too many instances of Irishmen betraying their fellow-compatriots. There was the notable instance of the treachery of Esmonde of Wexford in '98, when the noble Lord Edward Fitzgerald and the gallant Robert Emmett were bravely battling for independence. There was the notable instance of the treachery of Keogh and Sadlier in 1852.

Even supposing that the Rev. Isaac Williams, and his *confrères*, the 'four other Negro preachers,' are not men of the stamp of Sharp, Esmonde, Keogh, Sadlier, and others, we are quite satisfied that they in no way represented, or represent, the voice of Virginian people of the Ethiopian race, and were not—nor are they now—entitled to speak on this matter with any authority. It is idle to suppose that the Rev. Isaac Williams and his four colleagues knew 900,000 Virginian Africans intimately!

Some humiliating instances might be found of hypocrisy, in English political circles, which should keep us from undue surprise at what we suspect is the time-serving of this Rev. Isaac Williams and the four negro preachers who repeat after him. We sometimes see men who have been themselves condemned in an English High Court of Justice, and who have spent months in English gaols, active in their opposition to other men who have also been condemned for immoralities, and may have as good a cry that injustice has also been done them. A man basing his claim to purity on the *injustice* of his own legal condemnation, and then hounding from all possible return to political life a man who also declares the *injustice* of his own legal condemnation, is a strange revelation of the possibilities of human nature. And it may also be added, that there is now undergoing his punishment for immorality of an unusually disgraceful kind, a man who bears an honoured English name, and had taken a prominent part in the defence of the very class which he was privately inveigling to their ruin. The Rev. Isaac Williams, and his four countrymen and co-religionists, may or may not be hypocrites and pharisaical. If they are not pharisees, then we say that they have our humble but warm encomiums for thus manfully speaking in reproof of the conduct of some of our African countrymen. Yet if the reproof or rebuke was called for, the open confession—the confession in a published pamphlet—was wholly uncalled for. But if they are pharisees or hypocrites, then we say that they are offending sinners of the deepest dye, preaching with their tongues what they do not practise.

The Rev. Isaac Williams, moreover, tells us that 'a coloured man, only a few days ago, contended with me that the Negroes were right in certain of their practices, because the Lord Jesus Christ Himself said that "Seven women should lay hold of one man."'* Well, the African might have told the reverend gentleman the statement which he reports; but Mr. Williams does not tell us whether that man was fairly educated or an ignorant person; we

---

* This sentence belongs to the Book of Isaiah. They are not the words of Jesus.

infer that he was an uneducated person, and that, though blamable, his responsibility was less than a fairly educated man would have to bear. At any rate, if that man did say that 'Seven women should lay hold of one man,' we are quite satisfied that he could have been none other than an immoral man.

We have satisfied ourselves, then, that, whether the African under review was educated or an illiterate, he was of an immoral disposition. Like all other persons who are sincerely interested in the welfare of our African race, we are not behindhand in offering our rebuke to that man of the African race who may think as that African appears to do. Yet we do not hesitate to say that the reference made to this African in his pamphlet, by the Rev. Isaac Williams, which furnishes a weapon with which our enemies may strike at us Africans, was entirely uncalled for. Laird Clowes has thought it meet to fling the words of our countrymen, the Rev. Isaac Williams and the 'four other Negro preachers,' in our faces as sufficient proofs of African immorality; but we shall, and we *must*, by-and-by, pay him back in his own coin, by showing how Britishers and other Caucasians were in the past, and are in the present, also immoral. We propose to cite passages from the writings of his own British countrymen as proving whether Britishers are greatly immoral or not.

How many Caucasians there are who, although they may not *say* that 'Seven women should lay hold of one man,' actually carry out in practice everything embodied in the sentence. There are, we are certain, amongst Caucasians, those who have allowed themselves to exceed in practice the limit fixed by the 'coloured man's' motto; and there are also those who have nearly reached the limit. Such immoral practices have been, and are being, carried out by Caucasians, not only in this our civilized nineteenth century, but also in the times of the buried past. What a great contrast does the insignificant 'coloured man' present to the British Elizabeth, the last of the Tudors, who in practice carried out (in the days of Shakespeare) the 'coloured man's' saying, but in the reversed order! The one a black man, and an American African, and a subject (not a citizen, because the African in America is not allowed to exercise the rights conferred upon him by law!) of the United States of North America; the other a Caucasian and Britisher, and once Queen of England and Ireland. The one was presumably an illiterate man; the other was one of the cleverest women who ever sat on a throne, and was at least an accomplished linguist, speaking and writing five languages in addition to her native English. And yet Elizabeth, the greatest of the Tudors, was destitute of all moral principles; and here is our proof: 'The woman who despises the safeguards must be content to forfeit the reputation of chastity. It was not long before her familiarity with Dudley provoked dishonourable reports. At first they gave her pain; but her feelings were soon blunted by passion: in the face of the whole court she assigned to her supposed paramour an apartment contiguous to her own bedchamber, and by this indecent act proved that she was become regardless of her character, and callous to every sense of shame. But Dudley, though the most favoured, was not considered as her only lover: among his rivals were numbered Hatton and Raleigh, and Oxford and Blount, and Simier and Anjou: and it was afterwards that her licentious habits survived, even when the fires of wantonness had been quenched by the chill of age. The court imitated the manners of the sovereign. It was a place in which, according to Fount, 'all enormities reigned in the highest degree,' or, according to Harrington, 'where there was no love but that of the lusty god of gallantry, Asmodeus.'* Such was the reputation of Elizabeth Tudor, who is wrongly called the 'virgin-queen.' And this account is culled from the most impartial of British historians.

Whatever excuse could be accepted from the African could not be accepted from Elizabeth.

The Israelite, King David the psalmist, more than exceeded the 'coloured man's' suggestion, that 'Seven women should lay hold of one man;' for the second king of Israel had many wives and many concubines. His wise son and successor, King Solomon himself, with all his wisdom, could not exercise control over his sensual passions; and he even greatly surpassed his father David in the multitude of wives and concubines—seven hundred wives and three hundred concubines, making a grand sum total of one thousand women.† But Solomon and his father David were Asiatics; and we therefore pass on to Europeans.

A more immoral, depraved, and worthless monarch than the British Charles II. never sat on any European throne. When he died, this 'Merry Monarch' left several illegitimate children, of whom the best known were James, Duke of Monmouth, by Lucy Walters; Charlotte, Countess of Yarmouth, by Lady Shannon; Charles, Duke of Southampton; Henry, Duke of Grafton; George, Duke of Northumberland; and Charlotte, Countess of Lichfield, by the Duchess of Cleveland (*i.e.*, Mrs. Palmer, Countess of Castlemain); Charles, Duke of St. Albans, by Eleanor (Nellie) Gwyn; Charles, Duke of Richmond, by the Duchess of Ports-

---

* Dr. Lingard's 'History of England,' vol. xiii., chap. vii., pp. 500, 501, second edition.

† 2 Kings xi. 1-4. We do not, however, mean to say that King Solomon bore personal marital relations with them all. Many were merely nominal wives.

mouth (Madame Carwell); Mary, Countess of Derwentwater, by Mary Davies. Many more illegitimate children, by other women, the Merry Monarch had, who gained no such public prominence as these.* But we now turn to more modern times.

There are hosts of white Americans who believe, like the 'coloured man,' in the plurality of wives. The Mormons have for many years both believed in and practised polygamy; it is, indeed, a prominent article of the Mormon creed. If Mormonism be a religion at all, it is certainly an immoral one, sustaining immoral practices; a mixture of Protestantism and Mahommedanism, and abhorred by both Protestants and Mahommedans. The founder of American Mormonism, Joseph Smith, was a very loose-thinking and immoral man. From the leader we can form an estimate of his followers, and they are loose-thinking people on all the great moral questions, so much so that American law has had to be directed against the Mormon polygamic practices.

It may be mentioned here that though he (Joseph Smith) founded Mormonism in 1830, polygamy was not first practised amongst the Mormons, because it was not then included in the tenets of the 'Book of Mormon.' And though cohabitation was indulged in by Smith, it was only when he perceived that his licentiousness did not find favour with his followers, and when it was necessary to appease the just resentment of his lawful wife, that he suddenly declared, in July, 1843 (we believe that is the date), to his only too credulous and lax followers, that he had a 'revelation' from God, who, he said, not only sanctioned, but even commanded, the polygamic practice. It was then that polygamy began to fairly blossom among the 'Latter Day Saints.' And such was its rapid and general spread

* Lingard's 'History of England,' vol. x., chap. i., p. 115, fifth edition.

among the people that, when Brigham Young, Joseph Smith's successor in the headship of American Mormonism, died in 1877, he left seventeen wives and fifty-six children behind him to mourn his loss.*

Though Mormonism is mainly composed of Americans, there are Englishmen and Swiss, Germans, Norwegians and Swedes, Frenchmen and Danes, in the Mormon ranks, who perhaps number half a million.

The Mahommedans, too, believe in the plurality of wives; for when Mahomet died he left numerous wives and concubines behind him; and a part of the Mahommedan Bible, the Koran, actually deals with his (Mahomet's) loose relations with women.†

It is probable that had the Mormon Brigham Young lived a few years longer he would have died leaving not seventeen, but at least twice seventeen, wives behind him to mourn his loss; but in modern times he certainly yields the palm to the present Sultan of Turkey, Abdul Hamid II., who rejoices in having between eighty and one hundred wives and concubines in his harem at Stamboul, and, as if that number of women were not enough to satiate his immoral appetite, the 'Commander of the Faithful' is kept engaged in increasing the supply. The Shah of Persia, of living men, owns a superior only in the Sultan of Turkey, as far as the plurality of wives and concubines is concerned. Thus it can be seen that the Rev. Isaac Williams' 'coloured man' does not stand alone in the belief that '*Many* women should lay hold of one man;' for there were in other centuries, and there are in this century, men and women of position who were, and who are, just as immoral as this obscure and nameless 'coloured man.' We now dismiss the Rev. Isaac Williams and the 'four other Negro preachers,'

* 'Encyclopædia Britannica,' vol. xvi., p. 827, ninth edition.
† *Ibid.*, pp. 561, 599, ninth edition.

who in various ways furnished Mr. Clowes with a weapon to use, in accusing us Africans of immorality. When Caucasians come forward, like Mr. Froude, Clowes, Sir Spencer St. John, and others, and accuse us Africans of immorality, one would suppose that immorality never existed, and does not exist, to any extent, amongst the countrymen of these same Caucasians. But we shall show that immorality does prevail to a frightful extent amongst them. We briefly alluded, at the outset, to the immorality which is prevalent in the British Isles; now we propose to deal at some length with the British immorality, that is, with immorality as it exists in the country of Sir Spencer St. John, James Anthony Froude, and Laird Clowes. The actions brought in the Divorce Courts of every country testify to the immorality which is prevalent in that country. The British Isles have their Divorce Courts; and the large number of petitions annually filed in these Courts must testify to the widespread extent of immorality in Britain. Caucasians tell us Africans that we are immoral; we say that we, as a race, are *not* immoral. We say that immorality is as old as the world, and must be a force—a demoralizing, indeed, but not the less a powerful, force—in the world. It has marched with Caucasian civilization; it is marching shoulder to shoulder with civilization to-day. We say that immorality has had, and has, its abode amongst the Caucasians as fully as among other men; but it is our firm conviction that those who are responsible for the condition of the morals of the Africans who are living under Caucasian rule are his Caucasian rulers and governors. It is the business of the dominant Caucasian to watch over the morals of the subject African, because morality is part and parcel of civilization; and do not Caucasians pose as civilizers, as the civilizers of the African? Great moral responsibility, then, without doubt, rests on the shoulders of the Caucasians, while instruction and precept and example lie with him, and must originate from him who governs, and who is the great boasted civilizer. If the Caucasian rulers of us subject Africans fail to disseminate moral instruction, and, what is of much greater moment, if they fail to set their subjects a commendable example in the path of virtue and chastity; if, instead, they themselves plunge headlong into the abyss of vicious immorality, what effect must their derelictions and shortcomings, their wicked ways and bad example, have on us Africans? The ignorant African will be sure to follow in the footsteps of those above him. 'Example,' says Rogers, 'is a motive of a very prevailing force on the actions of men.' Have the British countrymen of James Anthony Froude and W. Laird Clowes set their African subjects the good or the bad example? We answer, without fear of contradiction, that they have decidedly set them not the good, but the bad example; and the following pages, we venture to say, will prove our statement. What was it that forced the Right Honourable Robert Bourke, G.C.I.E., Lord Baron Connemara, in the peerage of the United Kingdom of Great Britain and Ireland, ex-Lord Governnor of Madras, the second Presidency and Province in British India, to resign the Governorship of Madras early in the last year (1890)? Was it not immorality? Was he not caught, red-handed, in adulterous intercourse with his own Irish servant, and did he not thereby court a divorce suit at the hands of his wife, which was in fact instituted by her, and heard in court, with the result of a decree *nisi?* When the poor ignorant African hears that the noble lord, the Right Honourable Baron Connemara, G.C.I.E., ex-Lord Governor of Madras, a man of the greatest intelligence, and a legislator, has not thought it beneath his dignity to stoop to commit a disgraceful *liaison* with his own servant, where is he (the ignorant and benighted African) to take his good example from? Yes, we ask, where are his good morals to come from when a noble lord, the African's universal ruler (because he is a Caucasian, and a Britisher to boot) sets him a bad example? Mr. Laird Clowes evidently did not bear in mind the divorce petition (heard in July, 1890) of Lady Connemara *v.* Lord Connemara and Hannah Moore, a servant, when he was treating of the moral condition of the Africans, and quoting Froude as saying, in reference to us Africans, that 'morals in the technical sense they have none;' that 'there is no sign, not the slightest, that the generality of the race are improving either in intelligence' (we have dealt with the African's intelligence in the second chapter) 'or moral habits; all the evidence is the other way.' If their own countrymen are immoral, what right has either Froude or Clowes to expatiate on, or even refer to, the moral condition of the Africans to the detriment of their character? If the Caucasian does not practise what he preaches, how dare he pretend to moralize on the wickedness of the African?

What was it that forced the Right Honourable Sir Charles Wentworth Dilke, a Baronet of the United Kingdom of Great Britain and Ireland, author and editor, an ex-M.P. for Chelsea, ex-Under-Secretary of State for the Colonies, ex-President of the Local Government Board in Her Britannic Majesty's second Gladstonian Administration, and now presumptive Gladstonian Liberal candidate, with a view to the representation in the British House of Commons of the Forest of Dean, to retire into private life in the year 1886? Was it immorality? Did he figure as a co-respondent in the notorious divorce suit of 'Crawford *v.* Crawford and Dilke,' in January, 1886; and was he declared by judge and jury guilty of adultery with the petitioner Crawford's wife? Mr. James Anthony Froude never thought of the divorce petition of 'Crawford v. Crawford and Dilke' when he was treating of the morals of the West Indian Africans in his ' English in the West Indies'; nor did Mr. W. Laird Clowes give that case, or that of Lady Connemara v. Lord Connemara and Hannah Moore, a servant, a moment's thought when he was denouncing so vigorously the morals of the American Africans in his 'Black America.'

When the poor ignorant African—in far-off Georgia, Mississippi, Virginia, South Carolina, Alabama, North Carolina, Louisiana, Florida, or it may be in Cape Colony, Natal, the Gold Coast, Bechuanaland, Zululand, Mauritius, Jamaica, Trinidad, Sierra Leone, Barbados, Lagos, Gambia, or elsewhere — hears that his universal ruler, a Caucasian and an Anglo-Saxon, gives way to immoral practices; or, what is of even greater moment, hears of the scandal connected with a prominent Member of Her Britannic Majesty's Government of 1880-1885, how can we wonder if he falls into the sin of immorality, the very sin of which educated and high-ranked Englishmen are guilty? and is not that same African to be commiserated with rather than assailed by his Caucasian ruler?

Why do not Mr. Froude and Mr. Clowes, instead of treating of the morals of the African, treat of the morals of the Right Honourable Sir Charles Wentworth Dilke, Bart., G.C.B., and of the Right Honourable Robert Bourke, Lord Baron Connemara, G.C.I.E.? That would be a better occupation for them. We Africans tell the Caucasians to practise at home what they preach, and not play the part of the pharisee. At all events the humble subject-African's responsibility for sinning against and breaking the Sixth and Ninth Commandments is less than that of educated and cultured English gentlemen, who belong to the race that claims to be his rulers, his civilizers (?) and his legislators. It is recognised that the soldiers of an army have less responsibilities than their general, because their general is their ruler and director. We must confess that we cannot understand why it is that British writers are so hard on the African when they treat of African morals, while at the same time their own countrymen are grossly immoral.

There is the gravest aggravation of some of these English cases of immorality, in the fact that too often the licentious men have had wives actually living with them at the time of their wrong-doing, who are made by them to suffer the cruellest indignities.

Another case has occupied much public attention, but it need only be briefly referred to in further illustration of our argument. The Honourable Charles Stewart Parnell, the Member for Cork, who was sometimes spoken of as the 'Uncrowned King of Ireland,' brought irremediable dishonour on his name, and misfortune for his cause, by failing to appear in the divorce suit of 'O'Shea *v.* O'Shea and Parnell,' and letting judgment go against him by default. There were revelations of intrigues made at that trial which would have been regarded as utterly disgraceful if they had borne relation to the African, and yet there were many prepared to condone the moral offences for the sake of the talents of the offender. We are indebted to the 'Nonconformist conscience' for creating a healthy public opinion with regard to the official position of a convicted adulterer, which Mr. Gladstone emphasized by his famous and effective—though, as some people think, dictatorial—letter.

And to strengthen our case still more, and further prove that Immorality wields her sceptre, and has an undisputed sway over the Caucasian, two other cases of the greatest importance have just been made public. The offences of Sir Charles W. Dilke, Mr. Charles S. Parnell, and Lord Connemara, dwindle into insignificance when compared with the offences which must now be mentioned. Two British

Members of Parliament, both of them well-known men, have but recently (at least as known to the general public) fallen victims to the conquering power of immoral passions. One — the English Liberal Member, or, rather, the late Member, for North Bucks, has just (May 6, 1891) been sentenced to twelve months' imprisonment, he having pleaded guilty to half a dozen criminal counts of prurient immorality. But what seem to render his crimes more heinous, shameful, and disgraceful in the opinion of all right-thinking men, are the facts (1) that he has passed the middle age of life; (2) that he is a married man, and has a true and loving wife; (3) that he was at the time of his iniquities a Member of the British House of Commons, and also a Member of the London County Council; (4) besides these offices, he was a J.P., and Chairman of the Anglesea Quarter Sessions, administering the very law which he helped to legislate in the British Parliament; (5) moreover, he is a Captain in the Queen's Navy; (6) he is the eldest son and heir of a baronet occupying a high social position, and more than blessed with this world's goods; (7) and the females whom he sought to entrap were not women of twenty-one, or beyond that age, but girls of tender years, girls in their teens, and aged under and about sixteen.

The London *Daily Chronicle* of May 7, 1891, commenting on 'Regina *v.* Verney' (tried in May, 1891), and on British immorality in general, amongst other things, says: 'It is even more painful to reflect upon the spread of vice in the country. The heartless cynicism, which is ever quick to sneer at homely virtue, may well feel reproved by the spectacle of the widespread demoralization of which this latest scandal is an example; and there is hope in the fact, which has now been demonstrated, that the law of the land is still strong enough to reach one of the worst forms of scoial crime.'

Lloyd's News of May 10, 1891, also, commenting on the Verney case, and the widespread immorality existing in the United Kingdom, says : ' His ' (Captain Verney's) ' was not the crime of impetuous youth, nor even of mature manhood, whose mental balance had been disturbed by the force of a great passion. There was not a touch of even false sentiment to mitigate its utter baseness. It recalls in its callous concupiscence the stinging words of Byron : " Prurient, yet passionless, cold-studied lewdness." The head and front of Captain Verney's offending in the eyes of good men and women is, that he deliberately spread his net for any girls that might be caught by guile or by money. Behind innocent-looking advertisements, offering fair prospects of employment to the daughters of the ordinary newspaper reader, this man was lying in wait for his prey. And he has evidently been pursuing this course for years, all the while posing as a philanthropist, and even as a social purist. What amount of success he has had with the general seduction agency, which he and the woman Rouillier set up, it is impossible to say ; but so cruel and cunning a spider must have secured his share of human flies. From time to time piteous stories have been told, and have also been authenticated, of young English girls enticed abroad to Brussels, Paris, Havre, or some other Continental city, where they have speedily fallen a prey to the dealers in human flesh; for a young girl without money, in a city where hardly anyone speaks her language, is of all creatures the most helpless. But here was a man who caused his victims to be taken across the Channel, so that they might be more helpless, and apparently more easily cast off.' *Lloyd's News* continues: ' There are men of Captain Verney's stamp who have never yet been detected, and his fate will strike a wholesome sense of terror into their hearts.' It is only a small section of the English people who parade as social purists, and venture to attack their African fellow-creatures, who are frail as they; and their proceedings are sometimes unwise; but when a criminal like Captain Verney is run down, and it is made plain that he has been seeking to entrap any innocent girl that might be attracted by his agent, then we all become social purists, and, though we may be saddened at the spectacle of his humiliation, no right-minded man or woman can demur to the righteous retribution which has fallen upon him. His expulsion from the House of Commons should render him incapable of ever sitting again, or he may one day be seeking to prove his innocence by 'writing a pamphlet,' as has recently been done in behalf of the Honourable Sir Charles Wentworth Dilke.

It may not be too much to mention here, that the gallant gentleman, Captain Edmund Hope Verney, has just (May 12, 1891) been expelled the British House of Commons. And he richly deserved his expulsion. The other—the Irish Conservative Member for East Belfast, for whose arrest a warrant has been issued, has not yet ventured, as Captain Verney did, to direct his steps homewards to Britain to stand his trial for the immoral crimes of which he is accused, but continues living in ignoble and, let us say, constrained exile, because he knows only too well that the moment he sets foot on British soil he will be promptly arrested. Surely if he believes himself innocent, and the victim, as he alleges, of a political plot concocted by his political opponents—the Gladstonian Liberals and the Irish Nationalists—he would long ago have surrendered his person, taken his trial, and purged his reputation from the charge or charges of which he now stands accused ; but the Honourable Member for East Belfast prefers doing otherwise, and remains in virtual hiding on the Continent. It is worthy of mention that the Member for East Belfast, like Captain Verney, was accustomed to pose as a social purist; but, lo ! he is himself accused of worshipping at the shrine of Immorality! The Member for East Belfast is truly a fine specimen of a legislator fitted to legislate for the moral well-being of the Africans who are living under the British flag !

Immorality, we had occasion to mention before, exists as extensively in France as it does in Britain. It was the indirect, or it may be the direct, cause which led to the forced banishment of the French General Boulanger. It was his immoral nature which (though he was a married man) caused him to be inveigled into the toils of more than one woman other than his wife; and this it was that really brought on his exile and ruin and death. And it was a herculean task for him to shake off the yoke of immorality under which he had to toil even to the very end.*

There are many who believe that Léon M. Gambetta, tribune of the French people, a man of singular ability and of distinguished parts, once Minister of the Interior, and afterwards French Premier and President of the Council, was a very immoral man. The wound from the pistol-shot, which prostrated Gambetta and terminated his existence not many years ago, was, and is, by many attributed not to mere accident. It is thought to have been a self-inflicted wound, and his death was a suicide. While his friend, but supposed mistress, Mademoiselle Léonine Léon, is by many reported and believed to have goaded him on to the fell deed by her alleged misbehaviour. As this is a matter of uncertainty (in consequence of the conflicting nature of the reports that have been spread concerning the private character of Gambetta), we venture to do no more than refer to a passing suspicion.

* Boulanger's suicidal death on the grave of the woman who kept him is the final declaration of his shameless immorality.

Kings and queens have their little weaknesses in the matter of immorality, like other mortals. Immorality caused the graceless Servian Milan to perform his undignified escapades, which served to belittle him in the eyes of Europe and of the world. And when Queen Liliuakalani, of the Hawaiian Islands, attempted recently to force the recognition of her illicit son as her successor and heir-apparent on the Hawaiian throne, that attempt, or proposal, very nearly drove her subjects into open rebellion, which would have aimed at the establishment of a republic. At all events, the chocolate-coloured Sandwichers gave their queen to understand that they would have none of her 'full-blooded Kanaka' as her successor and their ruler. Austro-Hungarian Crown Prince Rudolph, the pride and hope of the Hapsburgs, became immoral, and because of the Baroness Vetsera committed suicide in 1888.

Reference may also be made to the dismissal of Captain Arthur Wybrow Baker from her Majesty's Service in Trinidad, the causes for that dismissal being well known to bear relation to other things as well as official untrustworthiness. Did he set the subject Afro-Trinidadians a worthy example?

Whatever immorality there may be in the West Indies, the West India Committee is largely responsible for it; and we are not alone in that belief; for the Trinidad *Public Opinion* of March 20, 1891 — a journal edited by a Caucasian—commenting on the morals of the St. Lucian Africans and the West India Committee, says: 'There is little or no incentive to the people to lead moral lives; and in many cases the example set them by those to whom they should look up (the example set the Trinidadian Africans by this Baker, for instance) is a deplorable one. To many people in England, in fact, everywhere but in the West Indies, the West India Committee represents the sublimated wisdom and morality of the Caribbean Archipelago. The members composing it should therefore, for propriety's sake, if nothing else, be able to point to efforts made and example shown for the moral elevation of the masses. As the twig is bent, so will the tree be inclined; and if the people see before them constant instances of unchastity on the part of those to whom they naturally look up for example, it is not surprising that they should follow suit.'

We are of opinion that the three countries where the grossest immorality is to be met with are the United Kingdom, France, and the United States of North America. London, Paris, and New York are the three cities in which the rankest immorality exists. But of these three capitals Paris and New York yield the palm in vice to London, which leads the van in the immoral race, the Metropolis of France and the Empire City being left far and away in the rear. Prostitution, rampant and prolific, with daring effrontery, stalks abroad unchallenged, greeting and elbowing you at every turn, walk where you may, in the streets of London, from the early morn of God's daylight to the hours during which stark night is permitted to exercise her sway.

Who, we ask, were the unfortunate Whitechapel victims of the East-end but loose, immoral women? It was their immoral nature which led them to their pitiable doom, and caused them to fall easy and pliant victims to the murderous knife of the Ripper-assassin.

We say that immorality prevails in London, as the capital of the British Empire, to a greater extent than it does in any other portions of the British Empire; and the reader may be reminded that, when the decision in the divorce cause of 'O'Shea v. O'Shea' became known, the Irish people, with an almost unanimous voice, gave it as their conviction that it was London which had corrupted the morals of Mr. Parnell their leader.

Vicious immorality predominates in both the West-end and the East-end of the British Metropolis more than it does in the other parts of London; but these other parts are in a sufficiently degraded condition. We referred briefly to the state of the East-end, and to the Whitechapel murders as the outcomes of immorality, considering that a brief reference would be sufficient. We shall now allow the Britisher to give us his opinion of the immorality prevalent in his own country and in London, and shall quote one of the daily newspapers published in London. The London *Daily Telegraph* of May 14, 1891, under the heading of 'The State of the West-end Streets,' tells us that : ' Mr. E. C. Keevil, a gentleman having business premises in Regent Street, attended (on May 13), in company with Inspector Shannon, before Mr. Hannay (Police Magistrate of Marlborough Street Court), to make a complaint respecting the congregation of immoral women in Regent Street and the neighbouring thoroughfares. Addressing the magistrate, Mr. Keevil said, "I desire, sir, to address you, on behalf of my fellow-tradesmen, in support of a complaint of one of the inspectors of the C Division, with respect to the state of Regent Street, caused by the number of prostitutes who frequent that and neighbouring streets, and seriously cripple the carrying on of business. I am not desired to come here as a purist, a philanthropist, or anything of that kind, but merely as one seeking protection for his business. We ask your assistance to have the present state of things remedied, and dealt with in the way such things are in Glasgow, Edinburgh, and other boroughs, where the police are under the control of the municipal authorities. There the evil, which I know always has existed and always will exist, is under decent control. We only want it to be under such control here that foot-passengers may not be openly molested, as they are now, if they stop for an instant to look at a shop-window."—Mr. Hannay: "I may say that you have my entire sympathy, and I am here ready to punish all such women who are brought before me. Your application should, however, be made to the Commissioner of Police. There are laws, and I am here to enforce them; but I have no control in the streets."—Mr. Keevil: "We went to a former Commissioner, Colonel Henderson, and he said that the law was imperfect, and that the state of things was not as much under his control as he would have liked it to be."—"There is the difficulty that private persons will very rarely come forward to support complaints against women of the class you refer to; while it has occurred, unfortunately, that the unsupported testimony of a policeman in charges of the kind has been viewed with suspicion. I may say that I always judge every case upon its merits; and if I see no reason to doubt the evidence of the policeman, I act upon what he says. It is a matter that I would rather not discuss in public, but I must say that our streets are really a disgrace to us."—Mr. Keevil: "It is our belief, sir, that shutting up the houses where these women were wont to congregate is only making matters worse."—"Mr. Hannay: "Now you are touching upon a delicate matter; and I would rather not discuss it."—Mr. Keevil then withdrew. A foreign woman, giving the name of —— was subsequently charged with annoying gentlemen outside the London Stereoscopic Company's premises. — Inspector Shannon handed to the magistrate a letter received by Superintendent Hume from the manager of that company, complaining of the customers being driven away by women. Gentlemen were caught hold of and spoken to, it was averred, while ladies would not stand beside women of the class complained of.—Inspector Shannon said that he had understood that the manager of the Stereoscopic

Company intended to appear and support the charge, but he was not present.—Mr. Hannay: "That is just the point. People make complaints, but will not come to Court to support them. Go down, and tell him that I am surprised that he will not come half the length of Regent Street to support his complaints."—Mr. Shannon: "But he will not come, sir."—Mr. Hannay: "They leave the police to do everything, and will not help themselves at all."— —— was fined 40s.'

What with the often occurring seductions, what with the legionary divorce causes annually heard, we surely have abundant public proofs of the immoral natures of Britishers and other Europeans in the United Kingdom.

We take it that it is more than sufficiently disgraceful and shameful that Members of Governments, Members of Parliament, Lords, Baronets, Magistrates, and Officers in her Britannic Majesty's Forces, should figure as respondents or co-respondents in divorce petitions, and figure as prisoners at the bar on criminal charges under the Criminal Law Amendment Act; while it is just as, or, may we say it? more disgraceful and shameful when Protestant clergymen or ministers of religion, preachers of the Gospel and morality, figure as respondents or co-respondents in divorce suits, as well as when they are put on their trial and proved guilty of immoral offences under the Criminal Law Amendment Act.

We say that British Protestant ministers of religion have figured either as respondents or co-respondents in divorce cases; and as we do not, like Laird Clowes and James Anthony Froude, allege anything against anyone without substantiating it, we refer the reader—the sceptic or unbelieving reader—to a well-known case tried in March of this year (1891), in which a British Protestant clergyman figured as the respondent. That one example, we hope and trust, will suffice for all. When a clergyman, a British clergyman and preacher of the Gospel, who is supposed to be chaste and pure, stoops to violate either the Sixth or the Ninth Commandment, and as a consequence figures either as the respondent or as co-respondent, according to the tenor of the case, in a Divorce Court, his example, already baneful, is likely to become contagious to the benighted African, who only too readily will follow suit.

We again say that British clergymen are even caught redhanded in criminal adultery, and convicted of indecent assaults under the Criminal Law Amendment Act. And as we do not (as we have already said), like James Anthony Froude and Laird Clowes, allege anything against anybody without substantiating our charge, we refer the doubting or unbelieving reader to the case (tried in June 24th, 1891, at the Berks Assizes) of a Protestant clergyman who was indicted for such immoral offences. That one instance, too, we trust, will suffice for all such.*

When we see Immorality affecting not only Magistrates, Members of the County Council, Officers in Her Britannic Majesty's Forces, Members of Parliament, Members of Government, Lords, Baronets, and also Ministers of the Gospel and of religion, is there not cause for wonder that the benighted African, if he happen to violate the Sixth or the Ninth Commandment, should be so closely and unremittingly run to earth and denounced by those very Caucasians who themselves violate both the Sixth and the Ninth Commandments?

* As an outcome of clerical immorality the British Clergy Discipline (Immorality) Bill, under the pilotage of His Grace the Lord Archbishop of Canterbury, has been read a third time and passed (March 20, 1891) the Lords in the Sixth Session of the Twelfth Parliament of Queen Victoria's reign, and there is every reason to hope and believe that that Bill will pass the 'faithful Commons' this (Seventh) Session and become law.

When those in high places sin, they must be held responsible for the sins of the lowly. When rulers—Caucasian rulers—are immoral, there will surely be those who are immoral amongst the subject Africans, though it is never the great majority of them. Like master, like man. We Africans, then, seeing how excessively rank Immorality is amongst the Europeans, and with what undisputed sway she holds her rule amongst all of European descent, tell the Caucasians to practise what they preach, because example produces more effect than precept. No white man is authorized to tell his black brother that he has a mote in his eye, while so big a beam abides in his own (the white man's) eye.*

Let the good example be set the subject African, living under Caucasian rule, by his governors, and it will have the desired effect; and let Caucasians put a stop to their hypocritical cant in complaining of African immorality.

How comes it, we ask, that there are to-day lawyers, doctors, clergymen, authors, engineers, artists, teachers, scholars, merchants, and what not, of African blood? We say that the true and only answer is, that the descendant of Ham has seen the examples set him by his rulers, has followed and continues to follow them, and, as a consequence, he is now to-day working out his own future, and is fast entering into keen competition with his Caucasian rulers in every kind of profession and occupation that the African is not debarred from. No sane man will for a moment entertain the thought that the British Africans, when they were liberated in 1838, and the American Africans, when they were liberated in 1863, were ever given a recompense for being so forcibly, unjustly, and with such diabolical cunningness and fell purpose, taken from their hearths and homes in beloved Africa, and held in servile bondage.

* Matt. vii. 3-5.

No. It is the force of example alone which is inspiring the freed men; for the African, when the Gift of Enfranchisement fell on his lap, had to toil on his way as a labourer up the ladder of civilization and general progress, without material and substantial aid; using his progressive and ascending powers—the resultants of the forces of example—to their present lofty pitch to the admiration of the world. Yes, commendable and worthy example, we may say, 'gives an impulse towards progress to the whole mass' of Africans all the world over.

Despite the fact that the Americans set their then African slaves a bad example, the standard of morals to-day is very high in Liberia, because the American Africans left behind the chrysalides of all the wicked and corrupting examples set them by the Yankees, to rot and stench in their own land; and as they were all innately pious, God-fearing men, as well as men of the greatest intelligence, they were enabled to easily civilize their aboriginal countrymen in Liberian Africa, and reclaim them from evil; the Liberian moral standard is as high as that of any other country in the world.

The standard of morals in Hayti, though high, yet falls short of that of Liberia. The Frenchmen, when they were forced to quit Hayti, and were driven into the sea, left behind them the unhallowed legacy of immorality, which pernicious legacy and example taxed all the energies of Toussaint the Great, Dessalines, Christophe, Boyer, and Pétion to drive away.

But it is not only in the present age that immorality has been a force and a power amongst Caucasians as well as amongst Asiatics. Immorality has been the means of changing the histories of peoples, and has altered the geographical boundaries of countries. More: it has been the chief cause of the effacement of more than one country from off the earth in bygone days. Immorality, the chief sin of Sodom and Gomorrah, brought down the anger of Heaven on those cities; brimstone and fire rained on them, and Sodom and Gomorrah were wiped off the face of the earth, and can never be restored.*

Unlawful fondness of Bathsheba, the wife of his officer Urias, caused the Israelite King David to break not only the Sixth and Ninth Commandments, but the Fifth as well. After debauching Bathsheba, the licentious Israelite resolved to put his devoted officer Urias to death. The king succeeded only too well in his dark design; but immorality transformed the hitherto stainless David into a murderer. His matchless wisdom availed his son and successor, King Solomon, but little, for it did not prevent Immorality from enveloping him in her unhallowed embraces. The adulterous Solomon, because of his being the slave of women—for he had, we are told, seven hundred wives and three hundred concubines, making a grand total of one thousand women†—from being a devout believer in the God of his fathers, Abraham, Isaac, Jacob, and David, swerved from the path of rectitude and truth, became an idolater, and fell to worshipping the idols of his women. But his sins involved the loss of ten tribes of Israel to his son and successor Rehoboam.

Immorality on the part of the lewd and licentious Trojan, Paris, and his innamorata, the equally lewd and licentious Helen of Sparta, King Menelaus' wife and queen, brought Mycenean Agamemnon and his myriads of embattled squadrons of fierce and bloodthirsty troopers of Old Greece (and in their train disaster and ruin) thundering for a decade before the gates of the ill-fated city of the valiant and mighty Trojans, which was finally taken, sacked, and wiped out of existence. It also lost Antony the decisive

* Gen. xix. 24, 25. † 2 Kings xi. 1-4.

battle of Actium, his great empire, and his possible chances of winning another equally great. And, moreover, it caused that brave and capable, but indolent and immoral, Marcus Antonius, the Mark Antony of Shakespeare, to fall into despair and to commit suicide.

Most of the British sovereigns have an unenviable and immoral reputation, beginning from the Red King, the Second Norman William, and ending with the so-called 'First Gentleman in Europe,' the Fourth Hanoverian German George. Very few indeed are free from the charge of immorality; the Third and Sixth Henrys, the Fifth and Sixth Edwards, the two Marys, the Third William, Anne, and the Third George, the Farmer, being the only exceptions, as, also, are Stephen, the Fourth Henry, and the First Edward, the 'Greatest of the Plantagenets,' but these last three are doubtful.

The immoral relations of the Second Henry with loose women, especially the Fair Rosamond Clifford, caused his wife, Queen Eleanor, to urge her sons to rebel against her husband and their father.* The Lion-hearted Richard,† the 'mirror of chivalry,' whom the great Sir Walter—the great Scott of Abbotsford—immortalizes in 'Ivanhoe,' and his Lackland Brother John,‡ who was bearded at Runnymede by his stubborn subjects, and from whose grasp Magna Charta was wrested by sturdy and plucky Britishers, were

* Lingard's 'History of England,' vol. ii., chap. v., pp. 382, 383, 434-436, second edition ; 'Dictionary of (British) National Biography,' vol. xxvi., p. 10 ; *ibid.*, vol. xi., pp. 75, 76 ; *ibid.*, vol. xxi., p. 139 *et seq.*; 'Student's Hume,' pp. 119-121.

† Lingard's 'History of England,' vol. ii., chap. v., p. 426 ; *ibid.*, chap. vi., p. 501 ; Morris's 'History of England,' p. 93 ; 'Encyclopædia Britannica,' vol. xx., pp. 540, 541, ninth edition.

‡ Lingard's 'History of England,' vol. iii., chap. i., pp. 91-93 ; Morris's 'History of England,' p. 99 ; 'Student's Hume,' p 144 ; 'Dictionary of (British) National Biography,' vol. xxix., p. 416.

just as dissolute as the Red King, the Second Norman William, and the First Henry.* Her licentious passion for her paramour, Roger Mortimer, caused the disreputable Queen Isabella† to wage unnatural and unjustifiable war on her henpecked husband, taking him prisoner. And finally, the same guilty passion was the cause of the brutal and cowardly murder of the weakling Edward II., while he was a close and defenceless prisoner at the Castle Berkeley.

The Third Edward, under whom the decisive and well-fought battles of Calais and Poitiers added to the lustre of British arms, in the winter of his life, and in the dotage of old age, yielded to woman's influence, and allowed his mistress, the imperious Alice Ferrers, to rule, or rather, to misrule, his kingdom;‡ just as the Second Henry of France, wedded though he was to a Catherine de Medici, suffered the fair but sinful Diana of Poitiers, his mistress, to control the affairs of his kingdom, from the beginning of his reign to the day of his death and the end of his reign.§ The Fourth Henry of France was an immoral man, and his excesses

* Morris's 'History of England,' p. 63; Lingard's 'History of England,' vol. ii., chap. iii., pp. 207, 212, 213; Freeman's 'History of the Norman Conquest of England,' vol. v., p. 155; 'Dictionary of (British) National Biography,' vol. xxv., pp. 450, 451; 'Student's Hume,' p. 101.

† 'Student's Hume,' p. 170; Lingard's 'History of England,' vol. iii., chap. iv., p. 449; *ibid.*, vol. iv., chap. i., pp. 9-19; 'Dictionary of (British) National Biography,' vol. xxix., p. 65 *et seq.*

‡ Lingard's 'History of England,' vol. iv., chap. ii., p. 142; 'Encyclopædia Britannica,' vol. vii., p. 684, ninth edition; 'Dictionary of (British) National Biography,' vol. xvii., pp. 66-69.

§ 'English Cyclopædia of Biography,' vol. iii., p. 350; 'Encyclopædia Britannica,' vol. xi., p. 670, ninth edition; 'History of France—from the Origin of that Nation to the Year 1702,' vol. i.; William Tooke's 'Monarchy of France,' p. 377.

hastened his death.* His early dissoluteness cut off the brilliant career in arms and administration of Henry V. of England, and sent him to an early grave.† His unrestrained indulgences brought the licentious and indolent Fourth Edward to his death at a comparatively early age.‡ The Third Richard,§ like his rival Henry VII., was of a disreputable nature, while the Eighth Henry was a royal Bluebeard, who stopped at nothing to attain his ends. When the Defender of the Faith, Henry VIII., married his brother's widow, he might have had at least a particle of genuine and lawful affection for her; but when he tired of her, and was captivated by the charms of the young and beautiful, but cunning and ambitious Anne Boleyn, who would not consent to be mistress but would only be his wife, the Bluebeard sought a divorce from his Queen Catherine—the wife who is admitted to have been 'without fear and without reproach.' When, in 1527, the reigning Pope, Clement VII., would not grant the prayer of his petition for a divorce from his wife, the Eighth Henry illegally divorced the stainless and devoted Catherine by a private scheme, and contracted an ecclesiastically unlawful marriage with Anne Boleyn. And when Clement remained as immovable as the sphynx, and kept pronouncing against his divorce, and declaring Henry's subsequent marriage with Anne null and void, the Second Tudor supported the doctrines of

* 'History of France—from the Origin of that Nation to the Year 1702,' vol. ii., p. 714; Chambers's 'Encyclopædia,' vol. v., pp. 316, 317; 'Encyclopædia Britannica,' vol. xi., p. 671, ninth edition.

† Lingard's 'History of England,' vol. iv., chap. iv., pp. 425, 426 *et seq.;* 'English Cyclopædia of Biography,' vol. iii., p. 365.

‡ Lingard's 'History of England,' vol. v., chap. iii., p. 317; Morris's 'History of England,' p. 171; 'Dictionary of (British) National Biography,' vol. xvii., p. 82.

§ 'English Cyclopædia of Biography,' vol. v., p. 89.

Luther, and proclaimed himself the head of the English Church, though but six (that was in 1521) years before he arrayed himself against Luther, refuted his doctrines, and earned the title of 'Defender of the Faith' at the hand of the Tenth Leo. When, however, Anne Boleyn's maid, Jane Seymour, caught the fancy of the immoral 'Defender of the Faith,' he, under the pretext of her supposed incontinency, beheaded Anne, surnamed of Boleyn, who was never his lawful wife, and married Jane Seymour the very next day.

After the death of Jane Seymour, Henry VIII. married, as all the world knows, Catherine Howard, and he put her to death on the plea that she had been unchaste before her marriage with him; and almost immediately after he had beheaded Catherine Howard he married Anne of Cleves. But after a brief period of cohabitation with his wife Anne of Cleves, the passionate and licentious monarch divorced, pensioned, and put aside his 'Great Flanders Mare,' and married Catherine Parr. The Eighth Henry was certainly one of the very worst kings whom the British people have ever had the misfortune to call their rulers. He was as vicious and licentious as he was suspicious, tyrannical, and cruel; but licentiousness was, without doubt, his predominant passion, his chief and ruling vice. It was deeply-rooted and ingrained, it was innate, and part and parcel of his vicious nature. He had many mistresses, as well as these wives, but the names of but few of these have been preserved. Elizabeth Tailbois and Mary Boleyn are the best known of a legion of them, the latter (Mary Boleyn) being the elder sister of Anne Boleyn, and the sensual king immediately repudiated her on seeing her fairer, younger, and more beautiful sister Anne.*

* See 'Dictionary of (British) National Biography,' vol. xxvi., pp. 76, 82-93; and, better still, Lingard's 'History of England,' vol. vi., chap. i., pp. 2, 3, 6; chap. ii., pp. 121-149; chap. iii., pp. 150-157, 161-185, 168-295; chaps. iv. and v.

We pass on, and come to James I., who was as immoral as any of his predecessors, who encouraged vice in his court, and was head instructor in the school of scandal in which Buckingham and Somerset were apt and foremost pupils.* Yes, in the reign of the 'British Solomon' National immorality flourished in Britain as it did in the days of Elizabeth and other sovereigns. James II.'s licentious passion for, and his subsequent betrayal of, the honour of, the Lord General Churchill's (afterwards Duke of Marlborough) sister, the ugly Lady Arabella,† were the real causes of the desertion of that nobleman (who was the first soldier of his patron), when the British monarch James II. was in sore straits, and his kingdom imperilled on its invasion by Orange William the Dutchman. Had Churchill remained loyal to James, and had not deserted him, we express a doubt whether the Dutchman William of Orange would ever have ascended the British throne; but, as Churchill deserted, and as he was James's right-hand man and first general, his example was contagious.‡ James's forces, as the world knows, went over to William's side, and the Fourth of the Stuarts had himself to flee the kingdom, the Dutchman mounting the British throne which he had abdicated.

The two First Georges were also as dissolute as their predecessors; for George I., when he came to mount the British throne, brought in his train a bevy of his German mistresses, who were so many burthens to the British taxpayers; while George II. was no better than his father, for his lips were steeped in immorality, and he made it his

* Lingard's 'History of England,' vol. ix., chap. iii., p. 321; 'Student's Hume,' p. 378.

† 'Dictionary of (British) National Biography,' vol. x., p. 307.

‡ Lingard's 'History of England,' vol. xiv., chap. ii., pp. 253, 254; 'Dictionary of (British) National Biography,' vol. x., p. 317; 'Encyclopædia Britannica,' vol. xv., p. 553.

business to get as much money as possible out of the British taxpayers' pockets for his German mistresses to squander.*

Under every British king who was noted for his depravity the court copied the example of the king, while the people in their turn followed the baneful and corrupting example set them by their superiors—the king and his court. The last British king and queen whose laxity of morals have come into unenviable prominence and attained notoriety were the dissipated George IV.† and his disreputable queen consort, Caroline of Brunswick ;‡ and these were certainly more depraved than the two First Georges. But the British sovereigns whom we deem to have been the most dissolute, depraved, and licentious, were undoubtedly the Merry Monarch, Charles II., and the 'Virgin' Queen Bess.

We now pass on to Charles II., the Merry Monarch, and we must dwell at some length on his career. Charles II., we may safely say, was not only the most depraved and licentious British monarch, but his compeer or superior in immorality amongst the European crowned heads has never yet been found. Immorality has perhaps never been more rife in the United Kingdom than it was in the days of the Second Charles. Virtue was laughed to scorn by the Cavaliers, while it was the belief of the Merry Monarch that every woman had her price. Unrestrained merriment ran wild, and indecency, gross and

---

* May's 'Constitutional History,' vol. i., p. 7; Whitaker's 'Almanack,' p. 89; 'Encyclopædia Britannica,' vol. x. ; 'Dictionary of (British) National Biography,' vol. xxi., pp. 146, 147, 150, 153-156, 163, 164, 170-172.

† Morris's 'History of England,' p. 479; 'Dictionary of (British) National Biography,' vol. ix., pp. 151, 152 ; vol. xxi., p. 204.

‡ *Ibid.*

unabashed, reigned triumphant in the land.* The Protector Oliver and his round-headed Puritans, bigoted and hypocritical though they were, sternly checked everything calculated to demoralize the British people, but when the great Protector Oliver and his son Richard were no more, and dissensions reigned in the ranks of the divided and leaderless Cromwellian army, and the dissolute Charles had ascended the throne of his fathers, there came in the train of Charles and the Cavaliers the reaction. For 'under the government of men making profession of godliness, vice had been compelled to wear the exterior garb of virtue; but the moment the restraint was removed it stalked forth without disguise, and was everywhere received with welcome. The Cavaliers, to celebrate their triumph, abandoned themthemselves to ebriety and debauchery; and the new loyalists, that they might prove the sincerity of their conversion, strove to excel the cavaliers in licentiousness. Charles, who had not forgotten his former reception in Scotland, gladly availed himself of the opportunity to indulge his favourite propensities. That affectation of piety and decorum which had marked the palace of the Protector Oliver was soon exchanged for a perpetual round of pleasure and revelry; and the court of the British king, if inferior in splendour, did not yield in refinement and voluptuousness to that of his French contemporary, Louis XIV. Among the females who sought to win his attentions (and this, we are told, was the ambition of several) the first place, both for beauty and influence, must be allotted to Barbara Villiers, daughter of Viscount Grandison, and wife to a gentleman of the name of Palmer. On the very day of the king's arrival in the capital she established her dominion over his heart and contrived to retain it for years, in defiance

* Morris's 'History of England,' pp. 344, 345; Lingard's 'History of England—Reign of Charles II.'

of the inconstancy of his disposition and the intrigues of her rivals. With her Charles generally spent several hours of the day; and even when the council had assembled to deliberate in his presence, the truant monarch occasionally preferred to while away his time in the bewitching company and conversation of his mistress.'* This Barbara Villiers, or Mrs. Palmer, who went by the title of Countess of Castlemain (her husband, Palmer, being Earl of Castlemain), was afterwards created Duchess of Cleveland in her own right. Such was the licentiousness and bare-faced indecency prevalent at the time, that though we presume Palmer was perfectly cognisant of his wife's infidelity and adulterous intercourse with the king, he took no steps to hinder his wife's doings; he did not try to divorce her, but, instead, basely connived at her conduct, and allowed himself to be raised to the Earldom of Castlemain, and to receive other emoluments, as the price of his wife's shame. Lingard, writing on the general depravity of the time of the Second Charles, again says: 'The present proved the most tranquil period of the king's reign, but it was disgraced by the extravagance and licentiousness of the higher classes. The gallants of the court shocked the more sober of the citizens by their open contempt of the decencies of life, while Charles laughed at their follies, and countenanced them by example. At the same time that he renewed his visits and attentions to the Duchess of Richmond, he robbed the theatres of two celebrated actresses, known to the public by the dignified appellations of Moll Davies and Nell Gwynne. Davies had attained eminence as a dancer; Gwynne attracted admiration in the character and dress of a boy. The former received a splendid establishment in Suffolk Street, and bore the king a daughter, afterwards married into the noble family of the Radclyffes. The latter became

* Lingard's 'History of England,' vol. xii., chap. ii., pp. 76, 77.

the mother of the first Duke of St. Albans. Charles never allowed her to interfere in matters of state, but he appointed her lady of the bedchamber to the queen, and assigned her lodgings in the neighbourhood of the court. She was so wild, and witty, and eccentric, that he found in her company a perpetual source of amusement, a welcome relief from the cares that weighed so heavily upon him at times in the subsequent years of his reign. Habit, however, still preserved to Castlemain the empire which she had formerly acquired. She suppressed all appearances of jealousy, and sought her revenge by allowing herself the same liberties in which her paramour indulged.

* * * * * *

'From the commencement to the close of his reign he was the slave of women; but though he tolerated their caprice, though he submitted to their intrigues, he was neither jealous nor fastidious, freely allowing to them that latitude of indulgence which he claimed for himself. His example in this respect exercised the most pernicious influence on the morals of the higher classes of his subjects. His court became a school of vice, in which the restraints of decency were laughed to scorn, and the distinctions which he lavished on his mistresses, with the bold front which he enabled them to put on their infamy, held out an encouragement to crime, and tended to sap in youthful breasts those principles of modesty which are the best guardians of female virtue. There may have been other periods of our history in which immorality prevailed, but none in which it was practised with more ostentation, or brought with it less disgrace.'*

Such was Charles's dissoluteness, such his licentiousness, that when Louis XIV. of France was desirous to wean off

* Lingard's 'History of England,' vol. xii., ch. iii., pp. 197, 198; vol. xiii., ch. vii., p. 381.

the Merry Monarch from the Triple Alliance, which was on the point of completion by the contracting parties, Britain, Holland and Sweden, the wily Sun-King, knowing only too well the depravity of the British Charles and his impressionable nature towards the fair sex—for he was the slave of women — sent over to the British court one Mademoiselle de Querouaille, better known to the Britishers as Madame Carwell—a woman as beautiful and witty as she was crafty and licentious—to carry out his matured plans; and it is a matter of common knowledge that his sending over so beautiful and yet so licentious a woman had the desired effect on the Merry Monarch. Charles was captivated by her beauty and caught in the snares of the temptress, and Louis, through her, succeeded only too well. Madame Carwell reigned triumphant at the British court, Charles adding her to the already large number of his mistresses. He created her Duchess of Portsmouth. She was the means of bringing about the secret Treaty of Dover (May 22nd, 1670). 'Le Grand Monarque' sent Charles's own sister, the beautiful and accomplished, but unhappy Henrietta, Duchess of Orleans, to carry out the terms of the alliance, but the way towards the accomplishment of his scheme had been paved by Madame Carwell.* The clauses of the Treaty are matters of history. By one of them Charles undertook to publicly profess Catholicism; but the shameful terms of the Treaty were that Charles should assist Louis with the might of his Three Kingdoms in the subjugation of Holland, though the British Ambassador, Sir William Temple, was at the very moment engaged (while Charles and his sister, the Duchess of Orleans, were arranging the preliminaries of the Dover Treaty) in getting the terms of the Triple Alliance ratified by the Dutch

* Morris's 'History of England,' p. 334, and Lingard's 'History of England.'

Government. The Treaty of Dover further set forth that Charles should give his active co-operation and assist Louis in his claims to the Spanish throne; while Louis, on his part, engaged to assist him with 6,000 troops in the event of the Merry Monarch finding himself embroiled in a revolution and his throne in jeopardy, and, what was more pleasing to his avarice and depraved nature, gave him an annual pension of £200,000, with which the Merry Monarch was to maintain and regale his legion of mistresses.

The patient reader will have observed that we have more or less confined ourselves, when dealing with British immorality from the time of William III. to the days of George IV., to the actions of the different Sovereigns and their courts, and that we have hardly insinuated that the vice of immorality was national. But we may say that from the depravity of each king and his court the reader can form a fair opinion of the morals of the British people; for we take it that what is true for the king and his court also holds true for the great majority of the people; and this was especially the case in the days of Charles II., and of the so-called 'Virgin Queen Elizabeth.' We know that then the manners of these sovereigns and of their respective courts were assiduously copied by their subjects.

Immorality has, then, prevailed to an enormous extent in Britain. We now direct our attention to France, to see whether it has not had just as extensive and unenviable a career in that country. We mentioned elsewhere that though the French Henry II. had a loving wife in Catherine de Medici, yet that did not prevent the fickle monarch from indulging in the grossest way in his favourite pleasures, for he had several mistresses, and many children by them. But the imperious woman who ruled the French people, with Henry II. as her medium, was his chief concubine, Diana of Poitiers, whom he created Duchess of Valentinois. Immorality, practised without any approach to moderation, brought death prematurely to Henry IV., to Louis XII., and to Louis XIII., all of them depraved and loose men, quite devoid of all proper moral principles.*

The Great Emperor of the West, Charlemagne himself (Lecky tells us in his 'History of European Morals'),† besides having two wives, indulged largely in concubines. Madame de Montespan was Louis XIV.'s ruling mistress, and through Louis she indirectly ruled France. In order to stand high in the king's confidence and favour, French noblemen had to ingratiate themselves with her. The Fourteenth Louis was certainly not as depraved as the British Charles II., but his great-grandson was the Merry Monarch of France, while we are satisfied that the morals of the Great Monarch were on a par with those of Elizabeth of England. Many mistresses were owned by Louis XIV., like the great majority of the French kings who went before him.

Of all the French rulers, however, the Fifteenth Louis was certainly the most licentious; his standard of immorality being a little less shameful than that of the Merry Monarch, the British Charles II. Dubois and Duke Philip of Orleans were leading lights in the school of shamelessness during Louis XIV.'s minority. When, shortly after the king attained his majority, and the Regency of Orleans terminated, the depraved Dubois died, the companion of

* 'Encyclopædia Britannica,' vol. ix., and 'English Cyclopædia of Biography.'

† Vol. ii., p. 343. We would recommend for the reader's perusal W. E. H. Lecky's 'History of European Morals,' from Augustus to Charlemagne, in 2 vols. We think it a pity that Mr. Lecky has not favoured the world with another 'History of European Morals,' say from Charlemagne to George or William IV.

his bosom in licentiousness and vice, Philip of Orleans, speedily followed him to the grave, he perishing through an illness brought about by his dissolute and intemperate habits; and after the deaths of Dubois and Orleans the conduct of the Duke de Bourbon, Louis' prime minister, and his mistress, the Marquise de Prise, did not conduce to raise the standard of French morals in the days of Louis XV. Surrounded, then, as he was, by low and lack-moral men and women, remembering the examples set him by Dubois, Orleans, and, afterwards, Bourbon, adding to these disadvantages his own innate depraved nature, it was not to be expected that when he found himself his own master he could have been aught but a licentious man. He was married, it is true, to one Marie Leczinski, but neither that circumstance nor her piety in any way tended to check his propensity to vice; they did not prevent him from plunging headlong into a career of debauchery and social crimes.*

History has preserved and transmitted to us the name of Madame de Mailly as Louis' first mistress, while De Châteauroux was another well-known mistress; but it was in the person of Jeanne Antoinette Poisson le Normant d'Etoiles, better known as Madame la Marquise de Pompadour, that immorality played an important part in French history. She was educated to be a king's mistress, thus testifying to the gross and universal licentiousness existing at the time. She, after vainly trying her utmost to attract Louis' notice, at last succeeded in meeting him at a ball given in Paris. She was presented to the king, and subsequently deserted her husband for Louis. In 1745 the licentious and ambitious woman and unfaithful wife became the king's mistress, and had apartments fitted up for her at

* 'Encyclopædia Britannica' and 'English Cyclopædia of Biography.'

Versailles near the court. It was De Pompadour who ruined De Maurepas, who made Belle-Isle minister, and afterwards made De Bernis, her favourite, the king's minister, under her guidance. She did more than this. She allied herself with Maria Theresa of Austro-Hungary against Frederick the Great, that alliance originating the Seven Years' War. She it was who was responsible for the loss of French North America, for the losses of Grenada, Dominica, and Tobago to France, as well as for the disastrous battles of Rosbach, Dettingen, and Minden, in which the French arms were utterly shattered, and their ranks demoralized, by the triumphant and conquering allies in the Seven Years' War. De Pompadour was the means of introducing the Duc de Choiseul to the French premiership, while it was with her co-operation that De Choiseul made the humiliating Peace of Paris, or Versailles, for France.* When Louis XV.'s fickle and inconstant disposition began to swerve from her, his unscrupulous and crafty mistress, De Pompadour, did not think it beneath her to superintend the arrangements of the king's debaucheries, and even minister to his sensual wants in her efforts to remain in the favour of the truant monarch; and she succeeded but too well.† She it was who made Clermont and Soubise commanders-in-chief, and at the same time it may be said that no man came into office, no man came into prominence and the king's favour, save through her as intermediary. She was, as a consequence, courted and flattered by all the depraved courtiers and others.‡ De Pompadour, who terminated her career in 1764, may be termed the Mrs. Palmer, or Duchess of Cleveland, of France, for the Duchess of Cleveland ruled Britain through Charles II. as long as the Merry Monarch

* 'Encyclopædia Britannica.' † *Ibid.*
‡ 'Encyclopædia Britannica' and 'English Cyclopædia of Biography.'

lived; while the Marquise de Pompadour, as long as she lived, did the same in France through the Fifteenth Louis. No one came into office, or was appointed to posts of trust, save through Mrs. Palmer; while Madame de Pompadour likewise was supreme in France, she exercising her imperious sway over the dissolute Louis, and, like Mrs. Palmer, remaining in her paramour's favour up to the last. After De Pompadour's death Louis XV. did not simply confine himself to selecting the ladies of his court as his mistresses, but plunged into more degrading habits, for he sought out vulgar women as well with whom to satiate his sensual appetite. The infamous Parc aux Cerfs, where many a woman was ruined, had the licentious Louis as its originator. It was arranged after the pattern of the harem of the 'Commander of the Faithful.' Vast sums were squandered upon the maintenance of this establishment, which fairly scandalized Europe. But it was in 1770, just six years after the death of De Pompadour, that the Archpriestess of the College of Immorality, the Parc aux Cerfs Institution, came upon the arena, who was none other than Du Barry. While Marie Jeanne Gomard de Vaubernier, afterwards Countess du Barry, was still in her teens she was an inmate of a French brothel, where Count Jean du Barry, a dissipated man in a dissipated age, met her. He was quite fascinated with her, and made her his mistress. He introduced her to the king's chamberlain, and he in turn presented her to the founder of the Parc aux Cerfs.*

When the captivated Louis wished to have De Vaubernier—who was as vulgar as she was beautiful—titled, in order that she might present herself at Court as his mistress-in-chief, such was the licentiousness and barefaced indecency prevalent at the time, that Count Guillaume, styled of

* 'Encyclopædia Britannica' and 'English Cyclopædia of Biography.'

Barry, brother to Mademoiselle de Vaubernier's former paramour, wishing to curry the favour of the licentious Louis, gladly and unhesitatingly offered himself to supply the title to the mistress of the immoral monarch, by marrying De Vaubernier, which offer Louis accepted. Du Barry married De Vaubernier, and she thus became Countess du Barry.*

It was in 1770, we say, that the Countess du Barry was fairly launched on the sea of courtly life. She was established at Versailles as the king's chief mistress. Like De Pompadour who went before her, Du Barry lost no time in entering upon the field of politics, and became the willing and pliant tool of the profligate courtiers. She was made much of because of the strong influence she wielded over the dissipated Louis. At the instigation of the intriguing courtiers she drove the able and talented De Choiseul and the Jansenists from office. Intriguers and office-seekers who succeeded in pleasing her obtained office through her, and became her passive tools. Du Barry made and unmade ministers, and Chancellor Maupeon, Marshal Richelieu, and other leading lights received their portfolios through her as intermediary; while many a French Parliament came to grief because of her. It was while acting under her protection that Maupeon, the Chancellor, dissatisfied with its proceedings, terminated the career of the then French Parliament in 1771.†

The profligate Louis, who during his whole lifetime had walked in the ways of the ungodly, and was the slave of women, died in 1774, an easy prey to a fell disease which he had contracted, after a very long but very inglorious reign. His grandson and successor, the Sixteenth Louis,

* 'Encyclopædia Britannica' and 'English Cyclopædia of Biography.'

† 'English Cyclopædia' and 'Encyclopædia Britannica.'

was destined to reap the bitter fruits of the evils the Fifteenth Louis had sown. When Louis XV. died he left behind an impoverished Treasury and an impoverished people; but he also left behind a debauched nobility and bourgeoisie, who were wealthy, tyrannical, and insolent at the same time. When the sovereign People of France rose in rebellion, they scattered to the winds Royalty, Nobility, and all other sorts of oppressors, and becoming their own masters, beheaded the Sixteenth Louis, who thus with his life expiated the sins of his immoral grandsire, and the beautiful Marie· Antoinette, his consort, shared his terrible fate. They did more. They beheaded most of the nobility; the guillotine, herself a daughter of the French Revolution, was kept busy at her sanguinary work. That guillotine was a dissatisfied Moloch, who kept demanding more victims. Ever more it would have. The all-powerful and frenzied populace of France sought out eligible victims for the all-devouring Moloch ; and nineteen years after the demise of the disreputable Louis XV., his mistress, the Countess du Barry, was pounced upon by the blood-thirsty Revolutionists. Short work was made in those days of dealing with the accused. To be accused was virtually to be condemned; and Du Barry was seized because she was accused ; was condemned because she was accused. In 1793 Louis XV.'s last mistress-in-chief perished at the hands of the Revolution, a victim and an expiatory offering thrown into the jaws of the all-devouring Moloch—guillotine.*

Immorality has been proved, then, to have prevailed both in Britain and in France to an outrageous extent. But, we may ask, are these the only two countries on the European Continent in which immorality has been thus rank? The truth is that immorality has existed *everywhere* on the European Continent ! Where, indeed, has it *not* erected its

* 'English Cyclopædia' and 'Encyclopædia Britannica.'

unhallowed throne? Do we turn to Russia and see whether immorality has been an active force in that colossal country? Why, Peter, the first Emperor of Russia, and the so-called 'father of his country,' with all his greatness, led—certainly at the commencement, if not to the end, of his reign—a life of profligacy; while his queen, Catherine (who afterwards reigned as Catherine I., Empress of Russia), was mistress to several Russian generals, the last and best known of whom was the Prince Menschikoff. It was in the house of that last-named personage that the First Peter was introduced to Catherine, whom he made his mistress, and then subsequently married. The conduct of Elizabeth, however, Peter's elder daughter, threw that of the Great Peter himself into the shade. Her court was pregnant with vice; there unbridled licentiousness careered wildly, while the morals of her nephew and successor, Peter III., were as low as those of Elizabeth. The Third Peter compelled his wife Catherine (afterwards Catherine II., Empress of Russia) to be his confidante in his numerous shameless amours with the Russian women. He forced her to confer on his principal mistress, the Countess Woronzoff, the distinguished Order of St. Catherine. But his wife and queen, Catherine, it is fair to say, surrounded as she was by a profligate court, equalled Peter in licentiousness even during Peter's life, and surpassed all other Russian sovereigns in immorality after the demise of Peter. It was with the aid of the two Orloffs, her disreputable paramours, that she succeeded first in dethroning Peter, then crowning her polluted brow with the imperial diadem of the Czars, and at last mounting the throne as Catherine II., Empress of Russia.*

It was during her reign that Poland was completely partitioned and disappeared from the rank of independent states. For the mere purpose of aiding the election of a

* 'Encyclopædia Britannica.'

former lover of hers, Poniatowski, to the kingship of Poland, Catherine hurled a Russian horde in battle array over the Vistula.*

The standard of Catherine's morals was as low as that of Elizabeth of England. Like Elizabeth, she encouraged wholesale and systematic immorality amongst the male and female courtiers and attendants by her example. Of course the people caught the infection, and copied the examples set them by their betters. Catherine made one favourite lover after another minister; dismissed one to-day and set up another in his place to-morrow *ad libitum*. Her most trusty and favoured, as well as her most crafty and unscrupulous, paramour was her minister Potemkin, who remained in office from 1775 to 1791. And he, when he saw that his mistress's eager passion was flagging (as De Pompadour before, when in a like predicament, artfully outwitted Louis XV.), had recourse to the contrivance of ministering to the sensual desires of the depraved Catherine. He got her fresh lovers, and he succeeded in retaining power and office through these creatures till his death. The great laxity of Catherine's morals caused the paternity of all her children (presumably by Peter, when that unhappy and eccentric monarch was alive) to be a matter of grave doubt, the paternity of her eldest son, Paul, being treated as a moot point.†

We do not propose here to enter into the history of the morals of other European countries, because we judge that in dealing, as we have done, with the morals of the British, French, and Russians, all Europe has been fairly represented. What makes Russian morals still worse to-day than they were a hundred years ago is the strange fact that the Russian law does not sanction divorce.

Though the Caucasian has an immoral record in the past,

* 'Encyclopædia Britannica,' vol. v., pp. 233-235.   † *Ibid.*

though he is now wallowing in the mire of immorality, he would fain take upon him to lecture the African on immorality.

Did Clowes, and his unenviable mentor, Froude, and the other calumniators of the African race, when treating of African morals, bethink themselves of the divorce case of Scott *v.* Scott and the Honourable Charles Lowther, which was heard in November, 1882; of the divorce case of the Honourable Wyndham Edward Campbell Stanhope *v.* the Honourable Mrs. Camille Caroline Stanhope and Adye, which was heard in May, 1883; of the divorce petition of Sir Francis MacNaghten *v.* Lady MacNaghten and Thornhill, which was tried in February, 1883; of the divorce petition of the Lady St. Leonards *v.* the Right Honourable Lord St. Leonards and another, which was tried in February, 1883; of the divorce petition of his Grace the Duke of Marlborough *v.* Her Grace the Duchess of Marlborough and another, which was tried in 1883; of the divorce petition of the Baron Henry de Worms *v.* the Baroness Fanny de Worms and the Baron Moritz von Léon, tried in July, 1886; of the divorce petition of the Lord Colin Campbell *v.* Lady Colin Campbell, His Grace the Duke of Marlborough, Shaw, Butter, and Bird, tried in July, 1886; of the cross-petition for divorce of the Lady Colin Campbell *v.* Lord Colin Campbell and another, which was also tried in July, 1886; of the Most Honourable the Marchioness of Queensberry *v.* the Most Honourable the Marquis of Queensberry and another, which was tried in January, 1887? Do the calumniators of the African race, when expatiating on the morals of the African to his detriment, also bethink themselves of the divorce petition of Crawford *v.* Crawford and the Right Honourable Sir Charles Dilke, Bart., which was tried in January, 1886; of the divorce petition of the Right Honourable Lady Connemara *v.* the

Right Honourable Lord Connemara, G.C.I.E., ex-Governor-General of Madras, and Hannah Moore, which was tried in July, 1890?

With between 1,500 and 1,600 divorce petitions, almost everyone based on moral unfaithfulness, which are annually heard in the United Kingdom, and in which not only noble lords and ladies, members of Government, members of Parliament, governors, baronets, knights, and honourables, but also parsons, figure as respondents and co-respondents, can the Britisher dare to deny that immorality prevails, to an enormous extent, in *his country?* With the immoral offences committed under the Criminal Law Amendment Act, for which one member of Parliament, the late member for North Bucks, has been sentenced to twelve months' imprisonment, and for which another member, the member for East Belfast,* is living in ignoble exile, on the European mainland, can the Britisher dare to deny that immorality prevails, to an alarming extent, in *his country?* With the bold front which immorality puts on as it stalks abroad, and greets them in the streets at every turn, not only in the small hours of the morning, but in the broad glare of daylight, and in the Cimmerian darkness of murky night, can the Britisher dare to deny that immorality prevails, to the rankest extent, in *his country?*

Yet, with their standard of immorality at such a high and unenviable pitch, the Caucasians — particularly the Britishers, Frenchmen, or Americans — would fain lecture, on the Sixth and Ninth Commandments, those Africans who are certainly a great deal less unclean than themselves!

Immorality has also been found the practice of great men, great national heroes; for even the immortal Lord Viscount Nelson, the hero of Trafalgar, the Nile, and many

* Since expelled from Parliament.

other battles, and the great Robert Burns, the Scottish poet, have gone down before the power of this evil, and have been found worshipping at this unhallowed shrine. It was the Lady Emma Hamilton, sometime mistress to Captain John Willet Payne, afterwards mistress to Sir Harry Fetherstonhaugh; afterwards mistress to the Honourable Charles Greville; then mistress to, and afterwards the faithless wife of, Sir William Hamilton, once British Envoy to the Neapolitan Court,* who caused her paramour, the great Lord Nelson, to refuse to recognise the Neapolitan treaty of Uovo-Nuovo, concluded between Cardinal Ruffo and the insurgent Prince Francesco-Caraccioli; and it was this Lady Emma Hamilton who urged her lover Nelson to have her enemy Caraccioli tried by court-martial, with his (the Prince's) personal enemy, Count Thurn, as president. Then Caraccioli was condemned to death. Though the unfortunate Prince petitioned for a second, but a fair, trial or for a free pardon; though he petitioned that should neither of these be granted, it was his desire to die a soldier's death by being shot; and though he was verging toward three-score and ten, the Neapolitan authorities refused all his requests, and resolved to carry out his death-sentence by hanging, by his being drawn and quartered, and by finally throwing his body into the sea, with a shot of 250 pounds' weight tied to their victim's legs. The preliminary proceedings and trial were unlawful; the subsequent condemnation was unjust; and the final act, the hanging, was not an execution but a judicial murder. And for these the Lord Viscount Nelson and the Lady Emma Hamilton were responsible.†

It is acts like these which are a sad blot on the great

* British 'Dictionary of National Biography,' vol. xxiv., pp. 148, 149.
† Southey's 'Life of Nelson,' vol. ii.

Nelson's reputation, and all these were brought about because of his unhallowed passion for this Lady Emma Hamilton, the wife of his friend, who urged Nelson on to the doing of them.*

Was not the great Robert Burns one of the most illustrious of British poets? does not he yield the palm, in the poetical arts, only to Sir Walter Scott among the poets of Caledonia? And was not he a keen worshipper at the shrine of Asmodeus? And did he not sing the praises of, and address odes to, his Clarinda, and other mistresses? †

George Noel Gordon, sixth Lord Byron, certainly a very celebrated British poet, was, as the world knows, a very immoral man. ‡

Caucasians therefore, having an immoral past and an immoral present, are not authorized to moralize over the Africans, because they are to some extent polluted and unclean.

Mr. Clowes, Mr. Froude, and others, are all acquainted with the good old adage, 'Charity begins at home.' Why do not they then, instead of moralizing over the African, moralize over their own far more degraded countrymen, these Honourables, these Knights, these Baronets, these Members of Parliaments, these Members of Government, these Governors, these Dukes, these Marquises, these

* Southey's 'Life of Nelson,' vol. ii. Also 'Encyclopædia Britannica,' vol. xvii., p. 323; vol. xi., p. 421.

† 'Encyclopædia Britannica,' vol. iv., pp. 568-570; 'Dictionary of National Biography,' vol. vii., pp. 427-434, 436.

‡ Macaulay's 'Essay on Moore's Life of Lord Byron,' pp. 143, 144 *et seq.;* 'Encyclopædia Britannica,' vol. iv., pp. 606-610; 'Dictionary of National Biography,' vol. viii., pp. 139, 140, 142-150, 153; Mrs. H. E. Beecher Stowe in *Macmillan's Magazine* and the *Atlantic Monthly* for September, 1869, and 'Lady Byron Vindicated ; a History of the Byron Controversy, 1870.

other lords, these parsons, who figure as respondents or co-respondents in divorce petitions in the Divorce Courts? If there was no immorality there would be no divorce petitions, and no need of Divorce Courts. Whatever holds good for the British people on the score of immorality, likewise holds true for the American white people. We are, indeed, convinced that the white Americans are *more* immoral than their British cousins. To quote a contributor to *Blackwood's Magazine* for May, 1891, 'Such heinous crimes as brought destruction upon Sodom and Gomorrah, indescribable and awful outrages upon women and girls,' are daily perpetrated in the United States of North America by the white Americans.

CHAPTER IV.

SUPERSTITION IN THE NINETEENTH CENTURY.

WHEREVER there is gross ignorance, there superstition will be found.- It has its seat in the region of ignorance, and exists in countries uncivilized and semi-civilized, though to some extent also in countries civilized.

When the 'suttee' immolated herself on the funeral-pyre of her husband, in half-civilized Hindostan, in the hope, and with the belief, that the doing of that act would secure her salvation and eternal happiness, as well as wash away the possible sins both of her husband and of his ancestors, securing their admittance into the kingdom of everlasting glory, we recognise superstition. When witches were burnt to death throughout the world, in bygone centuries, the then rulers who condemned them were 'superstitious.' James I., the 'British Solomon,' wrote his 'Demonology,' a book bearing on witchcraft, in which he ascribed the raising of storms and unpleasant winds, fell diseases, and other evils to the witches; and the superstitious British Solomon went in great fear of them. So great a hold had 'superstition' on the minds of Britishers, in the days of the British Solomon, that the statute 1 Jac. I., cap. 12, was easily passed against witches, or sorceresses, and their abettors. And that foolish and infamous statute was not repealed till the reign of George II. The laws bearing on witches, and their abettors, are set forth in sections 2 and 3 of the statute 1 Jac. I., cap. 12. In the words of a learned historian: 'With great parade of learning, he' (James I.) 'demonstrated the existence of witches, and the mischiefs of witchcraft, against the objections of Scot and Wierns; he even discovered a satisfactory solution of that obscure but interesting question, "Why the devil did worke more with auncient women than others." But ancient women had no reason to congratulate themselves on the sagacity of their sovereign. Witchcraft at his solicitation was made a capital offence; and from the commencement of his reign there scarcely passed a year in which some aged female or other was not condemned to expiate on the gallows her imaginary communications with the evil spirit.'

The Asiatic fakir, who practises severe austerities, and either condemns himself to a standing posture all the days of his life, with a stick under his armpits to support him, or lacerates his body with knives or with scourges, is deemed 'superstitious' by all Christians. The man who wears an amulet as a charm and preventive against diseases, mischiefs, and other evils, appended to his neck or attached to his waist, is 'superstitious,' though that superstitious custom is common to most of the countries of Asia, and especially where Mahommedanism prevails. The same custom, however, is to be met with even amongst Europeans and those of European descent, the Spaniards, and Spanish Americans, the Portuguese and Brazilians more particularly. Those Englishmen who ascribed the cause of the loathsome eruptions, which appeared on the face of the Bolingbroke Henry, to his execution of Archbishop Scrope of York, could not have been other than 'superstitious'; while the old custom of touching for the King's-evil, which originated with the Confessor and sank into desuetude in the days when Anne was queen, may truly be termed 'superstitious.'

But it was in ancient times that superstition played its most important part, when heathenism was most rife. Then men and women and children were butchered in the most barbarous manner, and sacrificed as victims to appease the anger or gratify the whim of a jumble of gods. In those times there was a universal belief in omens; and we know that when the great Julius, on landing in Africa, in his march against Cato Uticensis and the Numidian Juba, suddenly fell down, that incident was deemed an unlucky omen by his Romans, who were seized with consternation, which when the first and greatest of the Romans saw, he not only dispelled, but turned to his advantage, by wisely exclaiming, 'It is now, O Africa, that I take possession of thee!' A superstitious custom, which prevented the German Ariovistus (whose very name exercised unwholesome dread amongst the ranks of Cæsar's Romans) from fighting before the advent of the new moon, as Cæsar tells us in his first book of the Commentaries on the Gallic War, enabled that renowned general with the greater facility to shatter the German arms of Ariovistus. It was a superstitious custom, hundreds of years before the birth of the great Julius, which caused the stern and fighting Spartans to refuse to help the Athenians against the Persians at Marathon before the advent of the full moon. Superstition is gradually disappearing from the modern world with the advance of civilization, but it will be a long time yet before it finally disappears; for a belief in ghosts still exists even in the civilized world as it has existed in bygone ages.

In the Middle Ages witchcraft, alchemy, and astrology were universally believed in, just as there can be found men even in our own times, even in this nineteenth century, who implicitly believe in such things. Men who thirsted after knowledge, and excelled their countrymen in scholarly attainments, in the middle and earlier ages, were looked upon with awe, and had the notoriety of being leagued in secret compact with the Arch-enemy of mankind, who supplied them with the desired knowledge at the price of their souls, given over to him when they paid the debt of nature. Witchcraft was believed in, even by eminent men in Britain and other countries, in the days of Elizabeth and James I. And these sovereigns believed in it, as did also Louis XV. and others, but that belief is mostly confined to-day to the more ignorant classes of the people.

In the olden days old women were generally, but not exclusively, the victims of the absurd and superstitious belief in witchcraft. Even young girls were either hung, drowned, or perished by fire; because we know that when Joan of Arc appeared before the gates of Orleans, at the head of the French soldiery, so great and widespread was the superstition in the ranks of the demoralized British soldiers that, panic-stricken, they raised the siege without even striking a blow. And when they got her into their power, in the year following their disgrace, after subjecting her to a year's imprisonment, the superstitious English wreaked their vengeance on the young 'Maid of Orleans' by burning her at the stake, on the groundless charge that she was a witch, in league with Satan.*

Elizabeth, like most of her predecessors and successors, James I. foremost amongst these latter, was superstitious; she put implicit faith, we are told, in the utterances of the astrologers whom she consulted. The Hindoo devotee who, even in this nineteenth century of our era, takes an annual plunge in the Hooghly, in the hope that his act will wash away and purge him from his sins, and secure for him and for his descendants, down to the fourth or

* Morris's 'History of England,' p. 263. There is good reason, however, for thinking this account of the Maid of Orleans is legendary, not historical.

fifth generation, salvation and unending happiness in the next world, and who also believes that his plunge will cleanse the souls of his ancestors, and enable them to receive the glorious beatitude of the hereafter, is surely 'superstitious.' All Christians regard those Indians as superstitious who look upon the Ganges as a sacred river; just as they also apply the term 'superstition' to the fast from sunrise to sunset, and the ridiculously mysterious rites, performed by the fanatical Mahommedan Indians at their Mahradan, or Hosein festival, during which goats are sacrificed. But while the term 'superstitious' may safely be applied to the Hindoo worshippers of Brahma, Vishnu, and Siva, we may also apply the term to the veneration paid by the Asiatic Indians to the cow and the goat.

The excessive reverence and divine honour paid to the Brahmin priests by the Hindoos are by us Christians held to be superstitious and an absurdity. We ridicule, or at least make light of, the Indian custom of child-marriage, and the law against the re-marriage of widows. The British, unlike the French, being in the habit of interfering with the customs of their subjects, abolished the superstitious suttee-custom, in 1829, when Lord William Bentinck was Governor-General of India. But that legislation was accomplished only after a great struggle on the part of the Hindoos, who agitated and declaimed against what they termed the profane act of the Britishers. We say that the suttee was certainly a custom worth putting a stop to, and we hold the British fully justified in removing one of the many relics of Indian barbarism. Nevertheless, it is a fact that the British do not sufficiently respect the scruples of their subjects. It is otherwise with the French. But we are quite prepared to admit that the suttee-custom would, in all probability, have been put down by the French if they had been in possession of the peninsula of Hindostan.

The fact that the British made light of the religious scruples of their Indian Sepoys is supposed to have caused the famous Indian Mutiny of 1857-58. When, in 1856, Lord Palmerston's Government resolved to introduce the Minié rifle, which necessitated the use of greased cartridges among the Indian Sepoys, as they have done with such good result among the British army, both at home and elsewhere abroad, these Sepoys murmured, because they suspected and feared that the grease of the cartridge which was used for the Minié rifle was made of the fat of ox and pig. Now, the British Government, although they know right well that the Hindoo held ox-fat in the greatest abhorrence, because he believed that he would lose caste if he were to touch it, though they also knew that the Mahommedan equally abhorred the fat of the pig, holding the swine, after the fashion of the Jews, as an unclean animal, yet did not respect their scruples, nor did they take any precaution against exasperating the Sepoys, and driving them into active mutiny. They (the British Government) failed to allay the storm which they had conjured up, for the Indian Sepoys, from deep murmurings, burst into the now historical open Mutiny, which lasted twelve months, terminating only after thousands of lives had been lost and millions of money had been spent. Though the British Government were greatly to blame, yet we cannot help ascribing the Indian Mutiny to the superstition of the Sepoys, for their objection to the use of the greased cartridge, on the ground that it was made of the fat of ox and pig, could be nothing but superstition.

Those Hindoos, and particularly the Brahmins, who never leave India, on the ground that they would lose caste were they to do so, are by us deemed to be superstitious; while the same Hindoos, like their forefathers before them, only eat mutton of animal food, the Mahommedan doing the reverse, for he eats everything in the shape of animal food, mutton and pork being barred; while we Christians, who eat everything in the shape of animal food, deem both Hindoos and Mahommedans superstitious—the one for eating one thing and rejecting all others, the other for eating everything but mutton and pork. But it is not only the Asiatic who is superstitious, for the Malay is also superstitious; while the American, or Red Indian, who believes in the Manitow, and takes delight in ghost-dancing, is also superstitious. The Caucasians, who pose as civilizers, are themselves also superstitious; that it is our business to prove; and that we propose to do in the current pages.

Superstition exists in Europe to-day as it did in the days of the dead past.

The Balkan peasant of the Greek Orthodox Faith, who rubs himself all over with garlic during Holy or Passion Week, and other Fast-days, in the hope of keeping His Satanic Majesty at a distance, and, according to the peasant's belief, so that he may not have a chance of tempting him to swerve from the right path and commit mischief, must be called superstitious.

The Britishers who consult Gipsy fortune-tellers as to their prospects, and allow themselves to be defrauded of their money, are surely superstitious. And those Frenchmen and Germans, those Italians and Spaniards, who allow themselves to be inveigled and swindled of their last penny by the cunning fortune-telling Bohemians, Zigeuner, Zingari, or Gitanos, are also superstitious.

We call that person superstitious (not to say a hypocrite) who commits crimes in the course of his life, and yet practises rigid and excessive austerities; who will not work a horse on a Sunday, and objects to train, tram, omnibus, and carriage being used on a Sunday. Just as we term the women superstitious who will not thread a needle and do a little sewing, or other harmless things, for her husband or brother, on a Sunday, and objects to every sort of Music, save Sacred Music, on a Sunday. The Britisher to-day is, in some respects, as superstitious as his forefathers were before him in the buried past.

Wright, writing in 1852, tells us that there is a circle of stones in the county of Cornwall called the 'Dance Maine,' or the dance of stones, which the Cornish peasantry allege is a representation of a party of young damsels who, they said, were turned into stones because they happened to dance on the Sabbath. That circle of stones is therefore regarded by the Cornish peasantry with superstitious fear and reverence commingled. Wright also tells us that the superstitious Oxonian peasant, with charming simplicity and stolid belief, gravely avers that the party of soldiers who came to destroy Long Compton were changed into the Rollrich stones in Oxfordshire.*

Wright testifies to British superstition in 1852, it is true, but it is nevertheless true that it is in this nineteenth century that he writes; and we believe that the same superstition exists (in 1891) both in Cornwall and in Oxfordshire as it did in 1852, the year in which Wright wrote his book. It may truly be said that superstition exists to just as great an extent amongst Britishers as it does amongst other Caucasians. The British Lowen Pike, writing in 1876, that is, fifteen years ago, and twenty-four years after Wright, expresses the hope that the 'half-believers in witchcraft who are still amongst us (Britishers) may dwindle in numbers generation after generation.'†

* Wright's 'The Celt, the Roman, and the Saxon,' chap ii., p. 62.
† Lowen Pike's 'History of Crime in England,' vol. ii., chap. xiii., p. 592.

Sir Walter Scott, one of the greatest of British bards, and Caledonia's first poet, testifies to the superstition of the age in which he lived—and he flourished in the eighteenth and in the earlier part of the nineteenth centuries, that is to say, from 1771 to 1832—and particularly to the superstition prevalent amongst his British countrymen of those days, by writing his 'Letters on Demonology and Witchcraft.'

Because Robert Burns saw how superstitious his Scottish fellow-countrymen—his 'brither Scots'—were in his lifetime (and Burns flourished from 1759 to 1796), he immortalized superstition in his 'Address to the Deil,' and in 'The Deil's awa' wi' th' Exciseman.' And does not the English Samuel Rogers, who lived from 1763 to 1855, for a like reason immortalize it by addressing an 'Ode to Superstition,' thereby reflecting on the crude notions and absurd beliefs of the Englishmen of his day?

The celebrated but eccentric novelist, Charles Dickens, who flourished from 1812 to 1870, also testifies to the superstition of Britishers by writing his 'Wonderful Ghost Story.'

Hanovero-German George II. of Great Britain and Ireland, like many of those who went before him, 'remained to the day of his death an implicit believer in . . . . ghosts, witches and vampires.'* And the British Macaulay, in his 'Essay on Ranke's History of the Popes,' assures us that Samuel Johnson, 'incredulous on all other points, was a ready believer in apparitions. He would not believe in Ossian; but he was willing to believe in the second sight. He would not believe in the earthquake of Lisbon; but he was willing to believe in the Cock Lane ghost.'†

The Caucasian, who to-day believes in the so-called

* 'Dictionary of National Biography,' vol. xxi., p. 171.
† 'Macaulay's Essays,' p. 551.

'evil-eye,' and its imaginary harmful powers, is decidedly superstitious; and there are very many Caucasians who labour under that delusion. The belief in the 'evil-eye' is as rife to-day as it was in the days of yore.

When the British landlady absolutely refuses to allow her bed, or the beds of her lodgers, to be turned over on Sundays, under the absurd belief that mischief and disaster, grim and terrible, will befall her, and her kith and kin, if that act be done on the Lord's Day, she is a superstitious woman; and we also apply the term 'superstitious' to the British burglar, who arms himself with some mystic and questionable talisman, in the hope that it may serve as a charm against his being caught, red-handed, whilst burglariously storming and looting some wealthy mansion.

The belief in the banshee, or fairy, which ignorant Irishmen suppose attaches itself to a particular house, and presents itself to view at the approaching death of one of the inmates of that house, is gross superstition; while the canny Highland crofters, and other Highland men of Caledonia, 'stern and wild,' who believe in the second sight, and, like the ignorant Irishman, believe that an elf or fairy attaches itself to a certain house, and shows itself at the impending death of one of the members of that family, are superstitious.

More. There are Highlanders to-day who believe that, if the presentation of a tuft of the brown heather to their guest on his immediate appearance at their threshold be omitted, ill-luck and mischief will follow that omission and short-coming, while these same canny Highlanders have the belief that their aged relatives—the female ones in a greater degree—possess the gift of prophecy.

We say that all these superstitions, as above detailed, do exist nowadays in the United Kingdom of Great Britain and Ireland, and in other parts of the Caucasian world.

We have shown that superstition existed amongst Caucasians in the days of Burns, Scott, Rogers, Wright, and Dickens. But it is nevertheless our duty to produce, as evidences that superstition is still rife in Britain and France, what the Caucasian actually says of himself, in the year of grace 1891.

We shall quote Caucasian newspapers, and, if we prove that superstition exists both in Britain and in France, we should like to be credited with having virtually proved that superstition exists, not only in Europe, but also all the Caucasian world over. We may fairly urge this, because Britain and France are the pioneers and leaders of civilization—at least in the opinion of the great majority of the human race; and in the forefront rank of nations. If we should be able to prove that temples of superstition exist in the breasts of Britishers and Frenchmen, and that the British and French peoples have their Mumbo Jumbo, it may surely be taken for granted, that whatever is true for the British and French peoples, on the score of superstition, is also true for all other Caucasian peoples, who are less enlightened than they.

When we tell the reader that we have the authority of Lord Macaulay for saying, that the only true history of a country is to be found in its newspapers, he will understand why we are so concerned about quoting the newspapers. But we should not like it to be forgotten that we have already proved, more or less, that superstition existed, and does exist, amongst Caucasians.

What we have now to do is to produce more proofs of the fact that superstition exists in this nineteenth century, and even in this year of grace 1891. We must allow the Caucasian to speak for himself and for his people. *Lloyd's News*, a British Liberal Unionist newspaper, of April 26, 1891, says: 'During the week there has been considerable excitement at Deptford through the rumour that a ghost was to be seen at night time by the door under the portico of St. Paul's Church. Thousands of persons have assembled outside, and a special force of police had to be called out. The other night a man climbed over the railings, and ascertained that the scare was occasioned by some bills that had been posted on the church door, which were visible from the gate when the moonlight shone upon them, and disappeared when a cloud passed over the moon. Upon the removal of the bills no more was seen of the ghost.'

Just imagine the good people of Deptford believing in Junabaes! In Deptford there are Her Britannic Majesty's Naval Victualling Yard and Naval Dock Yard; there are several educational and benevolent institutions, the Royal Naval School included among the former, whilst the number of churches in Deptford is legion; and yet, with all these evidences of civilization in its midst, Deptford is superstitious.

What, in our humble opinion, makes Deptford's offence still more heinous, is the fact that it is a suburb and part and parcel of the British Metropolis. And do we not know that London is the capital and centre of the United Kingdom, the capital and centre of the British Empire, which embraces 12,000,000 square miles, and contains over 350,000,000 of inhabitants, the capital and centre of the greatest and largest Empire the world has ever seen? Does not London share with Paris the capitalship and centreship of civilization? And we might almost say that London is the capital of the world. And yet in that colossal and leviathan London there is this gross superstition —a belief in his Weird and Ghostly Majesty King Mumbo Jumbo.

The Star, a British Gladstonian Liberal newspaper, of April 28, 1891, says: 'Mr. Drury Wake, the chairman of the Northampton County Petty Sessions, whose death has just been reported, was a direct descendant of the famous Hereward Le Wake, and an uncle of the present Sir Hereward Wake, of Courteen Hall, Northampton. His mother, the Dowager Lady Wake, was a sister of the late Archbishop Tait, who was a frequent preacher at the pretty little church at Ritsford, in which village this branch of the Wake family have resided for many years.

'Both Mr. Drury and Colonel Baldwin Wake married the two only daughters of the late Mr. Henry O. Nethercote, the genial Liberal squire of Moulton, who was an intimate friend of Earl Spencer, and an eloquent speaker on behalf of the Liberal cause.

'This death in the Wake family closes a somewhat romantic story. Many years ago, when the brothers Wake wooed the squire's two daughters, Baldwin was a captain in the Hussars, and a very popular gentleman in the village. The night before his marriage he took a dose of medicine to induce sleep, which succeeded only too well, and he slept so long that his marriage had to be postponed for a day.

'Seven years ago Colonel Baldwin Wake discussed with the squire a question which brought ill-feeling. The unfortunate Colonel went to his room after the discussion, and by way of inducing sleep, from the want of which he greatly suffered, took an overdose of a mixture, from which he died during the night. Within the space of a year the squire himself was dead, a servant committed suicide in the lake, other deaths occurred, and *popular superstition and village gossip were much exercised.*'

We can readily believe that Northampton has superstition in its midst. If there is superstition in London, no one must wonder that Northamptonians are also superstitious. London is the chief city of the United Kingdom, and is supposed to be greatly enlightened, and quite the most civilized portion of the United Kingdom; and yet Londoners are superstitious: we must expect, therefore, that Northamptonshire, a county and country province of the United Kingdom, is less enlightened and less civilized than London, and that Northamptonians are more superstitious than Londoners. Where there is the greater ignorance, there the greater superstition will be found.

Northampton has educational and benevolent establishments like Deptford; it has Government, Grammar, and Bluecoat Schools, School-boards, and Hospitals, as well as Churches and Friendly Hospitals. It has more. For we are told that Northampton has flour and paper mills, breweries, foundries, churches, maltings, town-hall, corn-exchange, curryings, Government works, and is noted for its lace, boots and shoes, and various manufactures. Yet superstition, meet offspring of ignorance, is an institution among the good people of Northamptonshire. That Squire Nethercote perished within a year after the death of his son-in-law, Colonel Baldwin Wake, was nothing supernatural; nor can we understand why the Northamptonians should be so superstitious because, forsooth, as the *Star* tells us, a servant committed suicide in one of the lakes!

The *Daily Telegraph*, a British semi-Conservative Newspaper, of April 30, 1891, says: 'The churchyard of the Greyfriars was, previous to the Reformation, the most fashionable cemetery in London, no fewer than four British Queens having found sepulture there. The ghost of one of these female Sovereigns, Isabella, the disreputable consort of Edward II., was long supposed to haunt the cloisters of the (Christ's) hospital; but the phantom seems of late years to have been laid in the Red Sea, together with that of Nell Cook, whose apparition no longer terrifies small boys who venture on Friday nights into the dark entry of the Close of Canterbury Cathedral.'

We do not share the views of the *Daily Telegraph* when it says that 'the phantom seems of late years to have been laid in the Red Sea, together with that of Nell Cook,' because we are convinced that the same belief in, and dread of, ghosts or phantoms exists to-day amongst Londoners and other Britishers. A Huntingdonshire coroner's jury, which sat at Warboys, to inquire into the circumstances connected with the death of a young inebriated British tailor (named Andrews), who, on being pursued by the indignant husband of the married woman he had indecently assaulted, when he was returning homewards from the athletic sports held at Ramsay, fell into a reservoir, and after experiencing an undesirable *douche*, committed suicide by throwing himself in front of a passing train, returned a verdict to the effect that the said Andrews had committed suicide 'at the instigation of the Devil.' We find the *Daily Telegraph* of April 6, 1891, commenting on the silly verdict given by these superstitious Huntingdonshire jurymen only a few days before, expresses the opinion that, 'To declare the inebriated tailor, who threw himself, or accidentally fell, across the rails, and was cut to pieces by a passing train, was moved to the commission of the rash act by the direct " instigation of the Devil " argues an acquaintance on the part of the Huntingdonshire coroner's jury with the ordinary course of procedure of the Enemy of Mankind so familiar as to be, to say the least, remarkable. We are bound, however, in justice, to remember that Huntingdonshire is a very ancient county, in which, possibly, many old-world superstitions may yet linger : and in districts where mediæval traditions and folk-lore still obtain, it may with tolerable confidence be assumed that the Gothic Satan— horns, hoofs, tail and all—continues to play a conspicuous part in them. A fourth part of this fertile shire was formerly, according to old Fuller, Abbey land, belonging to monks and friars.

'The town to which the hapless tailor repaired was once known as "Ramsey the Rich," and in the palmy days of British monachism the income of its abbey, which had only sixty monks to maintain, amounted to no less than £7,000 a year. Now, Lucifer, we all know, was never tired of plaguing the monks. He set traps for them, he tempted them, he did his evil best to delude and beguile those holy men; although now and again the foul Fiend was caught in his own trap, as was notably the case with that malicious Demon who strove to interrupt the studies of the good St. Dominic. That excellent saint was sitting up very late one night, writing, by the light of a single candle stuck in a lump of clay, a sociable folio . . . when his cheerful task was sought to be thwarted by the Fiend, who made divers but ineffectual attempts to blow out the holy man's candle. St. Dominic, indeed, gained so complete a victory over the emissary from the nether regions as to force him to go humbly on his knees and hold the candle, while his sanctified opponent went on merrily penning his advocacy . . . until the socketless candle, burning down to the fag-end, began to grill the Devil's fingers, causing him to howl dismally; for Satan, we know from Milton, can feel and has felt pain. This may have been the kind of Demon who, in the thinking of coroners' juries in Huntingdonshire, goes up and down "instigating" tipsy tailors to throw themselves on the permanent way; and, for aught we can tell, the Warboys and Ramsey Devil may be the selfsame demon who strove to annoy St. Dominic, and got so soundly trounced for his pains. For Beelzebub, it is notorious, is ubiquitous. "Where are you damned?" Satan is asked in the Elizabethan play. "Everywhere," is the reply; and the Mephisto who was the perdition of Faust may be identical with the Fiend who, as the eccentric coroner's jury think, roams about the pleasant county of Huntingdon, "instigating" intoxicated youths to do desperate deeds. Only, in the lamentable case of the wretched young tailor, Andrews, the worthy jurymen do not appear to have given the Devil his due. He is credited with one act of instigation, whereas, if the strange hypothesis of the Huntingdonshire sages be a correct one, he must have been guilty of three distinct and consecutive suggestions of a diabolical character. First, he must have instigated Andrews to attend the agricultural sports at Ramsey, with the full knowledge and cognizance that the tailor would be led by the delirious excitement of wrestling, leaping, running, or football, to drink too much beer. Next, Andrews being fuddled, the Devil must have "instigated" him to assault the married female; and his final act of instigation must have been to whisper in the drunken fugitive's ear, "Throw yourself in front of the train and get smashed!"

'In one respect the Fiend seems to be open to the reproach of having committed a slight error of judgment. Why did he allow the flying tailor to fall into the reservoir? "Too much water," had poor Ophelia, for she was drowned; but Andrews was dragged, or managed to scramble, out of the reservoir. One would have thought that the abundant "douche" would at least have partially sobered him. Perhaps Mephisto, feeling sure of his prey, had momentarily flown away a few thousands of miles to see if there was anything or anybody requiring his friendly offices—say in the interior of Africa, or in Burmah, or in the State of Louisiana—and that, returning to Huntingdonshire, although drenched, still drunk, and still dashing across country, he addressed himself to his final act of instigation, and saw his victim comfortably under the wheels of the locomotive. It may be finally asked, by some inveterate sceptics, how the coroner's jury arrived at the knowledge that the miserable Andrews was instigated by the Devil at all? The reply to such a question might be a sufficiently simple one, " They are " ' (answers the *Daily Telegraph*, correctly and wisely) ' " a very old-fashioned people down in Huntingdonshire; and implicit belief in a personal and indefatigably prompting and suggesting Fiend is an extremely antique belief." ' That ' belief,' we say, is a *superstitious* one.

The *Daily Telegraph* for June 29, 1891, also says, ' There are probably vast numbers of foolish people (amongst Britishers), and not a few cultured and intelligent ones (not leaving out numerous clergymen, and a still larger number of ladies), who believe in astrology as firmly as the Chaldæans, the Assyrians, and the Greeks did, and as many Oriental nations continue to do to this day.

' Fashionable (British) society is just now infested by a number of female adventuresses, who, by means of various " subtle devices," are openly and insolently carrying on their trade as fortune-tellers for hire and gain. Let the police come down like a wolf on the fold on the well-dressed, well-installed, well-puffed, and largely patronized fortune-tellers of the West-end, and bring *them* to the bar of justice.'

The *Daily Telegraph* for October 7, 1891, good-humouredly asserts that ' New Kent Road affords a magnificent chance at this moment for a Mahatma. Hundreds of people in the neighbourhood are firmly convinced that a house in that busy thoroughfare is occupied by a ghostly inhabitant. Like the mysterious individuals of whom a great deal has been heard lately, the spirit is extremely chary of showing itself. Crowds assemble in front of the house, knock at the door, and ring the bell, in the hope of awakening the ghost to a sense of its public responsibilities, but without any result, except that of driving fanatic the good citizen who has the misfortune to live on the premises. Some weeks ago a young man was fined twenty shillings for creating a disturbance at the house. This does not seem to have had the desired effect, for now a dame named —— has been summoned before the Lambeth magistrate for a similar offence. A police-officer said there were about two hundred people assembled in front of the "haunted house" making a great noise, prominent among them being the accused, who appeared to be in a state of great excitement, and was demanding wildly to see the ghost. Mr. H—— fined her forty shillings—a tidy sum to pay for not seeing a disembodied spirit. It is refreshing to find that the inhabitants of New Kent Road remain genuinely unaffected by the materialistic tendencies of the age.'

Superstition, then, exists throughout the United Kingdom; yet it would seem that neither W. Laird Clowes nor James Anthony Froude pay due heed to it. It has been shown to exist not only in the Metropolis of the British Empire, but also in the provinces—Northamptonshire and Huntingdonshire affording striking examples.

We also apply the term 'superstitious' to those of the British people who believe in the so-called 'spiritualistic séances,' at which the 'spiritualistic' mediums give out that they have the power to summon the dead to appear, as well as absent living persons. The belief in such things is certainly to be classed 'superstition.' And it appears that this kind of superstition exists not only in Europe and in America, but in other parts of the habitable globe, where there are to be found these so-called spiritualists.

We are of opinion that the term 'superstitious' should be applied to all those Britishers and Yankees who are members of the Theosophical Society, which was founded, a few years ago, by Madame H. P. Blavatsky, who is regarded by many as nothing less than a fraud. Madame Blavatsky gave out that she had the power of performing miracles. But this same Madame Blavatsky is confidently asserted by some to have been of doubtful moral character. What is historically certain is that she deserted her own husband. Not much confidence can be placed in the extravagant pretensions of such a woman, when she claims to be inspired and to have the power of working miracles. 'Truth is stranger than fiction,' they say, yet she could reckon among her dupes eminent scholars and authors— like Mrs. Annie Besant, the friend and collaborator of Charles Bradlaugh, and 'pretty, piquant-looking,' little Mrs. Annie Wolf of New York, who writes under the *nom de plume* of Emily—who implicitly believed in Blavatsky's prophetic and miraculous powers.

The gift of prophecy was given to holy men like Isaiah, Jeremiah, Ezekiel, Daniel, and the minor prophets, by Jehovah; and the same Almighty Being gave the power of performing miracles to such holy men as Saints Peter, Paul and John; but we certainly cannot think that God ever did, or ever would give, the prophetic or the miraculous power to such a person as Madame Blavatsky, whose historical record will not bear investigation. What is the world coming to, when an impostor like Madame Blavatsky can so easily find believers?

We now pass on to consider Superstition in France. Wright, in his work, published 1852, says: 'In France, as in England, and, indeed, in most countries, they (the legends) are usually connected in the popular belief with fairies or with demons, and in England with Robin Hood. In France this latter personage is replaced by Gargantua, a name made generally celebrated by the extraordinary romance of Rabelais.

'The prohibition to worship stones, occurring so frequently in the earlier Christian ecclesiastical laws and ordinances, relates doubtless to these Druidical monuments, and was often the cause of their destruction. Traces of this worship still remain. In some instances people passed through the Druidical monuments for trial, or for purification, or as a mode of defensive charm. It is still a practice among the peasantry at Columbiers, in France, for young girls who want husbands to climb upon the cromlech called the *Pierre-levée*, place there a piece of money, and then jump down. At Guerande, with the same object, they depose in the crevices of a Celtic monument bits of rose-coloured wool tied with tinsel. The people of Croisic dance round a menhir. It is the popular belief in Anjou that the fairies, as they descended the mountains, spinning by the way, brought down the Druidical stones in their aprons, and placed them as they are now found.'*

These superstitious customs and beliefs, which existed in France thirty-nine years ago, still obtain to-day. Indeed, many a French damsel who is in need of that precious article, a husband, is in the habit of first partaking of a salted egg—water to allay thirst not being permitted to the fair candidate for matrimonial honours — and then retiring to bed in silence, without speaking to anyone, on every 24th of June, that is, on St. John the Baptist's Day.

A Correspondent of the *Daily Graphic*, a British Conservative organ, in a letter published on the 15th of April, 1891, says concerning a 'Haunted House,' at Nice: 'Some time ago Nice was in a ferment. A house in Le Port, at the foot of the quarries, in a terrace that has not the faintest look of the uncanny, was said to be haunted. Crowds often gathered outside it, though, I believe, the "experiences"

* 'The Celt, the Roman, and the Saxon,' chap. ii., p. 63, by T. Wright.

were strictly confined to those within. Sometimes there were two thousand "encumbering" the road, as the inhabitants put it. Sometimes there were three thousand! Mounted police were employed to prevent a hopeless block. Arriving at Nice the other day, the first person I asked, "Where is the haunted house?" said, "Why, to be sure, it is just at the corner of the harbour." I found that every cabman knew his way there. My "cocher" said: "You want to take views. No portraits of ghosts by daylight, té !" Besides, he's not there now." "Where is he?" I asked. "Who knows?" said cabby. "What was the explanation of the occurrences?" I inquired, for I fancied my man might be a sceptic. But he was no doubter at all. He averred that explanation there was none; and he laughed, shrugged his shoulders, looked sheepish and mischievous by turns. He seemed anxious to guard against possible disappointment, for he repeated the assurance that I had not a chance of seeing the ghost by day; but the house could be photographed.

'The ghost's conflict in this house was, to say the least, peculiar. Darkness would descend upon everything, and then the inmates would be beaten! No assailants were ever visible, and it was not the darkness which "could be felt," but blows — blows, too, which left bruises. The excitement caused by the recurrence of these mysterious assaults led to an organized inquiry by the police, but no explanation was ever satisfactorily established. Once twelve policemen searched the premises from roof to basement, while twelve other men of the force watched the house from the outside. No one left the house which was so carefully guarded, and inside nothing rewarded the search till the twelve men had examined everything, and were congregated at the foot of the stairs, on the point of leaving the place, when suddenly an ink-jar fell among them. They thought by the sound that it came from the very top of the house; and attached to the jar was a paper bearing the words, "Try as you will, you'll never catch me," or something to that effect.

'The police having utterly failed to unravel the mystery, and the nightly blows and unexplained darkness recurring, some of the bravest and strongest young men banded themselves together to investigate the matter. They prepared to sit up a night in the haunted house, and provided themselves with many lamps, and with cards to while away the vacant hours. Suddenly all the lamps throughout the house were extinguished, and blows were rained upon the hardy youths without their being able to guess whence they were assaulted, or who were the assailants. No one was any the wiser for this experiment, except the doughty champions, who were certainly sadder and sorer, if wiser, men next morning.

'Of course the usual explanations—coiners, illicit still, burglars' place of meeting—were offered to account for the mystery, but the premises do not lend themselves to any of these theories. One thing seems clear: there is now no ghost at the place, which is the factory of a marble-worker. But the manner of his passing is as little understood as was the manner of his coming; and it is not one ghost in a hundred that sets a city, the civic fathers, and their police all agog.'

Comment on this quotation is surely needless.

The Paris correspondent of the *Daily Telegraph*, writing to that journal, on the 2nd of June, 1891, also testifies to French superstition when he says: 'There has been great excitement in the neighbourhood of Saleix, situated in the Department of the Ariège, and the country people have been trooping to the spot to contemplate a girl who professed to have seen visions. She was asked by her visitors a variety of questions about the future; to which she appears to have replied to their entire satisfaction, for every day they arrived in increasing numbers. The small cottage which she inhabits with her parents was literally besieged, and at last the Maire, alarmed at the formidable proportions which this pilgrimage was assuming, called on the gendarmerie to interfere. The people were induced to return to their homes without more ado, and since their departure the girl gives out that she has not been favoured with any more visions.'

Superstition, then, having been proved to be prevalent amongst both the French and British people, and these two nations having been shown to be the leaders of modern civilization and progress, it may be taken for granted that superstition obtains to some extent amongst other and less civilized Caucasians.

The *St. Stephen's Review* of May 2, 1891, writing on the general incompetency and demoralization of the Portuguese, one of the most backward people in Europe, is of opinion that 'At home the "Portugee" is an ignorant, superstitious, unenlightened being.'

Lloyd's News of August 23, 1891, testifies to German superstition in this wise: 'The "army grub" or worm, a caterpillar which marches in procession of many thousands at a time, has created alarm in the Hurz district. There is a superstition in Germany that the appearance of this insect forebodes war, failure of the crops and famine.'

The Yankees, too, are just as superstitious as the British, French, and other peoples. Dalziel's Agency, telegraphing from New York, under the date of June 2, 1891, says: 'The New York *Tribune* publishes the following remarkable story: 'Two years ago a woman, whose name could not be learned, one Monday presented herself at the Manhattan Eye and Ear Hospital for treatment. She was found to be suffering with a bad case of nasal catarrh, and was placed under the care of Dr. Johnson. The patient received due attention, and went her way. Dr. Johnson died suddenly two days later. Six months passed before this patient went to the hospital again to be treated for the same trouble. The "cabinet" in which such patients are received, examined, and receive their treatment, was then in charge of Dr. Pond. That gentleman did everything possible for the patient, and she went home. Dr. Pond died within two days. His death was ascribed by the attending physician to the now common cause of "heart failure," though he had not been subject to trouble with that organ. The second death after attendance upon this patient caused a good deal of comment among the medical and nursing staffs of the hospital.

'The patient remained away, however, until last Wednesday, when, finding her old trouble again making her life miserable, she once more applied for relief. She said to the clerk that she feared the doctors might have some hesitation in attending to her case, as her previous visits had been followed by the deaths of Drs. Johnson and Pond. Her surmise was wrong, for she was promptly attended to by Dr. David Phillips, who had finally succeeded to Dr. Pond's department, and who had been made acquainted with the grim joke about the fatal patient, the woman being fully identified to him as the traditional individual.

'Dr. Phillips was dead the next morning. He went home after treating the patient, and dined with a few friends. He then made some professional visits. When he returned home from these, he complained of feeling ill, and went directly to bed. He did not make his appearance at the usual time in the morning, and his mother, who went to awaken him, saw him apparently in a sound and peaceful sleep. She did not disturb him, thinking a long sleep would do him good. No effort was made to arouse him until luncheon-time, when the family discovered, to their horror, that he was dead. A physician was called. When he arrived, and had examined the body, he gave it as his opinion that Dr. Phillips had died in his sleep of heart failure several hours previously.

'Dr. Phillips was regarded by his associates as an excellent throat and nose specialist, and a good general physician. He had great ability in diagnosis, and was always consulted when complicated cases came to the hospital. The officers of the hospital are reticent about the case. They admit that there is an extraordinary degree of excitement among members of the medical profession; and the staff of the Manhattan Hospital is being watched, with the expectation that another funeral may shortly take place, with one of its members as a subject.'

With all these superstitions prevailing among the Caucasians, which he is either ignorant of, or is aware of yet has overlooked, Mr. Laird Clowes, instead of attending to matters nearer home, which might so well interest him, prefers to attend to matters which do not specially concern him, and might well have been left alone until he had delivered the Caucasian world from its superstitions. Laird Clowes, on pages 112 to 114 of 'Black America,' says: 'Nor will I say much concerning the degrading superstitions and superstitious practices of the great mass of ignorant blacks. Two years ago the *Herald*, a respectable paper in Boston, published an article, five and a half columns long, the object of which was to demonstrate that Voodooism existed to an alarming extent among the African people of Boston and New England generally. Here are a couple of extracts:

' " No people are so prone, by nature and force of circumstances, to superstition as the blacks. Devout and easily excited, they are apt to accept, blindly and without reasoning, the traditions of their fathers; and even among those of reasonable education there are traces of idolatrous creeds and customs, which have always characterized the West India Negroes. Voodooism, of which much has been hinted, a little written, but almost nothing known—one of the blackest, cruellest, and most heathenish forms of idolatry the world has ever seen—exists to-day to an alarming extent right here in Puritan New England."

' " Perhaps the fact that the Negroes have always regarded themselves as a wronged people impels them to cultivate a revengeful spirit, and the prevailing object of their so-called spells is in the direction of working harm to their enemies. They pay more attention to vengeance than to the cure of diseases, although claiming wonderful power from their herbs and decoctions. The prevailing sentiment, if it may be so termed, of Voodooism, aside from idolatry, is revenge, and in their hatreds these people are implacable. No punishment is too horrible to be visited upon their enemies."

'Most white Bostonians believed,' continues Laird Clowes, 'that the article was full of exaggerations, but, to the general surprise, the Negroes practically admitted the impeachment.

'Here is part of a resolution which was passed in July, 1889, by the Coloured National League, sitting at Boston:

'" Whereas the Boston *Herald* has lately shown that the degrading superstition of Voodooism, as well as its practice, exists here in Boston, to some extent, among a few illiterate and ignorant persons of our race; and whereas the sentiment among the better class of coloured people is that no one should be swifter to condemn any kind of foolish race superstition or disreputable practice than the coloured people themselves; and whereas it should everywhere be the aim and desire of the coloured people to welcome any information that may show the need of greater race enlightenment, or that shall stir us up to more earnest efforts for the general elevation of our people ; be it resolved that the League places itself on record as being both anxious and willing to join hands with the *Herald*, or anyone else, in condemning, discountenancing, and stamping out Voodooism or any other 'ism' hurtful to the physical, moral, or spiritual elevation of the coloured people ; and that the League calls upon good coloured people everywhere to set their face like a flint against every kind of evil superstition, habit, practice, custom, or belief, whose tendency, if encouraged, might be to degrade, belittle, or harm the coloured people in public estimation."'

We are not prepared to deny that there might have been some sort of superstition amongst a few of the ignorant and illiterate American Africans of Boston some years ago, but this much we do say, that we certainly deny *in toto* Laird Clowes's statement that 'the great mass of the ignorant blacks' in America are superstitious, as we also give a general denial to the statement, as made by the Boston *Herald*, that 'no people are so prone (to superstition) by nature and force of circumstances as the blacks.' Nor is the statement, as made by the Boston *Herald*, and quoted by Laird Clowes, that 'even among those of reasonable education there are traces of the idolatrous creeds and customs which have always characterized the West Indian Negroes,' anything approaching to the truth. Neither the Boston *Herald* nor Laird Clowes attempt to support this accusation by any trustworthy evidence. It is one thing to affirm that some American Africans of 'reasonable education' have 'traces of the idolatrous creeds and customs' in their midst, but it is another and a very different thing to prove that they are in the generally demoralized condition which Laird Clowes and the Boston *Herald* allege they are? Such a statement as we have given from the Boston *Herald*, that 'idolatrous creeds and customs . . . have always characterized the West Indian Negroes,' can be only an opinion on which no authority rests. It is not given to the Caucasian to determine absolutely what are the characteristics of the Ethiopian races; such judgments are not within their right. They are better employed in determining the peculiarities of their own race. We Africans know ourselves better than Caucasians can ever hope to know us; and we take this opportunity of firmly declaring that 'idolatrous creeds and customs' have *never* characterized the West Indian Africans.

We turn the argument against our traducers. Caucasians know themselves better than we Africans can ever hope to know them; and we have quoted the statements of Caucasian authors and editors in order to prove that Caucasians are superstitious, in what is, unquestionably, a most demoralizing way.

Mr. Laird Clowes proceeds to tell us that American Africans, as represented by the 'Coloured National League' of Boston, 'to the general surprise,' 'practically admitted the impeachment.' What sort of impeachment did the 'Coloured National League' of Boston admit 'to the general surprise'? That which the National League admitted in July, 1889, was this: they admitted that 'the superstition of Voodooism, as well as its practice, exists (in 1889) here in Boston to some extent,' but they carefully added, 'among a few illiterate and ignorant persons of our race.' That is all that they admitted. They did *not* admit, and very properly and correctly they did not admit, that 'the *great mass* of ignorant blacks' were superstitious, because that statement, as made by Laird Clowes, was, and is, the reverse of the truth. Nay more, the 'Coloured National League' of Boston never admitted—and very rightly they did not—that 'no people are so prone by nature and force of circumstances to superstition as the blacks'; nor did they admit that 'even among those of reasonable education there are traces of idolatrous creeds and customs which have always characterized the West Indian Negroes'—for two very good reasons: (1) because amongst American Africans of 'reasonable education' idolatry and superstition do *not* exist, though it may be that 'a few illiterate and ignorant persons of our race' in America are superstitious: they are none of them idolatrous; (2) because their African countrymen in the West Indies have *never* been characterized by 'idolatrous creeds and customs.'

Men of more than 'reasonable education' amongst Caucasians have been unenviably distinguished for their superstitions. In Britain, for instance, almost all the British Kings, from Wessex Egbert (as well as his predecessors) to the First German George, were superstitious; and in France almost all the French Kings before and from Frankish Clovis to the Bourbon Louis XV. were superstitious. Did not James I. of England and Ireland, and VI. of Scotland, the British Solomon, himself write his 'Demonology,' in which he professed his belief in witchcraft? and did he not cause his Parliament to pass a law against supposed witches and their abettors? That unjust and disgraceful law was actually enforced year after year, and was not repealed till the reign of the second Hanoverian George.*

Sir Matthew Hale, a man of the greatest eminence and erudition, and a voluminous author, who lived from 1609 to 1676, and who was Lord Chief Justice of England during the maladministration of Britain by the Merry Monarch, openly professed himself in court as a believer, like Coke and Bacon, in witches and witchcraft, and when any unfortunate old women were standing their trial before him on

* 'Encyclopædia Britannica,' vol. vii., p. 63, ninth edition.

the charge of being witches, he was accustomed to bully the jury into returning a verdict of 'guilty.' And these wretched old women were condemned to perish either on the gibbet or in the fire.*

Even in this nineteenth century we have shown superstition to be found amongst Caucasians 'of reasonable education,' in London, Northamptonshire, Huntingdonshire, Cornwall, and Oxford, as well as among the people of Nice and New York.

As long as there are men of enlightenment and progress amongst us Africans, to organize our ranks and weed out unsound matter from our midst, the African race all the world over need never despair. Because of its manly resolution and outspokenness, in calling on illiterate Africans to abandon their superstitions, we congratulate and commend the 'National League of Boston.'

The Boston *Herald*, as quoted by Mr. Laird Clowes, also tells us that : ' Perhaps the fact that the Negroes have always regarded themselves as a wronged people impels them to cultivate a revengeful spirit.'

What, we think, the Boston *Herald* should have said is not that 'the Negroes have always *regarded themselves* as a wronged people,' but that 'the Africans *were* and *are still* a wronged people.' Does the Boston *Herald*, and does Mr. Clowes, forget how many myriads of unsuspecting Africans were pitilessly kidnapped by the white man, taken from their native home, and compelled to cross the ocean, and endure the horrors of the Middle Passage—during which many committed suicide, and many more perished from brutal and inhuman treatment—experienced at the hands of their oppressors? Are not the Africans a cruelly, shame-

* 'English Cyclopædia of Biography,' vol. iii., p. 256; Encyclopædia Britannica,' vol. xxiv., pp. 621, 622; *ibid.*, vol. xi., p. 382; 'Dictionary of National Biography,' vol. xxiv., p. 19.

fully wronged people? Does the Boston *Herald*, and does the Commissioner of the *Times*, want to forget the injustice, the cruelties, the unpardonable, unimaginable horrors attendant on African Slavery all the long years during which the white man forcibly held the black man in abject thraldom? Were the Africans *not a wronged people?* They are a wronged people to-day even as they were in the past. When the British Government of to-day deliberately passes over deserving and capable British Africans in order that the scum and refuse of the population of the British Isles may be provided with Colonial Government posts and other official advantages, must not Africans be considered still a wronged people? Does not the Government which withholds the franchise from the African inhabitants of Cape Colony, Natal, Gold Coast, Jamaica, Trinidad, British Honduras, and other places, wrong the Africans?

The Australian Africans have also their grievances in that—though New South Wales, Victoria, Queensland, South Australia, etc., are self-governing Colonies—the black aborigines do not enjoy the franchise; the alien colonists exercise the franchise, and are thus enabled to lord it over the proper inhabitants of the land. When the Yankees almost daily lynch the Africans and succeed in evading justice, must not the American Africans be spoken of as a *wronged people?*

In the South, as well as in other parts of the United States, the Africans, because they are deprived of the rights conferred upon them by the Constitution, can be none other than a wronged people. When the authorities of the United States fail to mete out justice to their African fellow-countrymen in the judicial courts, by refusing to give them a fair trial, or by failing to punish those of the white people in the States who oppress them, what must they (the Africans) be considered but a *wronged people*, and an unhappy people? The acts of injustice and the outrages committed upon them in America are notorious: they are a crying shame in a land which arrogates to itself the dignified name of 'Civilized' America!

There are many parts of the United States in which Africans are practically prevented from earning an honest dollar.

Some Africans had replaced some white miners who were on strike at the latter end of January of last year (1891), at the Carbon Hill Coal Mines, in Walker County, near Birmingham, Alabama, and this was made the reason why they (the Africans) were fiendishly massacred in their sleep by a Yankee mob. That outrage was barbarous, it was brutal; and yet the perpetrators of that fiendish massacre were not even so much as arrested; they continue to roam at large, unchallenged by the judicial executive, as if they had its approval. This is one of the many instances of the wrongs that are heaped upon the devoted heads of the unhappy Africans.

When honest Africans had been hired to replace the Cumberland mountaineers, who had given up work in the earlier part of last year (1891), a party of these mountaineers, well armed and equipped, marched to Tanbark Camp in the Cumberland mountains, where the Africans were at work, shot six of them dead, and wounded ten others. That is another instance of the wrongs heaped upon our unhappy people. And what makes the cup of misery the more bitter and the more galling, is the fact that the law takes no action in a matter where the African is the injured party, thereby exposing itself to the reproach of being an abettor of criminals and evil-doers.

With all these proofs before him, there is surely no man, unless he be an inveterate African-hater, like James Anthony Froude, who is evidently suffering from negrophobia; or unless he be a dullard, and not in full possession of his reasoning faculties, who will hesitate to admit that the Africans were, and are to-day, a cruelly wronged people. No, not even Laird Clowes will dare to deny that the Africans were, and are, a wronged people; for his book 'Black America' is, from beginning to end, replete with evidences of that fact.

Would Caucasian nations have needed to grant Africans Enfranchisement if they had *not* been a wronged people when in bondage? We Africans owe our Emancipation to the sympathies of the noble members of the great Caucasian nations throughout the world, to the force of Caucasian public opinion, to the will of the sympathetic and sovereign *people;* but we owe nothing to hard-hearted Caucasian Governments; the Governments have simply been forced to do what the people willed.

The Boston *Herald* says that 'perhaps the fact that the Africans have always regarded themselves as a wronged people impels them to cultivate a revengeful spirit.' The first part of this sentence we have dealt with; now the latter part of it claims our attention. If the allegation that some of the American Africans 'cultivate a revengeful spirit' be true, then we certainly condemn the cherishing of such a spirit. All good and true Christians abhor those who 'cultivate a revengeful spirit.' Yet if any Yankee has, or ever will have, cause to dread the vengeance of the African, he will only have himself to blame. The white man brought the black man against his will to America; and if the white man, with part of the money which he has amassed at the expense of the tears and groans of the black man in the days of slavery, will not send the black man away back to Africa, will continue to force him to remain in the United States, and will continue to oppress him there; then, if the black man should ever rise against his oppressors, the Yankee will have only himself to blame. He who 'sows the wind' must not wonder if, one day, he has to 'reap the whirlwind.'

How many people are there, nowadays, who do *not* believe that revenge is literally a feast for the gods! The good old maxim, 'An eye for an eye, a tooth for a tooth,' is still carried out in its entirety, in spite of the fact that those who do believe in retaliation are avowed Christians, and stand in the front rank of modern nations.

The French, because their arms were shattered in the Seven Years' War, and they were humiliated by the Treaty of Paris, which brought the war to a close, and deprived France of Canada, Nova Scotia, Cape Breton, Senegal, Dominica, St. Vincent, and Tobago, took their revenge when the American Colonists unfurled the standard of Independence; they threw their lot into the scale against the Britishers, and spent their treasure and ammunition, and even their blood, on behalf of the Colonists.

The Spaniards, because Havanna, Manilla, and much treasure and some ships were wrested from their grasp by plucky Britishers, in a spirit of revenge, joined the French against them, when the Britishers were warring with their American Colonists.

We may mention here, also, that when the Federal Republicans of the North crushed the Democrat Confederates of the South, they did not hang Jefferson Davis, the whilom President of the Southern Confederacy; they did not hang Robert E. Lee, the whilom commander-in-chief of the same Confederacy; but after the Irish Rebellion of '98 was nipped in the bud at Vinegar Hill, the Englishmen barbarously butchered their own Irish countrymen, slew the noble and brave Lord Edward Fitzgerald and hanged gallant Robert Emmett and Wolfe Tone and others in revenge, because they dared to battle for independence. The victorious Englishmen did not show the mercy to their vanquished Irish countrymen which the victorious Republicans of the North showed towards the vanquished South. And to-day, though Irishmen fight shoulder to shoulder with Englishmen, both by land and by sea, and even fought in the memorable battle of Waterloo, where the British commander-in-chief was an Irishman, the best of feelings cannot be said to exist between the majority of Irishmen and the ruling English. The barbarities perpetrated by Englishmen after Vinegar Hill have left an open sore in the breasts of the majority of Irish people. A rankling feeling, a feeling of animosity, still sadly exists. The majority of Irishmen in Ireland sing not 'God save the Queen!' but the bold and defiant refrains of 'God save Ireland!' and 'The Wearing of the Green.' Because of Vinegar Hill, and the atrocities attendant on that battle, the friendship of the United States of North America towards England is not as warm as it ought to be, because Irishmen, more or less, dominate the feeling and policy of the United States, and the Irish Americans have not forgotten how Englishmen butchered Irishmen during and after the Rebellion. It is truly said that 'blood is thicker than water.'

Ireland has been, and for a long time *shall be*, the 'Achilles-heel of England.' Who has not heard of the Clan-na-Gael, an association of Irishmen which originated, and still exists, in America? Who of the Fenian Brotherhood? Boyd's third edition of 'Wheaton's International Law,' pp. 586, 587, teaches us that 'England has on several occasions received annoyance from the formation of hostile Irish organizations in America. The first society for this purpose appeared in 1848, and was styled the "Irish Republican Union." . . . . This was succeeded in 1855 by another, named "The Massachusetts Irish Emigrant Aid

Society," whose chief function appears to have been the establishment of secret societies in various parts of the States. But both the head society and its secret branches remained in obscurity and insignificance until 1863, when they came forth at Chicago as "The Fenian Brotherhood." At the second congress of the Brotherhood, in 1865, the President of the society declared that they were "virtually at war" with England; and, to give a greater air of reality to this announcement, bonds were issued, "redeemable six months after the acknowledgment of the independence of the Irish nation," the bonds being payable "on presentation at the treasury of the Irish Republic." .... About this time the Canadian Government called out a few companies of militia to resist the threatened invasion of Canada by the Fenians, and if the language of the Brotherhood deserved any attention, precautions were highly necessary. Colonel Roberts, one of the ringleaders, promised "to have the green flag supported by the greatest army of Irishmen upon which the sun ever shone." General Sweeney talked of the large amount of arms and war material they had purchased, and threw out mysterious hints respecting a certain territory they were about to conquer, "from which we can not only emancipate Ireland, but also annihilate England." These and other threats were announced at public meetings, and though the project was absurd on the face of it, it was nevertheless a hostile organization against a State at peace with the Union. Matters became more serious towards the middle of the year. About 800 or 900 armed men actually crossed into Canada, and drove back a small number of volunteers. They retreated before another Canadian detachment, and on recrossing the frontier were arrested and disarmed by the United States forces. About sixty-five were made prisoners in Canada, and placed in the common gaol. The most remarkable event in connection with this raid was that, on the 23rd July, the House of Representatives resolved to "request the President of the United States to urge upon the Canadian authorities, and also the British Government, the release of the Fenian prisoners recently captured in Canada," and, further, that the prosecutions against those taken in America should be abandoned. In pursuance of this, the prosecutions against them were dropped in America, and some of the ringleaders released, after a day's detention, in bonds of $5,000. In October, the Government decided to return some of the arms taken from the Fenians, and the remainder were returned the following year. In November, 1868, the Fenian leader, O'Neill, marched in review through Philadelphia with three regiments in Fenian uniform, numbering, as reported, 3,000 men. In 1870 two expeditions crossed into Canada, but being repulsed, fled across the frontier, and were again disarmed, and their leaders imprisoned by the Union troops. Some of the leaders were fined and imprisoned, but were released two or three months after.'

Did not the Honourable Member for North Roscommon, Mr. James J. O'Kelly, in the early eighties, 'go to the Soudan for the purpose of joining the Mahdi's troops'* and measuring arms with the 'brutal Saxons'?

Because Sir Henry Arthur Blake, K.C.M.G., now Governor of Jamaica, in January, 1882, was 'one of the five special resident magistrates selected by Government to concert and carry out measures for the pacification of a large portion of Ireland,' on his nomination to the governorship of Queensland, in November, 1888, by Downing Castle, the Queenslanders, principally Irishmen, laid their veto on it, and 'Coercionist' Lord Knutsford was, with humiliation, forced to give in to the Queenslanders.

Because ex-President Stephen Grover Cleveland, when

* 'Men and Women of the Time for 1891,' p. 677.

in office, was suspected of being favourable towards Great Britain, he was beaten at the National Political Campaign of 1888, mainly through the preponderance of the Irish electoral votes, which went solid for his rival, Republican Benjamin Harrison; and, in revenge, no doubt, Democrat Cleveland gave British Ambassador Lord Sackville, on the 30th of October, 1888, 'the sack' and his passport.

That 'burning,' debateable, and, we may say, everlasting question of the Behring Sea, is now on the *tapis*. Let the Republicans yield an inch to Britain, and the Irish votes will go solid for the Democrats! Erin—yes, Erin!—is the 'Achilles-heel' of Albion, and holds the fort in the United States and in the United Kingdom!

The British, because the Spaniards made war on them while they were engaged in fratricidal conflict with their rebellious kinsmen in America, in revenge assisted the Spanish-American Colonies in every possible way, consistent with economy, when they were struggling to throw off the galling yoke of Spain. The same Britishers, because Frenchmen helped America to gain her independence, when Hayti rose against the French and drove them into the sea, revenged themselves on Frenchmen by giving the Haytians their sympathy and countenance, which excited the exceeding wrath of Frenchmen.

When the Yankees, not many months ago, rushed on to the shameful massacre of the Sioux Indian chief, Sitting Bull, and his ghost-dancing warriors, what was their war-cry? Was it not the revengeful slogan of 'Remember Custer!'? And the reason why the Yankees did rush on to the massacre of the inadequately armed Sioux Indians with the revengeful slogan of 'Remember Custer!' was this: General Custer met his death, many years ago, in battle with these very Sioux Indians, who successfully resisted him when he had ridden with his Yankee soldiers to effect the extermination of the ghost-dancing warriors of Sitting Bull. When, between the latter part of the year 1890 and the earlier part of last (1891) year, the Yankees marched against the Red Americans, their 'prevailing sentiment was revenge'; they showed how 'implacable' are 'their hatreds.' Again, Frenchmen, though they have always been in the front rank of civilization, and are professed Christians, nevertheless maintain the *Revanche* spirit towards the Germans. How the warlike Gaul is burning to wrest Alsace-Lorraine from the grasp of the not less warlike Teuton is matter of common knowledge! Frenchmen are leaving no stone unturned in their supreme effort to carry out successfully a *Revanche* war with the Teutons. They are trying their 'level best,' they are straining every nerve, to secure the alliance of Russia, and the co-operation of the Muscovite hordes of the White Czar, against the Germans, Austrians, and Italians in the war that cannot be very long delayed.

But to return to superstition. The Boston *Herald* does not seem to be aware of the fact that there was, and that there is, superstition amongst the whites in America, even in 'Puritan New England.'

In the olden days, how many old women, victims of gross superstition, and narrow-minded, sour-faced 'Puritan New Englanders,' were bound to, and perished at, the stake on the charge of being witches! The 'Puritan New Englander' to-day is as superstitious as his ancestors were who went before him.*

Laird Clowes brings his reference to African superstition to a close with these words: 'I may add that, not perhaps at Boston, but certainly in the South, and especially in Louisiana, Voodooism exists to-day.'

* See D. G. Brinton's 'Myths of the New World'; Bancroft's 'History of the Colonization of the United States,' vol. iii.; Hutchinson's 'History of Massachusetts Bay.'

Granted that the so-called 'Voodooism,' or, more properly, a harmless superstition, does exist in the Southern States of America amongst a very few of the illiterate American Africans, others of the African race, who know better than to be superstitious, have an apology forthcoming for those of their race who may be superstitious. It must be remembered that the American African received his freedom only on January 1, 1863—that is, but twenty-nine years ago. His civilization and Christianity began only with Emancipation, not in any proper sense before: those of the American Africans who may to-day be superstitious can only be a few ignorant men and women from among those Africans who actually experienced the yoke of servitude. The American whites are really responsible for any forms of superstition that may still lurk among a handful of Africans in America, because there was neither civilization nor Christianity for the African under the Slavery régime in the United States. It is Emancipation that has poured into the lap of the African Civilization and Christianity; and these powerful forces cause the African to seek after knowledge, and make great progress in Education. The Superstitions which the ancestors of every people have had amongst them disappear before Education, even as the chaff drives before the wind.

But does not Mr. Clowes himself tell us (on page 116 of his 'Black America') that 'educationally the coloured man has undoubtedly made great progress since his emancipation? In the slavery days ignorance was imposed by law upon the slave.' He says that the American African is superstitious; but he also tells us that, educationally, the African has undoubtedly made great progress since his glorious emancipation. And we fully believe that the superstition which does at all exist amongst the African Yankees will flee from their midst altogether, through the great and rapid progress which the Yankee Africans are making in education and civilization.

With a few more words we conclude this chapter.

Though the Roman Emperor Claudius and his lieutenants, Aulus Plautius and Vespasian, brought Civilization with the Roman soldiers into Britain;* though Fagan and Dervan, in the second century, brought Christianity into Britain, it is on record that the Britons retrograded and relapsed into barbarism and the idolatrous superstitions and practices of their ancestors; so much so that, when the Angles and Jutes, with the sovereign tribe of Saxons, landed in A.D. 449, England—degenerated and demoralized—fell an easy prey before the onslaught of these marauding hordes.† Matters continued in that low state until A.D. 596 or 597, when Benedictine Austin, or Augustine, brought his forty tonsured monks into Britain. These men reclaimed the degenerate Britishers from heathendom and superstition.‡ We Africans, then, can always hopefully rejoice, and can find our consolation in the fact that, if there be superstition amongst our people—a people who have not yet had sixty years of Civilization and Christianity —(these beginning with the Emancipation of the *British* African in August, 1838, and with the Emancipation of the *American* African in January, 1863), we are not so bad as the Britishers. Though the Britisher has had more than nineteen centuries of Civilization and over seventeen centuries of Christianity, he is *still superstitious;* and that he is so we have proved by referring to the writings of Sir Walter Scott, Robert Burns, Samuel Rogers, and Charles Dickens. We have done more. We have produced quotations from the works of Thomas Wright and Lowen Pike,

* Lingard, vol. i., chap. i., pp. 1-68.
† *Ibid.*, vol. i., chap. ii., pp. 103-105.
‡ *Ibid.*, vol. i., chap. ii., pp. 108, 109 *et seq.*

and from the *Daily Telegraph*, the *Star*, the *Daily Graphic*, and *Lloyd's News*, tending to show that the Caucasian is as superstitious to-day as his ancestors were before him, and had better see to the 'beam in his own eye' before he shows himself to be so vigorous over extracting 'the mote' of superstition out of his African brother's eye.*

* If the reader would like to have a more extensive knowledge of Caucasian superstition, we would refer him to J. F. Campbell's 'Tales of the Western Highlands'; J. Grimm's 'Teutonic Mythology'; Sir George W. Cox's 'Introduction to Mythology and Folklore'; H. Long's 'Custom and Myth,' also 'Myth, Ritual and Religion'; MacInnes and Nutt's 'Folklore and Hero Tales from Argyleshire'; J. Brand's 'Popular Antiquities'; W. Gregor's 'Folklore of the North-East of Scotland'; J. Napier's 'Folklore of the West of Scotland'; J. G. Dolzell's 'Darker Superstitions of Scotland,' 'Fireside Stories of Ireland,' and 'Legendary Fictions of the Irish Celts'; T. Crofton Croker's 'Fairy Legends and Traditions of Ireland'; G. L. Gomme's 'Manners and Customs, Superstitions and Traditions'; Miss C. S. Burne's 'Shropshire Folklore'; W. Henderson's 'Folklore of the Northern Counties'; Lowen Pike's 'History of Crime in England,' vol. ii., pp. 131-139; Stephen's 'History of the Criminal Law,' vol. ii., chap. xxv.; Lecky's 'History of Rationalism in Europe,' vol. i., chap. i.; and last, not least, we would advise him to look up the 'Encyclopædia Britannica,' ninth edition, vol. ii., pp. 744 *et seq.*; vol. vii., pp. 60-64; 293, 294; vol. ix., pp. 357, 358; vol. xv., pp. 199 *et seq.*; vol. xvii., pp. 135-158; vol. xxii., pp. 404-407; vol. xxiv., pp. 619-623.

CHAPTER V.

UNDER CAUCASIAN RULE.

WE do not propose here to dwell on the way in which the American Africans are defrauded of their votes by their white fellow-citizens, because the facts are sufficiently notorious. But we join our protest with that of Mr. Clowes, who has the courage to admit, in his third chapter of 'Black America,' that the trickeries practised on them (the American Africans) are infamous, cruel, and shameful. Laird Clowes, however, makes a great mistake when he quotes Mr. A. M. E. Church, of Vicksburg, an American African clergyman, as writing in the year 1866 : ' We will say . . . that the mass of Negroes would do themselves and their country more good if the ballot were out of their reach.'

The clergyman of Vicksburg's mere statement of opinion is of little or no importance. Does not Mr. Clowes know that the great majority of Irishmen, the Nationalists, have been agitating for Home Rule during many long years; and, at the same time, the small minority of Irishmen, the Conservative Orangemen, have been almost throughout, and they are even now, persistently opposing their countrymen in the demand for Home Rule ?

Is it not a known fact that, at the present time as in the past, certain Irishmen are put up on the floor of the British

House of Commons, and elsewhere, to denounce their brother Irishmen?

Do not Conservative and Liberal Unionist Scotsmen and Welshmen continually oppose the demand for Home Rule in Scotland and Wales, which is made by their countrymen, the Gladstonian Liberal Scotsmen and Welshmen?

When the Indian Hindoos, not many months ago, petitioned the British Home Government for a Constitution, did not the Indian Mahommedans immediately afterwards send a counter-petition to the British Parliament against the granting of a Constitution to India? We are of opinion, then, that the Rev. A. M. E. Church's opposition to the granting of the ballot and the franchise to his American-African countrymen and kinsmen is on a par with the opposition manifested by the Irish Conservative Orangemen, by the Conservative and Liberal-Unionist Scotsmen and Welshmen, to the granting of Home Rule to Ireland, Scotland, and Wales respectively. And this same opposition is also on a level with that displayed by the Indian Mahommedans to the conferring of a Constitution on India. Mr. Church's assertion that 'the mass of Negroes would do themselves and their country more good if the ballot were out of their reach' is nothing unusual from a political point of view. The clergyman of Vicksburg, however, ought not to interfere in politics; he should stick to his pulpit and to proper pulpit topics. Mr. Clowes, on page 88 of his book, has the following excerpt from Mr. James Anthony Froude's 'English in the West Indies': 'One does not grudge the black man his property, his freedom, his opportunity of advancing himself; one would wish him as free and prosperous as the fates and his own exertions can make him, with more and more means of raising himself to the white man's level. But left to himself, and without the white man to lead him, he can never reach it. . . . We have a population to deal with the majority of whom are of an inferior race. Inferior I am obliged to call them, because, as yet, they have shown no capacity to rise above the condition of their ancestors, except under European laws, European education, and European authority to keep them from war upon one another. . . . Give them independence, and in a few generations they will peel off such civilization as they have as easily and as willingly as their coats and trousers.'

The first part of this quotation which claims our notice is, that the African, if 'left to himself, and without the white man to lead him, can never reach it,' *i.e.*, 'the white man's level.' That is what Mr. Froude and Mr. Clowes believe ; but their belief is not soundly based. We have proved, in our Second Chapter, that the Haytian, though left to himself, has not only not 'retrograded and reverted,' but ' has raised himself to the white man's level '; and to that chapter reference should be made. The Liberian also, though left to himself, 'has raised himself to the white man's level.' Liberia is as prosperous to-day as it might be were it under a white man's Government. We will allow the white man to have his say on this subject.

The American Colonization Society, writing in the *African Repository* for April, 1890, says : 'The present condition of Liberia is evidenced :

'*First.*—By the increased agricultural industry of the settlers ; their extending cultivation of coffee, cocoa, and sugar, which is placing them in a condition not only of comfort, but of independence.

'*Second.*—By the growing commerce of the Republic, which is laying under cultivation all available products, spontaneous and cultivated.

'*Third.*—By the earnestness with which the people are

turning their attention to the interior, and pushing their settlements and agricultural labours to the healthy and fertile highlands in that direction.

'*Fourth.*—By the development among the Aborigines, especially the Kroo tribe, in imitation of, and through the teaching of, the settlers, of the knowledge and practice of civilized arts, mechanical and agricultural; also, their intelligence and their capital for the conduct of foreign trade. They have begun to ship their own products directly to Europe, and import thence merchandise suited to their localities.

'*Fifth.*—The erection by the settlers of schools and churches, by their own means, for the benefit of themselves and the Aborigines, without any prompting or pecuniary aid from the United States. Chief among the educational agencies recently established by the Liberians, is the Ricke's Institute, founded by the liberality of a Negro immigrant from Virginia, and supported by the Baptists, with no aid from America. It is conducted by three ministers, one educated at Liberia College; one at Shaw University, Raleigh, N.C.; and the other brought up in Liberia, without any special school-training. A Mahommedan convert, from the interior, has been employed to teach Arabic and the vernacular languages.'

The Liberians are more than ever awake to their privileges and duties on that Continent. Their influence upon the natives is everywhere increasing; and instead of the settlers relapsing into barbarism, as it is sometimes asserted, they are making effective inroads upon the physical, intellectual, and moral wilderness.

The re-captive Congoes, who were captured in slave-ships by United States men-of-war and landed in Liberia thirty years ago, have learned the arts of civilization, embraced Christianity, and become capable citizens, filling important offices in the Republic. Some of these people have been recently introduced into the Congo Free State, under the auspices of the authorities there, as elements of civilization, owing to their knowledge of agriculture and the trades.'

The American Colonization Society goes further in its eulogy of Liberia and the Liberians, and writes in the *African Repository* for April, 1891, that 'The action of the Legislature of Liberia, at its last session, regarding foreign affairs, was greatly in advance of anything in the past.

'The grant to an English company of the sole right to collect, manufacture, and export India-rubber, in and from that Republic, promises greatly to promote its industrial and financial interests. For this monopoly, £20,000 sterling, as a first instalment, was received on the 12th of June by the Government at Monrovia.

'The legislature has also granted to the same company the right to establish a bank under charter from the Government, and to construct telegraphs and one or more railroads from the coast to the interior.

'The educational advantages of the Republic are increasing. The Methodist Episcopal Seminary at Monrovia has been reopened, and the Episcopalians have not only enlarged their school facilities at Cape Palmas and at Cape Mount, but they are preparing to open a boarding-school on the St. Paul's river. The Ricke's Institute, an indigenous school established by the Baptists, is growing in influence and importance. It now contains over forty pupils, some of whom are Aborigines, mostly of the Bassa tribe.

'The facts are that the Government of Liberia attracts the social, commercial, and political economy of several millions of Africans, that for leagues about its settlements the kings and chiefs are friendly and even subordinate, and that its people have advanced in civilization and are successfully working out their destiny according to nineteenth century lights.'

No one out of Liberia is better qualified to speak of the condition of the Liberians than the American Colonization Society, and that society in every way testifies to the fact that the Liberian—an African—'has raised himself to the white man's level . . . without the white man to lead him.' For it further says that the 'Liberian people have advanced in civilization, and are successfully working out their destiny according to nineteenth century lights.' And yet, with all this progress standing to her credit, Liberia is (June, 1891) hardly forty-four years old as an independent Country.

Mr. Clowes quotes Mr. Froude as saying: 'We have a population to deal with the majority of whom are an inferior race. Inferior I am obliged to call them, because as yet they have shown no capacity to rise above the condition of their ancestors, except under European laws, European education, and European authority to keep them from war upon one another. . . . Give them independence, and in a few generations they will peel off such civilization as they have as easily as their coats and trousers.'

We have shown, in the case of Liberia in this chapter, and in the case of Hayti in the second chapter, that the African is not an inferior race, and that far from the independent African 'retrograding and reverting,' or 'peeling off such civilization as he has,' he is, in the words of the Caucasian Yankee, 'advancing in civilization, and is successfully working out his destiny according to nineteenth century lights.'

We must say a few words, however, in answer to Mr. Froude's statement that the Africans 'as yet have shown no capacity to rise above the condition of their ancestors, except under European laws, European education, and European authority to keep them from war upon one another. . . .'

Are the Independent People of Liberia waging war upon one another?* Is Hayti not at the present moment (June, 1891) quite peaceful and quiet?† And are the Liberians and the Haytians each living 'under European laws, European education, and European authority,' as Mr. Froude says they must do in order to keep from war?

But we have to ask this question: Did the Briton show any capacity to rise above the condition of his ancestors, and keep himself from warring upon his brother Briton, before the arrival of the Roman and his legions? Was it not Roman laws, Roman education, and Roman authority that kept the Britons from waging fierce war upon one another?

When the Roman eagle took its final departure at the head of the Roman legions, in A.D. 426, leaving Independence in the lap of the Britons, how did the Britons behave themselves? Did they not wage even fierce and unnatural war upon one another? Did not the partisans of Ambrosius and Vortigern cleave each other's skulls, and even drink each other's blood, and eat each other's flesh, like so many cannibals? The independent Britons, deprived of Roman laws, education, and authority, degenerated, and fell to slitting each other's throats; and, as division is always a source of weakness, the Pict-Scot savage was successful in his attacks upon them. The spear of the Saxons, Jutes, and Angles restored peace to the Britons for a time; but

* The Chief Magistrate of Liberia, His Excellency J. J. Cheeseman, is a *national*, not a *party*, President, having been elected by the *unanimous* voice of his countrymen.

† The same remark may be applied to General L. M. Fk. Hippolyte, President of Hayti.

then these Saxons (as the combined Saxons, Angles, Jutes, and Britons were called) fell to fighting amongst themselves, until the Danes, or Norsemen, succeeded in keeping them quiet. The Normans, in their turn, failed to keep England peaceful, for civil war broke out in the reign of the Red King, and there were civil wars in the reigns of Henry I., Stephen, Henry II., John, Henry III., Edward II., Richard II., Henry IV. One would think that Mr. Froude and Mr. Clowes have never heard of Jack Cade's Rebellion and Seven Oaks. Are not the Twelve Battles fought during the Civil Wars of the Roses a matter of well-known history?

The reigns of Henry VII., Henry VIII., Edward VI., Mary I., Elizabeth, and James I., each experienced civil war. Twenty Battles were fought in the Civil War between Charles I. and the Parliamentarians, when Cavaliers and Roundheaded Puritans smote each other, the last, the decisive battle, handing Charles over to his subjects, who subsequently beheaded him.

We have mentioned civil wars in England, but the sister kingdoms of Ireland and Scotland were each also subjected to the baneful influence of civil war. The children of Caledonia, 'stern and wild,' and the children of unhappy and distracted Erin, were almost continually levying war upon one another.

The British people had civil wars under Charles II., James II., William III. and Mary II., George I., and George II. In brief, it was only the battle of Vinegar Hill, fought in 1798, in the reign of the Third George, that put an end to Civil War amongst the British people. At Vinegar Hill Englishmen and Scotsmen were marshalled in battle array against their Irish countrymen, whom they then defeated. That conflict put an end to the story of fratricidal strife in Great Britain. From the time of that battle, fought in 1798, to the present time Britain has enjoyed only ninety-three years of freedom from fratricidal war.

It required Roman laws, Roman education, and Roman authority to keep the Gauls from war upon one another. The Romans civilized the Gauls; and, when the time-honoured but then effeminate Roman Empire was tottering and crumbling to pieces, after its long career of dominion and glory, the conquering Franks poured their irresistible legions from Germany into the heart of the Gallic country, gave the death-blow to the Empire of the countrymen of Cæsar and Cicero, brought Roman Gaul into subjection, gave their name to the country, and imposed Frankish laws, Frankish education, and Frankish authority on the necks of their subjects. But France, too, has had a long career of fratricidal strifes, the last civil war amongst Frenchmen, that between the Government and its adherents and the Social-Commune, only terminating in 1871, after the troops of Marshal Duke MacMahon of Magenta had marched to the slaughter of those of Eudes, Duval, Cluseret, Bergeret, Wetzel, Onolowitz, Dombrowski, Wroblowski, Cecilia, and sundry other 'Generals' of the Reds.

Would Germany be now one of the leading countries of the world if it had not had the beneficial effects of Roman civilization and Roman supervision? Yet Germany has had a long spell of civil wars, for there was a time when Teuton smote brother-Teuton, as arrayed against each other in the field.

The last Civil War in Germany ended at the decisive battle of Königgrätz, or Sadowa, on July 3, 1866, when Protestant and Hohenzollern Prussia, under Prince Frederick Charles, humiliated Catholic and Hapsburg Austria, under General Benedek, thereby giving the deathblow to the Germanic Confederation of 1815, and laying the foundation of United Germany under the headship of the

Brandenburg conqueror, while mortified and crestfallen Austria was forced to consent to pay a war indemnity of 20,000 thalers, recognise the severance of the erewhile Germanic Confederation, and consent to a new formation of Germany in which she should bear no part; and to complete her cup of sorrow, the Fatherland of Franz Josef was forced to resign all claims to Schleswig-Holstein, for which she had fought and bled, in conjunction with the Hohenzollern, in the Danish campaign of 1864, in favour of Prussia, and to behold with streaming eyes, and bleeding from many wounds, Hanover, Hesse-Cassel, Hesse-Nassau and Frankfort pounced upon as spoils of war, and in the pride of victory, by her successful rival, the eagle of Hohenzollern.

Austria-Hungary has also had her civil wars; the last terminating in 1848, during which Austria and Hungary were arrayed against each other. Russia, Italy, and Turkey have each had their civil wars. Denmark, Norway, and Sweden, and Holland have also had their civil wars. The Spaniards never would have been able to rise above the condition of their ancestors except under Roman laws, Roman education, and Roman authority. The Visigoths, who gave the finishing blow to the moribund Roman Empire in Spain, continued the work of civilization which the Romans had begun, but did the Visigoths and their subjects refrain from tearing one another to pieces? When the Moors (*i.e.*, the descendants of Asiatics and Africans) landed in the dawn of the eighth century, they were able, within the short space of less than three years, to thoroughly subdue the divided and faction-torn Iberian Peninsula, and impose their yoke upon the necks of the Spaniards. Nor did the Moors quit Spain till the seventeenth century. The story of Portugal is almost identical with that of Spain.*

* The last Civil and Carlist War in Spain terminated only in 1876, for which *vide* 'Encyclopædia Britannica,' vol. xxii., p. 346.

The dying Roman Empire, which had introduced civilization into Lusitania, being weak and feeble, easily yielded to the onslaught of the warlike Moors after these latter had fairly overrun Spain. But when the Moors were unfortunately divided amongst themselves, and were warring upon one another, the Visigoths were able to reduce them into complete subjection, and Portugal became their prize.

It was Roman laws and Roman authority that raised the Switzer from the condition of a savage to that of a civilized being. The Austro-Germans, and afterwards Frenchmen, continued to carry out the work of civilization which the Roman had begun in Switzerland, and they helped to make the Swiss what they are at the present day. Yet the Switzer has had civil wars in his country and amongst his countrymen. It was but recently that Switzerland treated the world to an exhibition of civil war on a small scale in the Ticino Rebellion. The Hellenes, or Greeks, after conquering the aboriginal inhabitants of Hellas, imposed, with their yoke, their civilization and institutions on the pliant necks of the Pelasgians, while they gave their name to the country and its inhabitants.

Greece was, indeed, the home of literature and the arts; her civilization, already at a high standard, receiving a greater impetus when it came into contact with the civilization of the Romans, when the rule of the countrymen of Cæsar and Cicero was supreme at Athens. The reason why the Greeks fell such an easy prey to the omnipotent Romans was their being divided among themselves, and carrying on war upon one another.

The Turks, too, who put an end to the tottering Græco-Latin Empire, which had succeeded that of the purely-Roman-Latin in Greece, contributed to the advancement and progress of the Greeks until Navarino and Greek Independence died away with the rule of the Osmanlis.

But what two nations are there that can boast of indigenous civilization? The civilization of every nation, almost without exception, has been imported. What country is there which has never known any civil wars?

Civil war has shown its many hideous heads in all the different countries of Asia and Europe. It was not only in those countries which have been already mentioned that the baneful curse of suicidal war has been experienced, for the two Americas with their Indian Isles have suffered under similar experiences.

The Yankee inhabitants of the United States were in the habit of boasting before their great and now historic internal war that their country, unlike other countries, was greatly favoured and peculiarly blessed by Heaven, because of a total absence of civil wars in their Fatherland. But in April, 1861, did not the world see the Yankees of the South pitted against the Yankees of the North? And were not the former finally crushed in May, 1865? That great suicidal struggle had the question of Africo-American slavery as its *fons et origo*; and it scattered Yankee vaunting to the winds. That American civil war was the greatest of modern times, since upwards of a million men are said to have perished in the struggle.

But where, in any of the two Americas, has civil war not shown its hideous head? What shall we say of the periodical convulsions into which they are thrown, which agitate Mexico, Costa-Rica, Honduras, Guatemala, San Salvador, Nicaragua, Columbia, Venezuela, Peru, Bolivia, and Ecuador? Do not all these historical cases of internal struggle testify to the fact that the Americas are still enslaved by the hydra-monster of Civil War, whose baneful influence they are unable to shake off?

Chili and Argentina, the greatest of South American Republics (and, with Mexico and Brazil, the greatest of

Americo-Latin Republics in the Americas), cannot boast that they have had no civil wars. The latter—Argentina—has but recently treated the world to a display of civil war, when the descendant of one conquistador made the descendant of another conquistador bite the dust. And Civil War is now, as we write, being carried on with the greatest vigour and animosity between the Government of Balmaceda and his opponents of the Congressional party in Chili.*

The statement, then, which Mr. James Anthony Froude makes in his 'English in the West Indies,' and which Mr. W. Laird Clowes slavishly quotes, to the effect that we Africans are an inferior race, 'because, as yet, they' (the Africans) 'have shown no capacity to rise above the condition of their ancestors, except under European laws, European education, and European authority to keep them from war upon one another,' seems to us, and surely it will to the unbiased reader, to be, on the face of it, foolish and ridiculous. Scarcely any nation under the sun has had indigenous civilization; and almost every nation under the sun has had experience of civil war in the past, and even in this century there are countries whose peoples periodically wage fierce civil and suicidal war upon one another.

On page 202 of 'Black America,' W. Laird Clowes writes: 'In no British colony, for example, is there any reason why a capable Negro should not raise himself to high position and honour. In no British colony, on the other hand, does the Negro govern. And I think it may also be said that in every British colony in which he is

* Decisive and sanguinary Placilla, on the 27th August, 1891, terminated fratricidal strife in Chili; Congressional General Canto, fresh from the slaughter of his opponents at Concon, crushing and slaying the Balmacedist Generals Orozimbo Barboza and José Miguel Alcérreca on that field.

to be found, the Negro is a fairly happy and contented person.'

Mr. Clowes does not seem to be aware that there is one reason, and that it is the head and chief of all reasons, why the African 'cannot raise himself to high post and honour in any British colony.' The truth is, that fat and lucrative berths in the Colonies, whether in British Africa or in the British West Indies, are sedulously kept for the *Europeans;* though too often these Europeans are incompetent and incapable. They are, sadly too often, the refuse and the failures, the bankrupts, the spendthrifts, and the scum of the British population; while deserving and capable Africans are uniformly and systematically kept in the background. Let the African work as he may, he reaps none of the harvest of his work by securing official positions in a British colony.

In our own island home of Trinidad we have known intelligent youths of African blood who have been compelled to leave school or college much earlier than they wished, because of their parents' inability to provide a suitable pittance to maintain them any longer. And the moment they are out of school, these young men, as a matter of course, always make it their business to apply for some appointment in the Civil Service of the Colony. But do they succeed? No, they seek quite fruitlessly; though the very moment the *white* boys, often of shallow and mediocre ability, get out of school, and no matter whether they come from the higher or the lower classes, they are made welcome to every remunerative post at the disposal of the Government, and promotion for them is as rapid as they could desire. It is the same cry all the British Empire over where the African abides. The African is resolutely kept in the background.

In this way, then, is the African 'stopped short,' and

prevented from occupying 'high position and honour' in the Civil Service. It is not a matter for wonder if the Gallic King Brennus's old but expressive saying of *Væ victis!* ('Woe to the vanquished!'), or the familiar poetic words,
> 'The good old rule, the simple plan,
> That they should take who have the power,
> And they should keep who can,'

should be forcibly called to the African's mind.

What African, we say, who has the welfare of his race at heart, indulges in the delusive hope that every talented countryman of his—being, as he is, a member of an unfortunate and subject (but not degraded and down-trodden) race—will always get his abilities recognised by the Government of a ruling race like the Caucasian? No; the African who has the welfare of his race at heart will counsel his reliant, self-respecting brethren to depart from the land where the Caucasian rules, and go to the land of his African forefathers, the land where the African rules. He will advise all his countrymen who are living under Caucasian rule to go to that land of liberty, the Republic of Liberia, 'The Lone-Star of Liberia.' If the degenerate Saxons held no honoured positions in England when they were smarting under the iron rule of their Norman lords and masters, that is no reason why those Africans who remain under British and Yankee rule should not hold positions of trust and honour, when they deserve them, in the Colonial Civil Service. Do not the European possessions in Africa and in the West Indies annually send forth their thousands of young Africans, who betake themselves to the various European centres of learning as students of law, medicine, theology, engineering, etc., etc., etc.?

The African indulges in a vain hope, indeed, who believes that his dark-skinned face will be given the preference when he competes for any Government appointment under the Caucasian flag if there happens to be a pale-faced candidate in the field.

It is true that, now and again, the abilities of the African do receive official recognition, and Africans are occasionally entrusted with posts of honour and trust; and yet, even then, those Africans are seldom, if ever, *promoted.*

One may find a black United States' Minister to Hayti; a black Chief Justice in Barbadoes; a black Magistrate in Trinidad; a black Chief Magistrate in Gambia; two or three black Magistrates in the Gold Coast, and perhaps one or two black Magistrates in Sierra Leone and Lagos, as well as one or two law and medical officials of Colonial Governments; yet these Africans are never promoted— they are 'stopped short.' And we are of opinion that the few appointments which British Africans hold in British West Africa are due more to the fact that the West African climate pervading British territory in that sphere is more or less unsuitable to the constitution of Britishers than from a wish to loyalize Goldcoasters, Sierra Leoneans, Lagians, and Gambians, and make them more and more amenable to British rule. But are the authorities blind to the fact that they have Frenchmen and Germans for neighbours in Africa? What with the contiguity of the Liberian Republic to the British possessions of the Gold Coast, Lagos, Sierra Leone, and Gambia—what if the African inhabitants of these possessions were to suddenly unfurl the flag of independence, and join the promising Republic of Liberia, their neighbour? We should not be sorry to see European West and Central Africa joining the Liberian flag, and we firmly believe and prophesy that it is the destiny of all West, and Central, and other Africans to become Liberians ! ! !

Mr. Clowes tells us that 'in no British colony does the

Negro govern.' We all know that to be so; but the assertion of the truth of that fact only declares it to be the more shameful.

But Mr. Clowes again tells us that 'in every British colony in which he is to be found the Negro is a fairly happy and contented person.' If getting educated, acquiring a profession, learning a trade, and building up wealth, and gaining through these things social independence, make up the sum-total of happiness, then many an African may be said to be 'fairly happy and contented' under the British flag. Africans living under the rule of the British are not contented; they would like to have their abilities recognised. They are longing to enjoy the franchise, and to be members of colonial parliaments and governments, and to hold positions of trust and honour wherever Africans are to be found, and especially where they predominate numerically. But what, we ask, does Mr. Clowes know of the 'fair happiness and contentedness' of the Africans in the British colonies?

Is it not singular, as well as anomalous, that the Bermudas and Bahamas, small West Indian Isles, with literally a handful of inhabitants, as well as the Leeward Islands, though to a limited extent, enjoy the franchise and send representatives to their respective legislatures, while the great Colony of Jamaica has hardly any representation; while the great Colonies of Trinidad and Tobago, British Honduras, and the Windward Group of Islands have no franchise and no representation?

Is it not singular, and an anomaly, that the Bermudas Islands, with 16,000 inhabitants, who are for the most part Africans, send thirty-six elected members to their House of Assembly; that the Bahamas, with 48,000 inhabitants, mostly Africans, send 29 elected members to their Representative Assembly; that the Leeward, with 120,000 inhabitants, mostly Africans, send but 10 elected members to their General Legislative Council; while British Honduras, with a population of 28,000, Africans for the most part —unlike the Bermudas, with 16,000 people—is a Crown Colony; while the Windward Islands, with a population of 96,000, Africans for the most part—unlike the Bahamas, with merely 48,000 people—are taxed, but are unrepresented; while Barbadoes, with 172,000 inhabitants, mostly Africans, sends 24 elected members to its House of Assembly; the Bermudas Islands, with 16,000 inhabitants, sending 36 elected members to their House of Assembly; and the Bahamas, with 48,000 people, sending 29 elected members to their Representative Assembly: while the United Colony of Trinidad and Tobago, with an estimated population of 205,000, mostly Africans, has the franchise and representation withheld from it, and is, in fact, governed, or, rather, misgoverned, as a Crown Colony? Is it not singular, and an anomaly, that British Guiana, with 282,000 inhabitants, mostly Africans, except that it sends 6 or 7 representatives to the Legislature, is practically a Crown Colony, while the Bermudas, Bahamas, the Leeward Islands, and Barbadoes, colonies of fewer inhabitants, and of less progressive character, are more adequately represented? Is it not also singular, and anomalous, that Mauritius, with 373,000 inhabitants, mostly Africans, sends only 2 representatives to the Council, and but 10 elected members to the Legislative Council, while Jamaica, with 581,000 people, mostly Africans, sends only 9 representatives to its Legislative Council? But 'truth is stranger than fiction,' they say.

It can thus be seen, therefore, that in every British colony where Africans preponderate to any great extent, that colony either has not received a Constitution, or the Constitution which that colony has is very limited and curtailed in its provisions.

There is every reason to expect that, on some future day, the Bahamas and Barbadoes (the latter with the greater probability and certainty) will be deprived of their Constitution by the Imperial Parliament, because of the rapid increase of Africans in those two colonies since Emancipation. Assuming, of course, that the Africans remain in Barbadoes and the Bahamas, and do not migrate to their Fatherland, Africa, as we earnestly hope they will do.

The original Jamaican Constitution, which had existed for 200 years (and which was 'Representative), was done away with in December, 1866. It consisted of a Governor, a Privy Council, a Legislative Council, a Legislative Assembly of 47 Representative Members, and a paid body, which went by the name of the Executive Committee, and were the responsible Ministers of the Crown in Jamaica

On the initiation of the Jamaican Assembly on the 20th December, 1866—and the resolution was unanimously confirmed on the 22nd December in the same year by the superior body, the Legislative Council, and assented to by the then Governor on the 23rd December, 1866 — the British Crown was invited to grant another Constitution to Jamaica, a Constitution suitable to the altered condition of the colony. A motion of this sort, coming, as it did, immediately after the Jamaican-African Gordon Rising of 1865, cannot but bring home the fact to the mind of the average individual, that the British authorities were filled with alarm on account of the Africans in Jamaica, and brought pressure to bear on the legislative bodies of Jamaica. And there are those who maintain, and we are with them, that Her Britannic Majesty's Earl Derby's Third Government actually interfered with and suspended* the

* Who knows what part that curse of civilization, Secret Service Money, played in Jamaica during Lord Derby's Third Administration?

Constitutional Government then existing in Jamaica in 1866. At the same time Lord Derby's Government contrived to secure the allegiance of the wavering in Jamaica, for there were not a few malcontents who had not unnaturally taken umbrage because of that unjust and arbitrary measure. And why should we not suppose that the Jamaican whites, remembering that it was not the first time that a part of the Jamaican Africans had risen in arms (some Jamaican Maroon slaves having risen in 1795* and 1832),† and not unmindful of the fact that the Africans were increasing to an alarming extent since Emancipation, were seized with panic, and gladly advocated the change in the Constitution? There was also the proximity of Jamaica to Hayti. Might not the Jamaican-Africans wish to follow Hayti's example, and make a bold effort to secure Independence? Agitated with feelings of personal safety and self-interest, this party did not hesitate (they commanding a majority in the Jamaican Legislature) to surrender the Constitution which had existed for 200 years?

As far back as 1830—that is to say, eight years before the generality of Africans thought that the justifiable and legitimate Act of Emancipation would have been granted them—the elective franchise was being exercised by such of the Africo-Jamaicans as were enjoying the blessings of freedom and citizenhood. When Emancipation or Enfranchisement, and in its train full and unqualified Citizenship, came in August, 1838, the Jamaican Africans were enabled, we are told, speedily to send some representatives

* 'English Cyclopædia of Geography,' vol. iii., p. 321. From 1655 'the slaves' (to quote the 'Encyclopædia Britannica,' vol. xiii., p. 550) 'called Maroons . . . who had fled to the mountains, continued formidable. Down to the end of the eighteenth century the disaffection of the Maroons caused much trouble.'

† 'Encyclopædia Britannica,' vol. xiii., p. 551.

of their own race to the Legislative Council or Upper House, and many more of their prominent men to the Legislative Assembly or Lower House of Jamaica.

Jamaica, at the present day, is under the baneful influence of a semi-Crown Colony system of Government; Jamaica sending, as it does, but 9 representatives to the Legislative Council, is but inadequately represented when its 581,000 inhabitants are considered.

The administration of justice as it is in Jamaica and Trinidad, can only be one-sided and corrupt under the degenerating and deteriorating influence of Crown Colony Government and its concomitant red-tapism.

Were the Jamaican Governmental Administration also composed of sound materials, would the bungling Jamaican Director of Public Works, Valentine Græme Bell (who, like his prototype of Trinidad, the blundering and extravagant Director Tanner of Public Works) have been allowed to sell and hand over the Jamaican Government Railway to an American Company? The British Government of Jamaica, when it handed its Railway over to the Yankees, sold its birthright for a mess of pottage. Only under a Crown Colony Government could such a mistake have been committed.

The Queenslanders, in November, 1888, would have none of Governor Sir Henry A. Blake on account of his previous bad record as a member of the Royal Irish Constabulary, he having been engaged in bâtoning his Irish countrymen because they differed from him in politics; and also as a Resident Magistrate, he having oppressed the Irish people. The Queenslanders petitioned Lord Knutsford to keep his *enfant terrible* at home, and then the authorities at Downing Street thought that the next best thing for them to do was to seek out a colony on which to foist their *protégé*. Jamaica was the colony they fixed upon, and the man who was not thought good enough for the Queenslanders was saddled on Jamaica, and appointed her Governor in the very next month, in December, 1888. The Jamaican-Africans offered no protest when the rejected of Queensland was foisted upon them. The countrymen of George William Gordon, the hero-martyr of 1865, might have done so, but they would have been simply bringing punishment and disability on their own heads; but when Queensland gave a veto to Blake's being appointed her Governor, the Home Government never seriously thought of enforcing obedience to its mandate. They, no doubt, bethought themselves of the lesson which the American colonies taught their fathers in the days when the obstinate German, the Third George, was King. They wisely refrained from annoying the Queenslanders. It is very probable that had the Jamaican-Africans, like the Queenslanders, protested, and been prepared to back up their protest by force, against the appointment of Sir Henry Arthur Blake as their Governor, a few British ships-of-war would have been promptly sent by Lord Salisbury's Government to Kingston and Port Royal, to help to keep the 'fairly happy and contented' Africans quiet, or, rather, 'suppress' them.

Absenteeism on the part of the sugar-lords (the same sort of absenteeism on the part of the British Crown and the landlords which is felt in Ireland, and which is responsible for much of the misery prevalent in the Emerald Isle, and for the constant and unremitting agitation which distracts that unfortunate kingdom, and is lashing the Irish people into disloyalty, as well as forcing them to migrate from their native land to the United States) is rampant in the West Indian Colonies, Trinidad, and Jamaica especially. This absenteeism, which paralyzes and cripples the progress of the colonies, is also ruining their people.

Is it not an injustice and an anomaly that the sugar—

the mainstay and chief staple of the colony—the sugar which is grown in Trinidad, and is worked and manufactured by the labour, the exertion, and the skill of Trinidadian Africans for British sugar-lords, is sold at $1\frac{1}{2}$d. and 2d. per pound in the British Isles, while the prices in Trinidad for Trinidadian sugar do not fetch a halfpenny less than 4d. and 6d. per pound?

As a matter of course, and as the result of the crooked policy of blundering red-tapism, that amount of sugar which many a poor man in the British Isles is able to buy and consume, the poor Trinidadian African is disqualified from procuring in Trinidad, though if he were living in Britain he could procure it with the greatest facility.

The British judges in Trinidad are now engaged in stirring up class against class, the poor against the rich, and all for the sake of winning a transient popularity; and we do not hesitate to say that the authorities at Downing Street made a grievous mistake when they sent Sir John Gorrie and his 'learned' brothers, Justices Cook and Lumb, to Trinidad.

Perjury prevails to an alarming extent in Trinidad, for many an indigent rascal and fortune-hunter looks upon the Trinidadian Law Courts as the best and surest places in which to make his fortune; and, relying on the fact that others before him have succeeded in the nefarious traffic, the perjurer, we say, does not hesitate to urge his spurious and fictitious claims against some wealthy men whom he has never seen, or has never spoken to in his life; or, if he brings an action against some wealthy man with whom he has transacted business, the chances are ten to one that he has no real claim whatever upon him.

The young brigade of briefless lawyers deliberately help

to complicate the position in Trinidad; because these (the young, *not* the old lawyers), being themselves indigent and out of work, take upon themselves the *rôle* of barrators, and are encouragers of litigation. There are several that we know of who, instead of helping to mitigate the evil, are simply a disgrace to the noble and honourable profession. And, as if to complicate matters still more, Sir John Gorrie, the Chief Justice of Trinidad, and the Attorney-General, the Hon. S. H. Gatty, Q.C., who began their feuds in Antigua (as if the world was not large enough for these two men!), have been sent to Trinidad, as to a better and fairer battling-ground. Such disagreements serve—when the Chief Justice and the First Law Officer of the Crown fall to loggerheads—but to create a judicial deadlock. As a consequence of such disagreements, the Attorney-General is generally conspicuous by his absence from the Law Courts when matters are brought forward which require his attention as Counsel for the Crown.

The administrators and expounders of the law should set a good example to the inhabitants of the colony by ceasing their bickerings, and concerning themselves with the business of the people; those high in office, especially those who administer the law, should be above reproach, and not indulge in party bickerings. But what will not happen under Crown Colony Government?

Also we may mention here that the same tyranny on the part of the judges, which stifles public opinion and gags the public press in Jamaica, Trinidad and Tobago, and elsewhere in the West Indies, is paramount in British Guiana. Mr. Louis de Souza,* a Barrister-at-Law, of Lin-

---

* This brilliant African claimed descent from no less a house than that of Royal Braganza.

coln's Inn, who was a distinguished African, had the moral courage to resist judicial tyranny, and beard the British Guiana judges in their own den; but he fell a victim to their resentment because of his just notions of liberty, and was by the Georgetown judges committed to the Georgetown Gaol for an alleged Contempt of Court, where he forfeited his life through no fault of his own. His imprisonment raised him a great many sympathizers—many more sympathizers than he had had when he first began his struggle with the judges; while his death, though it came as a surprise to his fellow-men because of its suddenness, made De Souza, already a hero, a glorious martyr.

Of the many white men of doubtful adaptation who have been foisted upon Trinidad, John Edward Tanner, the Director of Public Works; Stephen Herbert Gatty, Q.C., the Attorney-General; Samuel Leonard Crane, the Surgeon-General; John Cook, the first Puisne Judge; Henry W. Chantrell, the Auditor-General; Charles B. Hamilton, the Receiver-General; George Workman Dickson, the Assistant Director of Public Works; David Wilson, the Commissioner of the Northern Province and Sub-Intendant of Crown Lands; and William Robinson, K.C.M.G., the Governor and Commander-in-chief of Trinidad and Tobago, stand in prominence.

Trinidadians have an insufficiency of hospitals, an insufficiency of wards, nurses, and attendants, while the small and inadequate Port-of-Spain and San Fernando Hospitals are the only two benevolent institutions of the kind in the Island Colony worthy of note. Supposing there be a deficit in the Treasury of the Crown Colony of Trinidad which prevents the William Robinson Administration from meeting the needs of the inhabitants, and supplying them with more and better hospitals, more and better surgeons and physicians, more and better wards, more and better nurses and attendants, there is an alternative or a remedy forthcoming. And this is the remedy: let the British Secretary of State, the Right Honourable Lord Knutsford, reduce the salary of the Governor and Commander-in-chief of Trinidad and Tobago (who—will it be believed by him who is not *au courant* on the subject? —receives £5,000 per annum as salary for misruling Trinidad and Tobago, with 205,000 inhabitants; that is to say, he—the Governor—receives half as great a salary as his Excellency the President of the United States of North America, General Benjamin Harrison, receives annually for ruling 63,000,000 Yankees; that is to say, again, receives nearly half as much salary as the Vice-President, the Secretary of State, the Secretary of the Treasury, the Secretary for War, the Secretary of the Navy, the Secretary for the Interior, the Secretary for Agriculture, the Postmaster-General, and the Attorney-General of the United States of North America). We suggest allowing his Excellency Sir William Robinson* £2,000 yearly, instead of £5,000; and let the British Secretary of State for the Colonies reduce the salary of the Chief Justice of Trinidad and Tobago (who receives £1,800 per annum; that is, only £200 less than the Chief Justice of the Supreme Court of the United States of North America does), and allow Sir John Gorrie £1,000 instead of the £1,800 he receives annually; let the British Secretary of State reduce the salary of the Attorney-General, and allow him £700 instead of £1,000; let him reduce the salary of the first

* Sir William Robinson has since been promoted to Hong Kong, having been swept away from Trinidad by Sir Frederick Napier Broome, K.C.M.G. We wish the Chinese of Hong Kong joy of their gift of a Governor.

Puisne Judge, and allow him £900 instead of the £1,000 he is receiving annually; let him reduce the salary of the second Puisne Judge, and allow him £900 instead of the £1,000 he now receives; let him reduce the emolument of the Director of Public Works, and allow him £900 instead of the £1,500 he is now annually receiving; let him reduce the emolument of the Surgeon-General, and allow him £600 instead of the £1,000 he now receives; let him reduce the emolument of the Receiver-General, and allow him £600 instead of the £700 he now receives; let him reduce the salary of the Assistant Director of Public Works, and allow him £600 instead of the £800 he now receives; let him reduce the income of the Commissioner of the Northern Province, and allow him £700 instead of the £800 he receives; let him reduce the allowance of the Auditor-General, and give him £700 in lieu of the £800 he is now receiving. In brief, let Downing Street reduce the salaries of the officials of the Civil and Judicial establishments, and, with the joint proceeds of these reductions, enlarge and improve the existing hospitals and wards; build more hospitals; employ a more numerous staff of efficient nurses and attendants; get a more numerous staff of competent medical men, weeding out those who are not competent, in the behalf of the Trinidadian *people*.

But we fear that there is not the slightest likelihood of that being done, though the plan is feasible enough. It is the same cry all over the British Colonies where Africans are in a majority; and yet Laird Clowes would have us believe that 'in every British colony in which he is to be found the African is a fairly happy and contented person.'

After the Trinidadian people had sent a numerously-signed petition to the British Secretary of State for the Colonies (as the outcome of an enthusiastic mass-meeting

UNDER CAUCASIAN RULE.   207

previously held in the Queen's Park, in the capital of the Island-Colony of Trinidad, in 1886), Trinidadians of all shades of opinion were cajoled into believing that Responsible Government, even on a moderate basis, would be granted them, when a Royal Commission of ten men was appointed to inquire into the fitness of the people for the elective franchise. That Commission, which had for its chairman the Attorney-General, the Hon. S. H. Gatty, Q.C., sat for some months, during which time many witnesses were examined as to the fitness of the inhabitants for a Constitution.

On the conclusion of their labours in the examination of witnesses (who were almost unanimously in favour of the granting of Responsible Government to Trinidad), and immediately before closing their last Session and drawing up and sending their Report to the Secretary of State, the Chairman put it to the vote of the Members of the Royal Commission, whether they were of opinion that the inhabitants of Trinidad were fit and ripe for Responsible Government. On a division it was found that seven were for and three Members (the chairman included) were against the granting of a Constitution or Responsible Government to Trinidad. Those of our readers who are unacquainted with the fact—and we fear there are only too many—will find it strange perhaps when we tell them that the British Secretary of State abode by the decision, or vote, of the *minority*, the small minority of the three as against that of the *majority* of the Members of the Commission, and absolutely refused the Franchise and Representation to Trinidad and the Trinidadians.

It is but fair to say, we think, that that Commission, which was dignified by and rejoiced in the name of Royal, was but a farce and a mockery from beginning to end. The witnesses whom the Commission examined, and who after a severe cross-examination proved the fitness of Trinidadians for self-government, were set aside, and the mere opinion of three men, neither of whom had or has any real interest in the Island-Colony, was allowed to prevail. Their seven colleagues, who were, and are, almost to a man, bred and born in the colony, and have, or had, their interests in the colony, had their voice altogether ignored.

We make bold to say that though the British Secretary of State appointed a Royal Commission to inquire into the fitness of the Crown Colony of Trinidad for Home Rule, he never intended that the Constitution should be conferred on the Trinidadians. And why? Because of the great numerical preponderance of the African inhabitants over those of British blood in Trinidad. But on what ground or grounds do we base this statement, our readers may wish to ask? Only just recently (*i.e.*, in the earlier part of the year, 1891) Lord Knutsford, replying to a British Hondurian petition praying for a modicum of Responsible Government, made answer that the British Parliament never ntended that the colony in which the British inhabitants were greatly in a minority and were outnumbered by the people of a different race or nationality, should enjoy Responsible Government; that that was the case with the Colony of British Honduras, the number of the African inhabitants greatly preponderating over the British in that Peninsula-Colony.

Now, if the authorities at Downing Street refused British Honduras with 28,000 inhabitants Responsible Government, is there any right-thinking man who will say that the British Parliament will ever grant Home Rule to the united colony of Trinidad and Tobago, which has 205,000 people, and where the Africans greatly preponderate numerically, and in intelligence too, over those of British descent?

When the British Colonial Secretary of State, therefore,

appointed a Royal Commission to inquire into the fitness of Trinidadians for Responsible Government, well knowing that the British Parliament, or, rather, a British majority-party, would never consent to grant Trinidad a Constitution, because of the overwhelming majority of the Africans over the white inhabitants, he grossly insulted Trinidadians—Trinidadian Africans particularly—since he caused them to hope, and then disappointed them, in absolutely refusing to grant them what he had from the first (*i.e.*, from the receipt of the Trinidadian petition and his appointment of the Royal Commission) made up his mind not to grant them, viz., Home Rule or Responsible Government, which are, in fact, identical terms.

Again, was it not a British Conservative ministry, the Third Conservative Ministry of Earl Derby, which brought its authority to bear upon the Jamaicans, and pulled the Jamaican Constitution to pieces? Was it probable that a British Conservative Ministry like the present Second Conservative Ministry of the Marquis of Salisbury, which generally carries out the traditions and principles of former British Conservative Ministries, would have granted Trinidad (when it petitioned for Home Rule) the same Constitution which a previous Conservative Administration destroyed in Jamaica in 1866, inasmuch as there were in Jamaica, in 1866, as many Africans (the Africans in Jamaica being now more than twice as numerous as they were in 1866) as there are now (1891) Africans in Trinidad and Tobago? Like Jamaica, like Trinidad and Tobago.

The above, then, are the grounds on which we say that the British Colonial Secretary of State, when he appointed the Royal Commission to inquire into the fitness of the Crown Colony of Trinidad for a Responsible Constitution never intended that Home Rule should be granted to the Trinidadians.

What does the British Colonial Secretary of State do to meet, as he supposes, the needs of the Trinidadians? He appoints Louis Ant. A. de Verteuil, M.D., C.M.G., to represent Port-of-Spain, Jean Valleton de Boissière, M.D., to represent St. Anna and Diego-martin, Thomas Alex. Finlayson to represent Savana Grande, Mayaro, and Cedros, George Townsend Fenwick to represent Arima, Blanchisseuse, and Toco, George Fitt to represent Chagnan, Couva, and Montserrat, Charles Leotaud to represent Naparima, Eugene Cipriani to represent San Fernando, William Gordon-Gordon to share the seat in the representation of Port-of-Spain with De Verteuil, John Bell-Smyth to represent Tucarigua, John MacKillop to represent Tobago. How would the Australasians or the British North Americans have received and borne such a farce, such an insult? Canada and Newfoundland would have joined the United States of North America quickly enough, and the Australians would have established an Independent Republic. The men Lord Knutsford appointed to seats in the Legislative Council are all whites, and, it is needless to say, they do not represent the Trinidadian Africans in any way, because they have not been so elected by the Africans. They have all been foisted upon the Colony by the British Colonial Secretary of a British Government.

Trinidadians, however, still fondly indulge in the vain and chimerical delusion that on their assuming office the Gladstonian Liberals will be graciously pleased to grant them 'Home Rule.' That remains to be seen. But we firmly believe that no faith ought to be put in either a Conservative Ministry dominated over by Lord Salisbury, or in a Gladstonian Liberal Ministry under the leadership of Mr. Gladstone. We should have more confidence in the Irish Parliamentary Party, if there were any probability of their coming into office, inasmuch as they are passionately longing to have Home Rule themselves, and they would not be indifferent to the claims of Trinidad and Tobago for the same Home Rule.

That Crown Colony Government, hateful as it is, shall continue dominant in Trinidad and Tobago rather than that the white colonial or Europo-Creole inhabitants should enjoy the Elective Franchise and Responsible Government, and the sweets of power should be handed over to Messrs. Rostant, Damian, Lange, Guppy, Goodwille and their party, to the total exclusion of Trinidadians of the Ethiopian race from being participators and beneficiaries.

But has Laird Clowes heard of the Reform and Home Rule Movement in Trinidad? If the African 'in every British colony in which he is to be found is a fairly happy and a contented person,' would he sign and send a petition to the British Home Government praying that the old rotten Crown Colony Government of Trinidad should be done away with?

We, unlike Laird Clowes, know that 'in every British colony in which' they are to be 'found' the Africans are 'a fairly unhappy and discontented people.' Nevertheless, those Africans who have the welfare of their race at heart, can render thanks to the Almighty for founding Liberia, the Light and Hope of Africa and Africans, to which all 'fairly unhappy and discontented' Africans living under the Caucasian flag can resort.

Africans mainly compose the Police force of Barbados, Trinidad and Tobago, and British Guiana; the Jamaican Constabulary, which is modelled on the semi-military system of the Royal Irish Constabulary—a force which Sir Henry Arthur Blake, the Governor of Jamaica, knows, without doubt, only too well how to wield—is mainly composed of Africans; Africans form the strength and bulwark of the Jamaican Volunteer Militia; of the Volunteer Corps in

British Guiana, and Trinidad and Tobago, and yet in none of these organizations can the African be a Commissioned Officer, every place being usurped by the pale-faced Britisher. In the American Army and Navy, as well as in the American Militia and Police, Africans may be found, but, like their kinsmen living under the British flag, they may never be more than privates or non-commissioned officers.

Many of the Officers of the Royal Irish Constabulary who have batoned and broken the heads of many a fellow-countryman, and whom the majority of Irishmen are incensed against and dislike, have been thought good enough to be foisted upon the Jamaicans and Trinidadians by the authorities at Downing Street. When their own countrymen detest the men composing the Royal Irish Constabulary because of their cruel ill-treatment of brother-Irishmen, is it likely that the Officers of the Royal Irish Constabulary will ever entertain kindly feelings towards the dark-skinned Africans in Jamaica and Trinidad and Tobago?

It has been shown, then, that in every British West Indian Colony in which he is to be found the African is the reverse of 'a fairly happy and contented person,' but we now turn to other parts, and fresh fields and pastures new —to Africa, where Africans do most abound, and to those parts of Africa where the British hold sway. We ask, are the Africans' prospects and condition brighter in British Africa than in the British West Indies, or in the United States of North America? We say not, and maintain that they are on a par, as we shall presently endeavour to show.

The Gambia with 15,000, Sierra Leone with 62,000, Lagos with 100,000, and the Gold Coast with 1,472,000 progressive and intelligent inhabitants—the great majority

UNDER CAUCASIAN RULE. 213

of whom are Africans born and bred and by descent—do not enjoy Representation, and have not Responsible Government, while all the British North American Provinces and Australasian Colonies, with illiterate and superstitious men largely in the ascendant, make use of and enjoy both.

The Cape Colony, with 1,430,000 inhabitants, most of whom are Africans, although it has Responsible Government, and sends 22 Representatives to its Legislative Council, and has a House of Assembly of 76 elected Members, refuses the Franchise and full and unqualified Citizenship (in their own country, too!) to the Africans, while we positively aver that we are aware that the rulers of the Colony of Natal (which boasts of an estimated population of 5,300,000, the large majority of whom are Africans) deny the African the franchise and representation, although Responsible Government now obtains in Natal, that Colony sending 23 Representatives to its Legislative Council.

We shall mention one more leading British Colony in Africa, and that is Mauritius, which we had occasion to refer to previously. We say that with a population of 373,000, mostly Africans, Mauritius is permitted to send only 2 Representative Members to the Council of Government, and 10 to the Legislative Council, which is an inadequate representation. Yet, though the Mauritian people are inadequately represented, their Constitution is preferable to that of Jamaica, or to having none at all, as in the cases of Trinidad and Tobago, Gold Coast, Lagos, etc. Because we believe in the maxim that half a loaf is better than no bread.

The African is relegated to the background, though he does all the heavy work of the British Colonial Forces in Africa as in the British West Indies. There is the Police Force of Mauritius; there are the armed and mounted

Police and Volunteer Forces of Natal; there is the West India Regiment (composed of Africans from the Sergeant-Major to the private) stationed in the Gambia, Sierra Leone, and Lagos; there are the armed Constabulary Force, and part of the West India Regiment, in the Gold Coast; there are thirty Volunteer Corps, the Cape Police, and Cape Mounted Rifle Forces of the Cape Colony, and though the African predominates numerically in every one of these organizations, yet in none of these does the African hold a responsible position, or, in other words, in none is he a commissioned officer.

If Africans, like Caucasians, are sufficiently intelligent and talented to become proficients in the medical, legal, theological, engineering, and surveying professions, it stands to reason that they (the Africans) ought to be qualified for the posts of commissioners of police, army commissioned officers, magistrates, and judges, and, aye, Governors under the British and American flags.

But is it only the African Ethiopian in Africa, in the Americas (including the West Indies and elsewhere) who is labouring under disabilities imposed upon him by red-tape? By no means. The Australian Ethiopian, unlike his African cousin, is rapidly disappearing before the march of the White Man and 'Civilization,' and that inevitable concomitant of 'Civilization,' the Fire-Water, particularly the *eau-de-vie*, the constitution of the Australian being decidedly weaker than that of the African Ethiopian in every way.

It was expected that the reaction following on their sudden liberation would have exercised a disastrous and fatal influence on the African Ethiopians. A greater mistake was never made, for, on the contrary, Africans have increased and multiplied in an astonishing manner, and are marching shoulder to shoulder with Caucasians and Civilization, just as the rest of Europeans formerly did with their Roman civilizers. Not so the Australian African, however, for, as we said before, he is fast disappearing, like the American and West Indian, before the progressive march of Civilization. The Australasian Ethiopian in Oceania is dwindling in number, while the African throughout the world is increasing in number. There are not perhaps 60,000 Australian Africans, while they are extinct in Tasmania; there are only about 8,000 in New South Wales, and 7,000 in Victoria; but it is in Queensland that the greatest number are found. In none of the Australasian Colonies are they electors, or liable for election; and they are not allowed in any way to interfere in politics, nor do they have full citizenship. We sincerely pity and mourn over the misfortunes of the poor 'black fellows.'

At one of the sittings of the Australasian Federation Convention in Sydney in the spring of this year (1891), a resolution was unanimously passed by the Australasian delegates of the Convention never to allow the Australasian Aborigines or Africans to have anything to do with politics; they were not to be allowed to exercise their full citizenship.*

With all these facts before him, as related throughout this chapter, will any reasonable and conscientious man say that 'in every British colony in which he is to be found the African is a fairly happy and contented person'?

The 'British and Foreign Anti-Slavery Society'—an institution which was founded in 1839, with illustrious Thomas Clarkson as its first President—exists for two avowed objects; viz. (1), the universal extinction of slavery and the slave trade, and (2) the protection of the rights

* The most persistent opponent of the privileges the Australasian Aborigines are entitled to is Sir George Grey, K.C.B., to whom we owe no thanks.

and interests of the enfranchised population in the British possessions, and of all persons captured as slaves. It has, however, done but comparatively little service since its foundation, for both slavery and the slave trade exist at the present moment in Turkey, Persia, the Belgian Congo Free State, in the British South Africa Company's Territories, the British East Africa Company's Territories, as well as in Zanzibar and Pemba, the British Royal Niger Company's Territories, and in many other places in Africa, more especially in Portuguese Africa. Africans in every part of the British Empire are still labouring—and very probably, as long as they remain under the British flag, will always labour—under disabilities, notwithstanding the so-called 'protection of the rights and interests of the enfranchised population in the British possessions, and of all persons captured as slaves,' by this society.*

Does or did this society ever protect 'the rights and interests of the enfranchised population' in Trinidad? It does not, and never did; while we venture to say that it never heard of the agitation for Responsible Government by the Trinidadians, and the manner in which Lord Knutsford insulted them.

We may safely say here again that Mr. Clowes, when he gives out that the African 'in every British colony in which he is to be found is a fairly happy and contented person,' argues on his ignorance of material facts. The St. Lucian African, far from being 'a fairly happy and contented person,' is nearly always falling to loggerheads with the Administrator and Colonial Secretary, the Treasurer and the Chief Justice of Lucia. The African in St. Vincent, Grenada, and all the British Colonies has some

* We personally decline with thanks the 'protection' of the 'British and Foreign Anti-Slavery Society,' or any other 'philanthropic' society.

grievance or other, and is consequently far from being 'a fairly happy and contented person.' Laird Clowes tells us, on pages 156 and 157 in his 'Black America,' that the *New York Tribune* says 'with truth'—what is 'truth' and what is *not* 'truth' the reader will see for himself—that 'there may be one faith, one baptism, and one Name under Heaven whereby men may be saved, but in South Carolina there must be a white man's church, high-toned and very respectable, and a place somewhere outside where the Negroes may herd together without disturbing the pious meditations of their superiors. Simon of Cyrene, who carried the cross, was a Negro, but that passage in the Gospels can be bracketed, if need be, and not read in the white churches of Charleston during Holy Week. The Ethiopian eunuch baptized by Philip could not have had a white skin, but that chapter can be omitted in the liturgical order of second lessons. The white saints will kindly consent to pray every Sunday for all sorts and conditions of men, provided "the niggers" are taught to remain in their own place, and not to intrude where they are not wanted. They will live and die in the faith and communion of their white fathers and white grandfathers, with no Negroes on the sacred premises, except possibly the coloured sexton, who must not under any circumstances be a communicant, but merely a sweep. What arrangements will be made for their benefit in the next world they cannot tell, but they may at least indulge the pious hope that there will be a separate "nigger heaven"—an adjunct, like their own coloured convention, to the white man's paradise—a separate missionary jurisdiction, with swarthy angels and combination Negro melodies.'

That there is 'one faith, one baptism, and one Name under Heaven whereby men may be saved'; that Cyrenean Simon, who carried his Saviour's Cross, was an African;

that the Ethiopian eunuch hailing from the distant realms of Queen Candace, who was baptized by Philip, was an African, are the only 'truths' which obtain in that article of the *New York Tribune*, which is in every respect coarse and brutal; it displays the narrow-mindedness of the writer, while its quotations reflect that of Laird Clowes. The article is, on the whole, so puerile and farcical that it hardly deserves consideration.

The fact that Simon the Cyrenean carried the Saviour's Cross reflects great honour on the African Race; for while Asiatics and Caucasians were persecuting the world's Saviour, the African, who was present from being a sympathizer and mourner, was forced to take upon himself the task of carrying the cross; and from being an imposed burden, it became a pleasant duty and an undying honour to African Simon, and through him to the whole Ethiopian race. How many millions of Christians of all shades of complexion have wished they had been in the Cyrenean's place! The Asiatics, in the persons of the Jews, persecuted the Lord Jesus Christ, Himself a Jew; and the Caucasians, in the persons of the Roman Pilate and his soldiers, rendered them active assistance, joining with the Jews in the crucifixion of our Lord; but the part which the African, in the person of Cyrenean Simon, took in that painful drama did not consist in persecuting, or helping to persecute, but it consisted in succouring his Saviour when He was unable to carry His Cross, in alleviating His pains when He was too weak to bear, and could hardly even walk. And is it because of Simon's achievements, and because Simon was an African and a 'blameless Ethiopian,' that the sapient *New York Tribune* would have all references to him omitted 'in the white churches of Charleston during Holy Week'?

But that was not the only triumph which Africa experienced in connection with our Lord; for Africa must be congratulated on the fact that, when the Infant Jesus, the future Saviour of the world, was being sought out for slaughter by the tyrant King of Judæa, Idumæan Herod, and could not be kept safe in His own country, Asian Palestine, Africa gave Him and His saintly relatives, Joseph and Mary, a home and a shelter in that time of need. They remained in safety in Africa until the cloud had disappeared from the horizon, and they could return to their own land.

The *New York Tribune* goes on thus : 'the Ethiopian eunuch baptized by Philip could not have had a white skin, but that chapter can be omitted in the liturgical order of second lessons.' The *New York Tribune* and Mr. W. Laird Clowes are evidently suffering from Africophobia, and they are, at the same time, very vain on account of the colour of their skin. Caucasians, however, while they are not unmindful of the fact that the Lord Jesus Christ was not an African, indulge in the delusion that He was a *white* man, seemingly forgetting that Our Saviour was an Asiatic of the Semitic Race. Yes, we say that Our Saviour, though He was not a descendant of Ham, was not a descendant of Japheth either, but a descendant of Shem; and we affirm that the descendants of Shem are nearer the Hamitic than the descendants of Japheth.

St. Peter, the First Head of the Christian Church, and the other Apostles and the Jews were not Africans it is true, but neither were they Caucasians ; they were all of the Semitic Race. Whence arises, then, the Caucasian vanity for his white skin?

After telling us that 'there may be one faith, one baptism, and one name under Heaven whereby men may be saved,' the *New York Tribune,* as quoted by Laird Clowes, adds : 'What arrangements will be made for their benefit in the next world they cannot tell, but they may at least indulge the pious hope that there will be a separate "nigger heaven" —an adjunct, like their own coloured convention, to the white man's paradise—a separate missionary jurisdiction, with swarthy angels and combination Negro melodies.'

We say that if there be one faith, one baptism, and one church, there can only be one God, and, therefore, one Heaven, not two. Yet, even supposing that the Africans in Heaven will be 'swarthy angels,' and not 'white angels,' neither the *New York Tribune*, Laird Clowes, nor any other man is able to prove that the King of Heaven is Himself white. What is in a colour of skin? Is not black as good as white? Is not black the favourite colour princes and peoples wear?

'What arrangements will be made for their benefit in the next world they cannot tell, but they may at least indulge the pious hope that there will be a separate "nigger heaven" —an adjunct to the white man's paradise,' are the *New York Tribune's* words. We tell the *New York Tribune* that the same ' arrangements will be made for our benefit in the next world ' as for the Caucasians and all other peoples, and that there shall and must be one Heaven for all ruled over by one King, one God ; while it is not given to the Caucasian, nor to any race other than the Ethiopian, to fix what place the African shall occupy or shall not occupy in Heaven. And it seems to us that the statement that ' there will be a separate "nigger heaven"—an adjunct to the white man's paradise,' is, to say the least, absurd on the face of it, and a cruel and shameful taunt.

' Dogma and Descent, potential twin,
   Which erst could rein submissive millions in,
   Are now spent forces on the eddying surge
   Of Thought enfranchised. Agencies emerge
   Unhampered by the incubus of dread
   Which cramped men's hearts and clogged their onward tread.

UNDER CAUCASIAN RULE. 221

Dynasty, Prescription ! spectral in these days,
When Science points to Thought its surest ways,
And men, who scorn obedience when not free,
Demand the logic of Authority !
The day of manhood to the world is here,
And ancient homage waxes faint and drear.

. . . . . .

Vision of rapture ! See Salvation's plan
—'Tis serving God through ceaseless toil for man !*

---

* The above quoted lines were written by our late esteemed and distinguished countryman, John Jacob Thomas, author of The Creole Grammar,' and ' Froudacity-Froudacity,' in a reply to Mr. James Anthony Froude's ' The English in the West Indies.' Mr. Thomas coined it from the historian of Henry the Eighth's cognomen, Froudacity being synonymous with mendacity. Hence, an Africo-American, a West Indo-African, or other African would term the assertions made by W. Laird Clowes and other calumniators of the mighty and wonderful Ethiopian race, *froudacious.*

CHAPTER VI.

AFRICA GOVERNED BY THE AFRICANS.

WE said, in the first chapter, that we did not propose entering on a discussion respecting the excesses said to have been committed by the white American Republican Liberal leaders and their American African following during the Reconstruction period in the Southern States of the Yankee Union, because we are convinced that all the particulars to hand which have been furnished to Laird Clowes, a Conservative, have been furnished *by Conservative Democrats*, and are all one-sided. All such particulars are greatly magnified by Laird Clowes, and we are satisfied that if any excesses were committed by the Republicans of the North during the Reconstruction in the South, those excesses could only have been committed by the white Republicans, and the responsibility, therefore, would lie on them only.

These are the reasons, and these only, which actuate us, and prevent us from entering on a discussion of the doings of that period in the South; but when Laird Clowes, writing on 'Reconstruction in Mississippi,' proceeds to quote the Southern Conservative Democrat, Ethelbert Barksdale, of Mississippi, as 'employing the language of a Northern statesman and Union soldier, that " in the whole historic period of the world the Ethiopian race had never established or maintained a Government for themselves,"' the situation is, as a matter of course, altered, and facts known to many must be put in the scale as material evidences, and brought to bear as such against the misstatements of the 'Northern statesman and Union soldier,' of Ethelbert Barksdale, of Mississippi, and W. Laird Clowes, with a view to showing that, on the contrary, the African Race has had Governments, capable Governments, of its own from time immemorial, as it has them now.

We have already had occasion to point out that Mr. Clowes's knowledge of Africans and their affairs is very limited, and by endorsing the statement of Ethelbert Barksdale, of Mississippi, he brings into greater prominence his ignorance of African history. For the African race, we are happy to be able to say, can boast that ancient Ethiopia, now modern Nubia, had a Government of her own, composed exclusively of African Ethiopians. It is a matter of common knowledge that the ancient Ethiopians imparted their religious arts, civilization, and form of Government to the Semitic Egyptians.* Ethiopia boasted of having enjoyed the best of Governments under Azerch, Arnen, and Piankhi-Meiamen; while from the reign of the latter King, and for several generations, Ethiopia domineered over Egypt.† Kashta, Shabak, Sabacus, Tuhraka, Urdamen, Nouat-Meiamen, Arkamen, are also celebrated Ethiopian Kings under whom Ethiopia flourished because they were capable governors.‡ Queen Candace, and King Zoskales, and other Ethiopian sovereigns who succeeded them, ruled

* Niebuhr's 'Lectures on Ancient History,' vol. i., pp. 59, 68, 72, 126, 137; 'Encyclopædia Britannica,' vol. i., p. 65; vol. vii., pp. 742, 743, 737, 740, 741; vol. viii., pp. 611-613; 'Herodotus,' vol. i., book iii.; Smith's 'Dictionary of the Bible,' vol. i., pp. 248, 588, 589.
† *Ibid.* ‡ *Ibid.*

their subjects wisely, causing Ethiopia to flourish. All these sovereigns were aboriginal or indigenous Ethiopians, and they were independent, owning no foreigner as their lord. These Ethiopians not only established but maintained a Government for themselves.*

Abyssinia, a State which was closely allied to the ancient and formidable State of Ethiopia, had an independent Government of her own. Auxum, its ancient capital, was its most flourishing town and the seat of its Government. It was in the sixth century, near about 552, when King Caleb, or Elesbaan, directed the destinies of the State, that the Abyssinian power attained the zenith of its early greatness, and wrested Yemen, in Arabia, from the grasp of the Arabians, after inflicting on this latter nation calamitous defeats.† And from about 1255, when Icon Amlac was Emperor, till the sixteenth century, the Abyssinians had capable and stable Governments of their own, and, consequently, Abyssinia was in a flourishing condition.‡ All these capable governors were indigenous Abyssinians.§ The Emperor, or King, Theodore, who reigned from 1855 to 1868, and who revived the ancient greatness of Abyssinia, must be treated as belonging to the Hamitic race, and everybody knows that Abyssinia enjoyed a good and stable Government under him till 1863, when he got into complications with the British, was defeated by them, lost his

* Niebuhr's 'Lectures on Ancient History,' vol. i., pp. 59, 68, 72, 126, 137 ; 'Encyclopædia Britannica,' vol. i., p. 65 ; vol. vii., pp. 742, 743, 737, 740, 741 ; vol. viii., pp. 611-613 ; 'Herodotus,' vol. i., book iii. ; Smith's 'Dictionary of the Bible,' vol. i., pp. 248, 588, 589.

† 'Encyclopædia Britannica,' vol i., pp. 64, *et seq.;* 'English Cyclopædia of Geography,' vol. i., p. 47 ; and *vide* Job Ludolf's 'Historia Ethiopia,' and Lacroze's 'History of Abyssinian Christianity.'

‡ *Ibid.*   § *Ibid.*

throne, and perished in 1868.* A Britisher thus eulogizes His Imperial Majesty, the Emperor Theodore of Abyssinia: 'The late King Theodore of Abyssinia, of whom we are not perhaps disposed to take the most favourable view, was a ruler of no ordinary ability. After his accession to power he began to inaugurate a series of reforms which, it has been said, had he lived in another country, or had suitable advisers at his side, would have gained him a reputation equal to that of Peter or Frederick the Great.'†

Who is there who has not heard of the greatness of ancient Egypt in politics, arts, literature, etc.? And can anyone disprove that the ancient Egyptians were of the Ethiopian Race?‡ The whole world knows that the Babylonian and Assyrian were mighty Empires, whose people were of the Ethiopian Race.§

We Africans also claim consanguinity with the Carthaginians, and were not the Carthaginians distinguished governors? There are a few who maintain, as we had occasion to point out before, that the Carthaginians were of the Semitic race, and could not have belonged to the Ethiopian race. With that question we have dealt in our Second Chapter. No doubt the Carthaginians differed from the Ethiopians or Nubians, who perhaps, in their turn, differed

* 'Encyclopædia Britannica,' vol. i., p. 64, *et seq.*; 'English Cyclopædia of Geography,' vol. i., p. 47; and *vide* Job Ludolf's 'Historia Ethiopica,' and Lacroze's 'History of Abyssinian Christianity.'

† *British Workman.*

‡ Smith's 'Dictionary of the Bible,' vol. i., pp. 588, 589, 741-744; *ibid.*, vol. ii., pp. 389-391, 868, 869; 'Herodotus,' vol. i., books ii. and iii.; Volney's 'Travels,' vol. i., chap. iii.; Catafago's 'Arabic and English Dictionary'; Dr. Hartmann's 'Encyclopædic Work on Nigritia,' 1876.

§ Smith's 'Dictionary of the Bible,' vol. i., p. 127, *et seq.*; pp. 149-154, *et seq.*; *ibid.*, vol. ii., p. 546, *et seq.*

from the Abyssinians, but all these three African nations were Ethiopians, and boasted of a common ancestor in Ham. Do not the Teutons and Celts differ from the Græco-Latins and Slavs, though these all claim a common ancestor in Japheth?

Africans, like Afro-Canadian Samuel Kinggold Ward and Americo-African G. W. Williams, however, do not stand alone in claiming the Carthaginians as having belonged to their race. The majority of Caucasian writers who refer to the Carthaginians and their history support the Africans in their claim. Mommsen does in his 'History of Rome.' Mrs. Harriett Beecher-Stowe, the celebrated novelist, and writer of many able works, also supports that claim. For, writing on page 78, chapter xvi., in 'Uncle Tom's Cabin' (her best known work), she says of Uncle Tom, a typical African, and the hero of her work, that 'Tom, in his well-brushed broadcloth suit, smooth beaver, glossy boots, faultless wristbands and collar, with his grave, good-natured black face, looked respectable enough *to be a bishop of Carthage, as men of his colour were in other ages.*' We take Mrs. Harriett Beecher-Stowe to mean, then, that the Carthaginians were not only Africans, but that they were Ethiopians also.

As Mrs. Beecher-Stowe, who is still alive, has never thought fit to alter the statement she made thirty years ago, we must conclude that she firmly believes that her statement is the correct one, and the judgment of so eminent a writer must receive due weight and consideration.

What unusual interest is awakened in the breast of the average African when reading about Carthage and her struggles, and her three Punic wars with Rome! What deep and joyous emotion fills him as he reads of the successes of the Hamilcars, Hannibals, Hasdrubals, Maherbals, Hannos, Himilcos, Magos, Sapphos, and Giscos! He takes exultant pride in their victories in Africa, Spain, Italy, Sardinia, Sicily, and Corsica. The African sorrows with the Carthaginians when he reads that they suffered defeats and experienced disasters. He grieves when the great, the glorious, the ancient Carthage was sacked and reduced to ashes. Do the sentiment and opinion of the African count for nothing? Are they not on a level with those of the Caucasian?

Now, to speak of the Carthaginian Government. We all know that Carthage boasted of a Constitution which was remarkable for its stability and firmness; one that made the people happy and contented and prosperous. The great Aristotle, in his 'Politics,' praises the Constitution of the Carthaginians, because few revolutions were known to have ever taken place in Carthage before its declining years. Carthage was wealthy and prosperous everybody knows; but how, we ask, could her wealth and prosperity have been attained save under a good Constitution and an able Government?

Carthage, too, like Ethiopia and Abyssinia, gave birth to a number of great men. But the five great chieftains and governors who overtopped the rest, and threw them all into the shade, were Hamilcar Barca, the hero of Ercte and Eryx (who was second only to his son, Hannibal the Great, in renown and ability, in the field and in the cabinet); his son-in-law Hasdrubal; and his three sons, 'the lion's broods,' the Brothers Barcidæ, viz.: Hannibal the Great (a man who takes his place with Napoleon the Great, and Caius Julius Cæsar, and Alexander the Great), Hasdrubal, and Mago. We do not propose to enter into the details of their achievements, because they are sufficiently known to the average reader. The reader will have observed that we have elected to confer the surname of 'the Great' on Hannibal, the greatest of the Carthaginians, and Toussaint-

L'Ouverture, the Liberator, and greatest of the Haytians; but we did not do this without good reasons, and hold ourselves justified in so doing. They are admitted by all writers who deal with the subjects to have been celebrities. Livy, Plutarch, Niebuhr, Mommsen, Church, Ward and others, eulogizing Hannibal the Great; while Caucasians like Samuel Whitchurch, Wordsworth, Whittier, Wendell Phillips, Lamartine, Métral, Dr. Beard, Sir Spencer St. John, Armistead, Rainsford, Schoelcher, Gragnon-Lacoste, Dubroca, and Haytians like Isaac Toussaint-L'Ouverture, St. Rémy, B. Ardouin, T. Madion, A. Firmin and others, with Liberian Professor Blyden and Afro-American Colonel Williams eulogize Toussaint-L'Ouverture the Great. We see no reason, then, for withholding the surname of 'the Great' from Hannibal Barca the Carthaginian, and Toussaint-L'Ouverture the Haytian, who were both African and Ethiopians. If we Africans do not recognise the abilities of and honour our countrymen, who will recognise and honour them? If we Africans do not perpetuate the greatest of the Carthaginians by christening Hannibal *the Great*, if we Africans do not perpetuate the greatest of the Haytians by chr stening Toussaint-L'Ouverture *the Great*, who will do this for them, the children of the 'Land of the Mighty Dead'? Will the Caucasians do it for us? No Caucasian writer has as yet conferred the surname of 'the Great' on Hannibal Barca or Toussaint-L'Ouverture, the greatest Africans who have ever lived.

Leaving Carthage and the Carthaginians we turn to modern times. And, we ask, have not the Moors established, and do they not now maintain, a Government for themselves? Did not the Moors, in 710 and 711 of our era, burst into Spain and Portugal and overrun that joinr Peninsula, reducing the Iberian and the Lusitanian provinces to subjection?

Would the Great Napoleon have been able to bring all Europe, save Britain and Russia, to his feet if he had not had a strong Government at home? Would the British Wellington have been able to gain the battle of Waterloo if his Government at home had not been a strong one? Would the Yankee Washington have been able to drive the Britishers into the sea, and wrest Independence from the impotent grasp of stubborn George the Third, the German King of Britain, if his Government had been a weak one? And we say that the Moors never would have reduced the Spaniard and the Portuguese to submission if they had not had a strong Government at home in Morocco. They did not quit Spain and Portugal until the dawn of the seventeenth century.

But who were, and who are, the Moors save the descendants of Africans and Asiatics? The Moors, we say, have not only established, but they maintain, a Government for themselves, though the Britishers, Frenchmen, and Spaniards are doing their best to partition Morocco, just as the Italians are doing their utmost to grasp Abyssinia, which enjoys and maintains a Government of her own and is independent. Morocco and Abyssinia, however, still continue to flourish.

The State and Kingdom of Ashantee was not in the past what it is to-day. It is true that Ashantee possesses a Native and Independent Government of her own; but fifty years or so ago a better, more capable, and more progressive Government sat at Coomassie. It is on record* that King Osai Tutu, who flourished in the early part of the eighteenth century, was the real founder of the great Ashantee Empire; the countries lying on the east and west of his Kingdom yielding to his powerful arms. His successor on the Royal Ashantee throne, Osai Apoko, made

* 'Encyclopædia Britannica,' vol. ii., p. 681.

further acquisitions of territory to the already vast Ashantee Empire. No sane man will for a moment suppose that kings or military leaders will venture to go on distant expeditions of conquest, and stay away months, perhaps years, together from their dominions, unless they leave a firm Government behind them at home, which can command respect and enforce obedience to the laws of the land. No man in his senses, we say, can turn his arms abroad if his Government be weak at home. And Kings and Emperors like Osai Tutu and Osai Apoko, renowned Ashanteans, never would have ventured on warlike expeditions on their own initiation, as they did, and have left their throne tottering behind them at Coomassie. Judging by these facts and these results, the unbiased man is bound to admit that Ashantee must have enjoyed an excellent and firm Government under Osai Tutu and Osai Apoko, the celebrated Ashantean Kings.

Also, so organized, capable, and orderly a Government had the Ashantees under King Osai Tutu Quanima, 'a most capable and indefatigable man, who directed the destinies of his country from the year 1800 to the year 1824, that they were able with their well-disciplined soldiers not only to meet and cope with, but also to inflict a crushing and paralyzing defeat on, the British General Sir Charles MacCarthy and his army at Essomaco, off the banks of the Adoomansoo, in 1824,* that is, only nine years after the historic Waterloo, when the Frank went down before the Britisher, and when Britain's name was as formidable as it is at present.

We now pass on to Dahomey, and say that this country is not now what it formerly was. The Dahomans are but a

* 'Encyclopædia Britannica,' vol. ii., p. 681; Spencer Walpole's 'History of England,' vol. ii., chap. vii., pp. 148-150; 'Annual Register for 1824,' pp. 206-208; *ibid.* for 1826, p. 223.

AFRICA GOVERNED BY THE AFRICANS. 231

wreck of their former selves. When King Guadjor Trudo, a man of talent and energy, wielded the destinies of Dahomey, the Dahomans had a Government to boast of. And when he died in 1732, Trudo left Dahomey in a flourishing condition, with peace at home and victories abroad.*

Gezo, who ascended the Dahoman throne about the year 1818, and presided over the destinies of Dahomey for forty years, raised the Dahoman power to its highest pitch. King Gezo, the most capable governor that the Dahomans have ever had, died in 1858 full of years and honour, and a glory to the African Race and to Dahomey.† He was as renowned a Dahoman as Osai Tutu Quanima was an Ashantean.

From Dahomey we pass on to Sokoto; and this country also has had a Government of her own. It was Sultan Othman dan Fodio who founded the Empire of Sokoto; and his son, Sultan Bello, who reigned from 1819 to 1832, raised the Sokoto Empire to its greatest height.‡

Again, West Africa also boasts of the States of Gandu and Bornu, the power of the latter dating back from the ninth century.§

Passing on to South Africa we come to Zululand, which was the Metropolitan State of the Great South African Empire of the Zulu Kaffirs. The early history of Zululand and Southern Africa, like the early history of Carthage, Ethiopia, Abyssinia, Morocco, Ashantee, Dahomey, Sokoto, Bornu, Gandu, Sahara, Senegambia, Sierra Leone, Soudan, Congo, Wadai, Darfur, Mozambique, Zanzibar, Sofala, Madagascar, and Africa generally, is very largely unknown,

* 'Gazetteer of the World,' vol. ii., p. 799.
† 'Encyclopædia Britannica,' vol. vi., p. 766.
‡ Ibid., vol. xxii., p. 248.
§ Ibid., vol. iv., pp. 61, 62.

much of it is buried in oblivion. And, unfortunately, the little that we know of Africa and Africans is derived from those opponents, if not enemies, of Africans, the Caucasians. We are informed, however, that in 1780 Sanzangakona directed the destinies of the Zulus with the greatest ability, and with honour to himself and his African and Zulu countrymen.* And after Sanzangakona's demise, his illustrious son King Ishaka, or Chaka, at the beginning of the nineteenth century, brought the Zulu, the South African, Empire to the zenith of its greatness, for he conquered all the States of South-Eastern Africa, stretching from the River Limpopo to the Cape Colony, and comprised Natal, British Basutoland, a large portion of the Orange Free State, and the Transvaal Republic.† Chaka, or Ishaka, the great founder of African dominion in South Africa, died in 1828.‡ His brothers, Mhlangana, Dingaan, and Panda, who succeeded him and one another, though able, were greatly inferior to Ishaka in administrative ability and in military talent.§ With the accession of King Cetewayo, the son of Panda, Zululand was bidding fair to rise again from the condition in which his uncles Mhlangana and Dingaan, and his father Panda, had thrown it, to the condition at which his mighty uncle Chaka had left it.‖ But the days of Zulu Independence were numbered, and the Zulu Kingdom succumbed before the attack of her powerful enemies the British and the Boer.¶

We do not propose to treat here of the Liberian Republic. We reserve it for the next chapter, where it can be dealt with at greater length.

From Africa we pass on to the Independent Americo-Ethiopian Republic of Hayti, and of it we must say a few words. Everybody knows how the Haytians rose in insur-

* 'Encyclopædia Britannica,' vol. xxiv., pp. 828, 829.
† *Ibid* ‡ *Ibid.* § *Ibid.* ‖ *Ibid.* ¶ *Ibid.*

rection in August, 1791, under their leaders Jean François and Biasson, and defied the might of France. Everybody knows also that when Toussaint the Great put himself at the head of the army of his Haytian countrymen in 1793, within a comparatively short space of time he became the Liberator of San Domingo. How he was treacherously seized by perfidious Frenchmen ; how he was conveyed to France a close prisoner, and how he perished, almost of starvation, in 1803, in a cold Alpine dungeon, are matters of history. The Government of Toussaint the Great was firm, wise, and progressive, and under Toussaint the Great the Haytians were prosperous, thriving, and wealthy. 'Under his government the Island was restored to more than its former prosperity.' The indefatigable Emperor Jacques I. (Dessalines) continued the struggle for Haytian Independence, and the Frenchmen, after suffering punishment at his hands, yielded to his conquering arms. After he drove Frenchmen from his country, the Island of San Domingo, Britishers and Spaniards tried hard to reduce the Haytians under their yoke, but they were prevented by the might of Dessalines, and were driven into the sea. Who is there who does not know that Hayti flourished under the Imperial Government of Jacques I. ? Hayti was also happy and contented under the Emperor Henri I. (Christophe), and under Presidents Pétion, Boyer (who governed Hayti or San Domingo for thirty-one or more years), Boisrond Canal, Geffrard Solomon, the Emperor Faustin I. (Soulouque), Salmave, while we have proved that Hayti is now flourishing, having a capable, wise, and vigorous Government, under the headship of the President, General L. M. F. Hippolyte. When, therefore, the *Times* Commissioner deliberately quotes Ethelbert Barksdale, who in his turn quotes 'the language of a Northern statesmen and Union soldier,' that '"in the whole historic period of the world the Ethiopian race had never established or maintained a Government for themselves,"' not only Laird Clowes, but the other gentleman referred to, say not only what is erroneous and misleading, but they display a sad ignorance of African history.

Laird Clowes, on pages 158, 159, of his 'Black America,' quotes James Anthony Froude, who writes in 'The English in the West Indies':

'There is a saying in Hayti that the white man has no rights which the blacks are bound to recognise. . . . They can own no freehold property, and exist only on tolerance. They are called "white trash." Black Dukes and Marquises drive over them in the street, and swear at them. . . . Englishmen move about Jacmel as if they were ashamed of themselves among their dusky lords and masters. The presence of the European in any form is barely tolerated.'

Apart from the fact that the statement that 'there is a saying in Hayti that the white man has no rights which the blacks are bound to recognise,' and that 'they can own no freehold property, and exist only on tolerance,' as made by James Anthony Froude and by W. Laird Clowes, is questionable, and will not bear investigation; it is, probably, the reverse of the truth. If that be as they are trying to make out, then we say that there is nothing strange or peculiar about foreigners not being allowed to own freehold property in the country of the Haytians. It is not unusual; it is not unique. Were not foreigners incapacitated from holding landed property in the British Isles until so late as the year 1870? It was the Naturalization Act of 1870, the 33rd and 34th Statute of the Reign of Victoria, chapter xiv., which removed many of the disabilities that aliens were labouring under in Britain. Even now it is still impossible for an alien to own a British ship, while he cannot hold shares, or be trustee of shares, in a British ship.*

What could be more singular, more unjust, and more severe and arbitrary than that on the death of every foreigner who had any property in France, that property was confiscated to the French crown, in accordance with the provisions of the *Droit d'Aubaine?* But that is now done away with, to the credit of Frenchmen. All foreigners were labouring under disabilities in Germany, Austro-Hungary, Italy, Russia, Denmark, Holland, Spain, and in other countries of Europe, and in the United States of North America, before 1860 or thereabout, and were forbidden to hold landed property therein, or, if they did, were confiscated to the State in which the property was situate.

Boyd's Third Edition of Wheaton's 'International Law,' pp. 132, 133, says: 'It is only of late years that the right of holding lands on the same conditions as subjects has been conceded to foreigners by most countries. In Belgium this was effected by the law of the 27th of April, 1865. Russia† conceded the privilege in 1860. Some of the Swiss cantons do not even now permit foreigners to hold real property without the express permission of the Cantonal Government, unless there be a treaty to that effect. Austria, the Netherlands, and Sweden only accord the right on condition of reciprocity in the foreigner's country. The constitution of the German Empire provides that every person belonging to one of the confederated States is to be treated

---

* 33 and 34 Vic., c. 14; Undèrhill's 'Trusts,' p. 361.

† But *Lloyd's News* for November 15th, 1891, says that 'The local [Warsaw] press announces that a law will shortly be levelled at foreign colonization of the Russian steppes, making the acquisition of farms and holdings by alien settlers illegal in future, and compelling such settlers as have already acquired grants of land to become Russian subjects within three years.'

in every other of the confederated States as a born native, and to be permitted to acquire real estate. But, as regards other countries, the laws of Bavaria, Prussia, Saxony, and Wurtemburg exact for their own subjects, when abroad, the same rights they extend to foreigners in their own dominions. In Italy, Denmark, and Greece aliens are under no disabilities in this respect. The ownership of land in the United States is regulated by the laws of each individual State of the Union. Some of the States impose no restrictions on foreigners; others require residence and an oath of allegiance; in others a declaration of an intention to become a naturalized citizen of the United States is necessary. Feudal principles were maintained so long in Britain, that until the year 1870 an alien was incapable of holding land for more than twenty-one years; that is, he could not purchase a freehold. This, however, was remedied by the Naturalization Act, 1870 (33 and 34 Vic., c. 14), which relieved aliens of most of their disabilities, and, as regards land, placed them on the same footing as [British] subjects.' The French, however, were the first to break through ancient prejudices in respect of foreigners, and to set the example of a more liberal and enlightened legislation, by removing many of the disabilities aliens were labouring under in France prior to 1791.* The British formed a treaty with the Yankees in the years the Naturalization Acts (33 and 34 Vic., c. 14, and 35 and 36 Vic., c. 39), 1870 and 1872, were passed, permitting the Yankees, if they felt so inclined, to hold property and have other rights in the British Isles and their dependencies, whilst the Yankees, in their turn, were to concede the same privileges to British subjects. Yet it is strange that no Canadian can own a Yankee ship as a British subject; only if he (the Canadian) consents to become a Yankee,

* Lord Chief Justice Cockburn's 'Nationality,' pp. 152-160.

under the protection of the Stars and Stripes, will he be qualified to own a Yankee ship. What is more severe than that the captain of every vessel, on arriving in the British Isles, is bound to furnish a list of all his passengers who are foreigners; and non-compliance with, and infringement of, this rule is visited with a heavy fine?

Even amongst themselves Britishers are unjust and severe.

What can be more unjust or more severe in this nineteenth century than that, whilst Englishmen and Scotsmen have each a volunteer force, Irishmen can have none in Ireland, though they can be volunteers in Scotland, England, and the British colonies? Not even the above can be more unjust or more severe than the law that, whilst no Protestant, orthodox Greek, Jew, Mahommedan, Agnostic, Idolater, Atheist, is debarred from the office of Lord Chancellor of England, and from the Lord-Lieutenancy of Ireland, a Catholic is disqualified from holding either of these offices; and this condition of things is aggravated by the fact that the majority of Irishmen are Catholics.

To return to the Haytians. We say that it is not a fact that whites 'can own no freehold property,' and that 'they exist only on tolerance' in Hayti. Froude tells us, and Clowes quotes his words, that 'Haytian Dukes and Marquises drive over them' (the whites) 'in the street, and swear at them.' This we also deny. We are again told that 'Englishmen move about Jacmel as if they were ashamed of themselves among their dusky lords and masters.' We should like to know why the 'Englishmen who move about Jacmel' should comport themselves 'as if they were ashamed of themselves.' If life is hard for the Caucasian (the Britisher) to bear amongst the Haytians, why does he not take his departure thence? Why should he remain in a place that is irksome to him? Why does the Englishman continue living 'among his dusky lords and masters,' as Froude contemptuously calls the noble Haytians, when he 'moves about Jacmel as if he were ashamed of himself'?

When Britishers, Caucasians, take up their abode in Hayti, it must or it ought to be with the full consciousness that they are to yield full allegiance to the majesty of the Constitution and Laws of the Haytians, and if they violate or transgress they will have to put up with the consequences which their infringement entails; they must expect that swift and effectual punishment will be meted out to them by the Haytians, as it would were they in their own country or dwelling amongst any other civilized people.

Laird Clowes, on pages 114, 115, and 116, referring to the criminality of the United States, states that the American African is many times more prone to criminality than his white countryman. Of course, as usual, Laird Clowes makes a statement which he does not prove. We all know that there are, and are sure to be, criminals everywhere, amongst every people. Where there are more Africans than Caucasians in the United States, there will be more African than Caucasian criminals, and where there are more Caucasians than Africans there will be more Caucasian than African criminals.

Whilst Mr. W. Laird Clowes, in one part of his book, speaks disparagingly of the 'material position' of the Afro-American, he admits, in another part of his 'Black America,' that 'there is no doubt that they are gradually acquiring property, and, in a few cases, accumulating capital. It was recently declared that coloured people owned a million acres of land in Texas alone, paying taxes there on twenty million dollars' worth of property, and there were in the State twenty-five coloured lawyers, one hundred coloured merchants, five thousand coloured mechanics, and fifteen newspapers conducted by coloured people.' Add to all this, that there are not half as many Africans in Texas as there are White Americans, and the fact that only twenty-eight years have elapsed since the American African received his Emancipation. Laird Clowes should be consistent, and not eccentric, for while he runs the African down to earth in one page, he eulogizes him in another.

This is how Laird Clowes eulogizes the Africo-American, by quoting a journal which shows that: 'Georgia's coloured people are making a good record for thrift and industry. In 1879 their property was valued at \$5,128,398, but in 1887 the valuation was \$8,939,479, showing a gain of $72\frac{1}{2}$ per cent. during the nine years. In the same time the valuation of white men's property had risen from \$229,777,150 to \$332,565,442, a gain of only 44·6 per cent. approximately. These figures simply prove what the intelligent representatives of the Negro race have said about the progress made, and they go to illustrate anew that the Negroes are working out their own future. The richest coloured woman in the South, Mrs. Amanda Ewas, who has a snug fortune of \$400,000, lives in Atlanta.'

By Clowes's own showing this is the hopeful result of only some twenty-eight years of freedom.

CHAPTER VII.

REPATRIATION AND LIBERIA.

WE now enter on our last chapter, and in it we propose to solve the African Race Problem in the United States.

Like the Africans, the Honourable Professor Edward Wilmot Blyden, LL.D., ex-Liberian Minister to the Court of St. James's; the Right Reverend Bishop H. M. Turner, of Atlanta, Georgia; Dr. H. M. Tupper, of Shaw University, Raleigh, North Carolina; the Rev. Mr. T. S. Lee, of Charleston, and other of our countrymen and kinsmen, we counsel emigration from America and immigration into Africa.

Yes, and like Laird Clowes we say there must be another exodus from Egypt, another restoration of the captive tribes. But what part of Africa shall the expatriated African go to? Shall it be to a country in Africa where the Caucasian rules, as Laird Clowes suggests? We think not, for the same Race Problem which is puzzling and agitating the United States would soon perplex and agitate that country where the 10,500,000 of American Africans are transported. There would be greater race jealousies than ever in that particular country. There are even now race jealousies between the Caucasian and the African, though they are not a great deal talked of and commented on out of the pale where they exist, which is wherever the

Caucasian rules, whether it be in Africa, in the West Indies, or in the Americas.

Laird Clowes lays down three conditions which must be offered to the expatriated African in order to accomplish his removal, and he suggests that—

(1) The emigrating African must be offered a country in which he may pursue high aims, enjoy a prospect of improved political, social, and financial *status*, and find climate and employment suited to his needs.

(2) He must not govern, but be governed. At the same time he must not be oppressed, either physically or morally, and there must be no restraint upon his improvement and advancement.

(3) His emigration must be assisted, either by those who owe him a debt, or by those who will benefit by his migration, or by both.

Whilst agreeing with every one of Laird Clowes's propositions, believing them to be sound and reasonable, we must take exception to one part of the second condition which he lays down, viz., that ' He (the expatriated African) must not govern, but be governed,' because that statement, to say the least, is absurd and ridiculous, being based on Ignorance and Prejudice.

We say, in our turn, and with emphasis, that the expatriated African *must not be governed, but must govern.* He must be independent, as his forefathers, 'the Mighty Dead,' were before him, otherwise the Race Question, which is now preying on the vitals of the United States of North America, would prey on the vitals of the particular country where our expatriated African should be sent. And have we not proved that the African Ethiopian, indigenously civilized, was able to govern? Have we not proved that the African States of Assyria or Babylon, Canaan and Phœnicia, in Asia have flourished? Have we not proved and shown that the indigenously civilized African Negro States of Carthage, Ethiopia, Abyssinia, Sokoto, Gandu, Bornu, Zululand, and others have flourished and have been mighty empires? And are not Liberia, Hayti, Morocco, and Abyssinia all independent African States that are flourishing and progressing? Therefore do we say that we Africans *must govern ourselves, and not be governed.*

Laird Clowes suggests that the expatriated African in the United States should be sent to the Congo Free State as 'the country in which he may pursue high aims, enjoy a prospect of improved political, social, and financial *status*, and find climate and employment suited to his needs.' That is *his* 'Ideal Solution.' But we say that no man could have made a greater blunder, no man could have failed more lamentably in solving, or rather in trying to solve, the African Race Problem in America than Laird Clowes does in suggesting emigration by the Africo-Americans into the Congo Free State. An 'Ideal Solution' indeed! Laird Clowes has not only failed, but blundered, in his scheme for solving the Race Problem in the Land of the Yankees; and this we shall endeavour to show, taking care to give reasons for *our* 'Ideal Solution' of the difficulty.

Our 'Ideal Solution' will be, we are confident, nothing unsound, nothing that can be likened to the fruit of the tree which grows by the banks of the Dead Sea: it will be nothing illusory, nothing incapable of realization, as is Laird Clowes's solution.

We now propose to show how Laird Clowes has failed and blundered. Their transportation from the United States would free the Caucasian Yankees from the incubus of the Americo-Africans, it is true; but it is not less true that the transplantation and repatriation of the 10,500,000 of Africo-Americans into Africa, into the Congo Free State, would give rise to another Race Problem in the latter country. We ask, Are not the rulers of the Congo Free State, King Leopold II. and his Belgians, all Caucasians, all white men? Would that circumstance not, then, occasion a Race Problem in the Congo Free State?

Yet this is not Laird Clowes's only mistake; he has committed other and greater blunders by suggesting that the Africans in the United States should make the Congo Free State their home.

We ask, Is it not a well-known fact that *the* official language of the Congo Free State is *the* official language of Belgium, *and that* is the language of the French, and is not Flemish also *an* official language in the Congo Free State as it is *an* official and *the* national language of Belgium? Can the Americo-Africans speak the French or the Flemish language? If there are those who do, how many do?

Laird Clowes, we are aware, is a Britisher, and, like the great majority of his countrymen, he cannot be said to be very politic and judicious. Is it not the prayer and the boast of every Britisher, and his Yankee cousin, that the Anglo-Saxon tongue shall and must become, in no distant time, the prevailing cosmopolitan tongue? We ourselves believe it must be so.

Yet Laird Clowes and Henry Morton Stanley, of Yambuya and Manyuema unenviable notoriety, forsooth! would send, if they could, the Americo-Africans into the Congo Free State, that they might discard the Anglo-Saxon tongue and adopt the French language instead.

We ask, Is it not also a well-known fact that the Constitution of the Congo Free State, while it agrees with that of Belgium, which is modelled on that of France, differs from the Constitution of the United States of North America—the very Constitution which the Afro-Americans are used to?

We ask again, Is it of no moment that the headship of

the Congo Free State is filled by a King who is the King of the Belgians also? And are not the 10,500,000 Americo-Africans in the United States of North America all republicans to a man? Why should we not also ask, Is it not a well-known fact that the Belgian rulers of the Congo Free State brutally ill-treat the Congoes, and hold them in a condition of servitude? Is it false to say that the Congo Free State is at a standstill and non-progressive under the sickly and incompetent Belgian Administration sitting at Boma?

So much so that Belgian Leopold and his Janssen Administration of the Congo Free State, tormented by the zymotic disease of incompetency and incapability, sent envoys in 1884 and 1889 to the United States of North America, praying that they might be allowed to take as many Africans as were willing to go, and whose services they were able to pay for, to the Congo Free State, to act as an antiseptic, and a panacea for the Belgian maladies in their maladministration of the Congo Free State?

Surely Laird Clowes cannot be serious when he proposes to send the Americo-Africans to the Congo Free State, a State where the rulers are whites; a State where *the* official language is French; a State where the Constitution (including the Laws) is Belgic French, and the Chief Magistrate a King; a State where the African is ill-treated and slavery exists; a State which, because its rulers are incompetent and incapable, is at a standstill and non-progressive.

Would Laird Clowes have the Americo-Africans killed by inches or killed outright?

Were the Africans in the American Union to leave the United States for the Congo Free State, they would be quitting the frying-pan to get into the fire.

These are, then, Laird Clowes's blunders.

With the Congo Free State backward and in every way unsuitable for the Africo-American, where must he betake himself, since he is oppressed in the United States? As he must necessarily be independent, so as to steer clear of all Race Problems, where must he go to?

Though Africa is almost partitioned, and under the so-called sphere of influence of Britain, France, Germany, Italy, Spain, and Portugal, yet there is room for not only the Americo-Africans, the West Indo-Africans, but for all other African expatriates, in that very continent.

We propose to send all Africans who are living out of Africa, and who are willing to go, to the Independent Republic of Liberia. This is *the* country all Africans except the Haytians should go to. We have shown why the Africo-American should not be sent to the Congo Free State. Now we propose to show why the returning exile should march into Liberia.

The expatriated African must not be sent to that part of Africa where the Caucasian rules, for then there would arise a Race Problem of higher dimensions and of a more virulent type than is perplexing the United States of North America, and that is undesirable.

The expatriated African must not be sent to some country in Africa where the aboriginal inhabitants are not only independent, but have never come into contact with Caucasian civilization, and particularly where the white man has not been seen; for the returning exile would have an uphill work in his attempt to subdue the African aborigines, and that is also undesirable.

It is also undesirable that the expatriated and civilized African (civilized under Caucasian influence) should have an independent country of his own other than Liberia, for the obvious reason that division, no matter in what form, is always weakness.

Did not the Magyars easily conquer Hungary, because Hungary and Europe were divided amongst themselves? These same now dwell in and possess the land they conquered centuries ago. Did not the Turkish Mussulmans easily crush and pull to pieces the moribund Eastern Roman-Greek Empire? And what was it that accelerated the success of the conquering Osmanli Crescent? Was it not the fact that Europe was divided against itself, and so was impotent to help the Greeks? And are not the Turks, though, like the Magyars, an Asiatic race, still in Europe?

The Moors pounced upon Hispania and Lusitania in 710; and because the rest of Europe was hopelessly divided, and because dissension and bickerings reigned supreme among the Spaniards and the Portuguese, their subjugation by the omnipotent Moors was not a hard task, but was easily accomplished, the turbulent and fratricidal Spaniards and Portuguese experiencing violent shocks and disastrous defeats at the hands of the conquering Moors when they took the field and joined battle with their enemies.

We repeat again that every sort of division is weakening to a nation, and is to be deprecated.

The African race is already, unfortunately, too widely scattered apart, and we Africans must concentrate, as much as possible, those of our race who are able and willing to be concentrated. All Africans, therefore, who have the welfare of their race at heart rejoice and seek consolation in the fact, that the Mexicans and Argentines protested, in 1889 or thereabout, against the projected settlement of the Africans in America in their respective countries. The protest by the Mexicans and Argentines threw cold water on the American African Colonization Scheme, and for this we sincerely thank the Mexicans and Argentines.

The Americo-Africans would, forsooth! quit the United

States of North America, and settle in Mexico or Argentina, leaving their Africa and their Liberia neglected. Is Liberia our Liberia, the Pride and Hope of Africa, and of true-born and true-hearted Africans, such a scarecrow that Mexico or Argentina should be preferred? We are glad, we say again, that the Mexicans and Argentines absolutely refused to receive the Africo-Americans in their respective countries. May they do so again if another opportunity presents itself!

Division is weakness, we say. Christianity, though the true religion, and though professed by the great majority of civilized humanity, is despised and ridiculed by the believers in the Law of Moses, by Islamism, by Hindooism, by Brahminism, by Buddhism, by Atheism—and why? Because these latter, these non-Christians (though they fail to see how hopelessly divided and faction-torn they are amongst themselves), with truth, with emphasis, and with the pointed finger of scorn, say to one another: 'See how these Christians love one another! See how they are always ready to tear one another to pieces, and they, forsooth! would fain preach to us on our ways and forms of worship!'

The fact that the Christian Religion is divided and split up into three great branches—Catholicity, Greek Orthodoxy, and Protestantism—without the shadow of a doubt places it at a disadvantage when it has to deal with non-Christians, and prevents us Christians from reclaiming and converting the heathen, the non-Christian, from his evil ways and practices.

In bygone ages Protestants fought Catholics and Catholics Protestants, while the enmity and jealousy between these last two, and also between Catholicism and the Greek Orthodox Church, still flicker, their traces being evident enough amongst Caucasians. But we Africans, a truly sensible and non-bigoted race, never had, have not, and never shall have, such religious enmities and jealousies as have existed, still obtain, and, we fear, will always obtain, amongst Caucasians up to the consummation of the world.

So much for religious divisions.

To turn to secular divisions—to return to the point which we have left—we assert that it is undesirable that the civilized and subject African should have any independent country of his own, either in or out of Africa, other than Liberia. Some day the Liberians and the new would-be independent Africans may fall to fighting one another, and the object of the fighting may be the headship of the whole or part of Africa.

The world and Europe saw, in 1866, the Hohenzollern German hurling his marshalled hosts at the embattled squadrons of his cousin, the Hapsburg German; but it was the crushing and decisive defeat at Sadowa which gave the headship of Germany to the Prussian Hohenzollern, driving away the crestfallen Austro-Hungarian Hapsburg from the leadership and membership of the Germanic Confederation.

Liberia must never have to measure arms with, and rush to the contest with, a kindred and civilized country that may be its neighbour in Africa, speaking the same language with the Liberians.

Did not Britishers and Yankees, though cousins, carry on war one against the other in 1812-1814? When Napoleon the Great issued his Berlin and Milan decrees against Britishers, and all Europe except Britain and Russia lay humbled at his feet, and slavishly obeyed the Frenchman's behest, did the Americans in any way help their British cousins in their need? Instead, they obeyed the order of Napoleon, and gave battle to the British in 1812-1814.

The Yankees in 1846 snatched the 'Oregon country,' and in 1871 wrung millions of dollars from their British cousins because of the 'Alabama' and 'Florida.'

Even now Britishers and Yankees are not as friendly as they ought to be. Jonathan envies his cousin of Britain the possession of British North America, the Dominion of Canada portion particularly, and is longingly looking forward to the day when he will be able to wrest it, by a *coup de main* or otherwise, from the tenacious grasp of his British cousin, John Bull.

Do not Britishers also envy the Yankees their possession of Alaska? Are not Britishers and Yankees always wrangling over the pearl fishery off Alaska? When will the 'burning' Behring Sea question be solved?

We maintain that the unity, the federation, of the Anglo-Saxon Race is as far-off as ever, the claims of Britain and the United States being hopelessly irreconcilable? Are not Frenchmen more or less jealous of the French-speaking Belgian Leopold for having the headship of the Congo Free State.

Again, take Spanish America, in a first instance. Did not Argentina and Uruguay, although professing the same religion, although having a common derivation and the same nationality, although speaking the same language with her (Paraguay), with the co-operation and under the leadership of Lusitanian Brazil, wage fierce and long-continued war from 1865 to 1872 with her, and finally, and as the outcome of the humiliating and disastrous defeats she experienced at their hands, strip Paraguay of an enormous slice of territory and impose upon her a heavy national debt as war indemnity?

In a second instance, did not Chili, although professing the same religion, although boasting a common origin and the same nationality, although speaking a common language with her sister-neighbours, declare war upon Peru and Bolivia on April 5, 1872, and, after the infliction of sundry and paralyzing defeats on the Peruvian and Bolivian *soldados*, and in the pride of victory, tear huge slices of territory from their grasp, Bolivia losing her only seaport, Antofagasta, in 1884 to her conqueror, exultant Chili, the land which boasts of having given birth to Juan San Martin de José, the comrade and brother-in-arms of the British Cochrane, Scottish Dundonald, who, next to his countryman, the British Nelson, was the greatest admiral who ever saw the light; while the equally crestfallen and equally unfortunate Peru was forced to relinquish absolutely, on the 20th of October, 1883, the rich province of Tarapaca, as well as to conditionally yield fertile Tacna and mellifluous Arica to her Chilian *conquistadores?*

In a third instance, did not San Salvador and Guatemala, although speaking the same language, although having the same origin and a common ancestry, although professing the same religion, war upon each other, the Salvadorian and the Guatemalan rushing to the shock of the contest and meeting each other in deadly embraces in fair and open field in 1890-1891?

But these are not the only instances. The Columbian Confederation—which the Libertador, Venezuelan Simon Bolivar, founded in 1819, and which formerly consisted of Columbia, Venezuela, and Ecuador—was dissolved in 1829-1830; but what has been the outcome of the untying of that knot, of that separation or dissolution? Their separation or dissolution from one another, we say, has caused the so-called Republics of Venezuela, Colombia, and Ecuador to sink considerably in the estimation of civilized humanity. They all three are periodically subject to revolutionary changes and internecine, and therefore suicidal, strifes.

Because the Government of each has been and is incompetent and extravagant, the three Republics have been and are mismanaged and misgoverned, their commerce has suffered and is suffering, heavy debts have been and are being contracted, their population has thinned and is thinning, their armies teem with 'generals,' who outnumber the *soldados*, and who (the 'generals') delight to fight with their tongues only, and whose swords, having never been unsheathed, are, as a consequence, quite innocent of blood.

And, to make matters worse, those three so-called Republics, Venezuela, Colombia, and Ecuador, have been for years wrangling with one another as to their respective boundaries, *i.e.*, to the east of Colombia, the west of Venezuela and the north of Ecuador, and south of Colombia. Such are the fruits of disunion and separation or division on the part of kindred and sisterly States.

More. Were Colombia and Ecuador united with Venezuela, *i.e.*, were they members of the Colombian Confederation which existed in 1829-1830, would ·Britain continue bullying, if not harassing, Venezuela, with respect to the Britannico-Venezuelan Guinese boundary debateable?

We trow not; for Venezuela, as a member of the Colombian Confederation, would have had Colombia and Ecuador at her back as allies and as sharers in the national interest and danger, and in the defence of the common Fatherland. And does not *l'union fait la force* against all outsiders and oppressors? The Colombian and the Ecuadorian would have been a *par nobile fratrum* to the Venezuelan. But disunion or division or separation is, as a rule, weakness.

Honest and well-meaning men like the American Colonization Society and Liberian Professor Blyden will sometimes say things which on second thoughts they would not say.

Liberian Blyden, in his book 'Christianity, Islam, and the Ethiopian Race,' would scatter the Africo-Americans in different parts of Africa. And in his pamphlet, 'The Return of the Exiles and the West African Church,' p. 23, he says: 'Imagine the result of one hundred thousand Africans from

America settled in the Yoruba country, with their knowledge of, and practice in, the use not only of the implements of peace, but of the implements of war.' To us such a proposal or imagination seems unwise. Because Caucasians are scattered, Liberian Blyden would further scatter the already widely-scattered Ethiopians, forgetful of the fact that in his 'Christianity, Islam, and the Ethiopian Race,' p. 429, he tells the Yankees 'not to wait until they have trained the Africo-Americans *to their ideal—in their peculiar modes of thinking. They cannot make them Anglo-Saxons. They never will make them so in spirit and possibilities*, if I interpret the providence of God aright.' And, despite this, he would scatter the English-speaking Africans; is it because the Anglo-Saxons are scattered? But the Anglo-Saxons are now studying concentration. Witness the Imperial and Colonial Institute and Imperial Federation. What we think a distinguished and talented man like Liberian Blyden 'should imagine,' or rather work for, is the unity and concentration of the Ethiopian race—at least, the English-speaking portion of it. If a brilliant man like Liberian Dr. Blyden cannot be a Guiseppe Garibaldi, he can be a Camillo Benso di Cavour or a Guiseppe Mazzini. We do not want a man who will *scatter*, but one who will *unite*, the already scattered race. Let a talented man like Liberian Blyden unite the Ethiopian race in Liberia. The American Colonization Society, in its seventy-fourth annual report (January, 1891), page 11, says: 'It appears to us that the most comprehensive, far-reaching, and productive plan for bringing that vast continent within the operation of civilization and under the influence of Christianity would be to scatter and to settle four millions, or about one-half of the African population of this country, in the land of their fathers. Place a million in Liberia, a million in the Niger districts and Yorubaland, which latter country seems now open to receive them, a million on the Congo, and a million in East Africa.'

With all due respect and deference to the organization which has done, and is doing, the Ethiopian race such yeoman services, we must beg leave to hurl our unqualified protest against that proposition of the American Colonization Society.

Members of the American Colonization Society and Liberian Dr. Blyden, are you unaware that the present tendency of the European and Yankee world is towards concentration? Have you never heard of General Count Ignatieff and Panslavism? Have you never heard of M. Delyannis and Panhellenism? Have you never heard of British Imperial Federation, Australasian Federation, and —tell it not in Gath and proclaim it not in the streets of Ascalon!— Anglo-Saxon Confederation, which would include the United States? British Imperial Federation, like Panslavism and Panhellenism, is both possible and probable. But while it is possible, Anglo-Saxon Confederation is improbable. Two kings, or, rather, queens, of Brentford, like Colombia and Britannia, cannot sit on the same throne. Were Britain and America, however, united, what European power would dare draw the sword without the Anglo-Saxon's consent?

But Lord North has prevented what might and could have been, to the exceeding joy of Frenchmen, Russians, and other rivals of Britishers.

Members of the American Colonization Society and Liberian Blyden, are you forgetful of the fact that Germany, like the United Kingdom and France, is now united? Are you unaware that united and regenerated Italy is the work of Guiseppe Garibaldi, Camillo Benso di Cavour, and last, not least, Guiseppe Mazzini? We ask you, Could not Russia and Austro-Hungary pour their legions, and snatch portions of Africa like other European nations? You will agree with us that they could do so if they chose. Surely, if Italy, Spain, Portugal, and Belgium can be in Africa, mighty empires like the Russian and Austro-Hungarian could be there too if they chose. But these modern Augustuses are wise in their generation; they know that division is weakness, and are engaged in the work of concentration and consolidation.

We would ask the American Colonization Society and Dr. Blyden, Would Texas have been so easily annexed in 1845 by President Polk, the defeats of Palo Alto, Resaca de la Palma, and Buena Vista inflicted on the countrymen of Iturbide, Santa Annæ, and Porfirio Diaz by Yankee Taylor so crushing and humiliating, the State of California and territories of Utah, Arizona, and New Mexico so coolly ceded by the Treaty of Guadalupe Hidalgo (1848) to the United States by Mexico, were the Spanish-speaking states of Central and South America united and allied with the latter country (Mexico)? Their selfish and insatiable greed for the sweets of power will one day, we fear as much, enable the earth-eating Yankees to easily swallow up all the Spanish American republics. If Spanish America were joined to Spain, that power would be more powerful than it is.

The Yankees could easily carry their arms into the bosom of our Africa if they felt so inclined; but the dread of the weakness of division and the power of unity rather than the Monroe doctrine prevent them from 'rushing' and bleeding our sorrow-stricken and unhappy Africa to death.

Have the American Colonization Society forgotten with what determination for four consecutive years their sires of the North fought their sires of the South? And wherefore? Was it merely because of Africo-American slavery? or was it rather that the North wished to retie the 'untied' states, to save and maintain the Union? That pseudo-philanthropist Yankee, Abraham Lincoln, writing on August 22, 1862, said: 'My paramount object is to save the Union, and not either to save or destroy slavery. If I could save the Union without freeing any slave, I would do it; if I could save it by freeing all the slaves, I would do it; and if I could do it by freeing some and leaving others alone, I would also do that.' But Abraham Lincoln saved the Union, *not when he freed the slaves, but when he armed them*, as the seceding white soldiers of the South learnt to their cost.

We would urge upon the American Colonization Society and Liberian Professor Blyden* the necessity of occupying themselves *only* with colonizing Liberia with African expatriates. From Liberia missionaries and other civilizers of Liberian nationality can pour into the heart of Africa.

These are, then, our reasons for saying that there should not be two or more independent civilized Ethiopian States in Africa or elsewhere, and in that all true-hearted Africans, we are sure, will agree with us.

Liberia and Hayti will never draw the sword against one another. Hayti, being small, cannot contain as great a number of people as Liberia, but may some day need Liberia's assistance; and we are sanguine that the friendship of Liberia and Hayti for one another will endure till the end of time.

The Republic of Liberia is the country we suggest should be offered as a home to all the Africo-Americans. And Liberia, the Land of the Free, the Light of Africa, has her arms ever open and ever ready to welcome all Africans who are willing to become citizens of her Republic, and

* If Dr. E. W. Blyden and the American Colonization Society should persist in their endeavours to send the Americo-Africans to anywhere else than Liberia, then it would be our business to oppose them most energetically.

to submit to her authority. There are twenty millions or more of Africans—the Haytians do not come under consideration because they are independent—who are expatriates, living under Caucasian rule, who, should they wish to be independent, ought to betake themselves to Liberia and there find a home. And should the hundreds of millions of African natives on the African Continent who are living under Caucasian rule also desire independence, they also should join the Liberians.

Liberia must become a mighty nation, and she must astonish the world. She must march and grow as fast as the United States of North America have done. She must crush and expel all oppressors of the Africans in Africa. Were the Liberian nation a mighty one, would the perpetrators of the Yambuya and other Stanley horrors in Africa have gone unpunished, and continued roaming at large? Justice, 'even-handed Justice,' retributive Nemesis, would surely have overtaken them.

Was it not the duty of the British Government to have tried Stanley and his filibustering companions? They did not, and their conduct in this matter was suspicious. Very likely the British Government was directly interested in Stanley's expedition; at any rate, Stanley and his freebooters have escaped in this world the severe punishment which is their due.

That the Liberian Republic is the only suitable Fatherland for the Americo-Africans and for all other Africans can be exemplified and attested. The Liberian Constitution is modelled on that of the United States, which is a Constitution copied not only by the Liberians, but also by Mexico, Chili, Argentina, Peru, Colombia, Venezuela, Ecuador, Bolivia, Paraguay, Uruguay, Nicaragua, Honduras, San Salvador, Guatemala, and Costa Rica also, this fact testifying to its excellency and wholesomeness.

It is that Constitution, then, that the Americo-Africans are used to in Liberia; but in Liberia there is no mob rule, no lynch law; there are no lynchings, no oppressions. Justice, 'even-handed Justice,' prevails and is paramount in Liberia.

No Race Problem can possibly exist in Liberia, because no man who is not of African descent can be a Liberian citizen.

The Liberian rulers are not whites, as in the United States and the British Colonies; they are blacks.

The official language is not French, as is the case in the Congo Free State, but English, the language which the Africo-American uses daily and exclusively, and has as his adopted mother-tongue.

Unlike the Congo Free State, Liberia is progressing. The Chief Magistrate is a Liberian, but the Chief of the Congo Free State is a foreigner.

These are the advantages she possesses over the Congo Free State, and these show that she is in every way the suitable and indeed, the only, country for the Africans from the United States of North America.

Liberia rejoices in having three distinct and separate powers of Governmental Administration, viz., the Executive, the Legislative, and the Judicial.

The Executive power is vested in the President, Vice-President, Secretary of State, Secretary of Treasury, Attorney-General, Postmaster-General, etc.; the Legislative power is vested in the House of Senators and the House of Representatives; and the Judicial authority is vested in a Supreme Court and in several inferior courts, with a Chief Justice, certain other judges, and divers magistrates.

Liberia has in her all the elements of progress, and, embracing as it does at least 150,000 square miles of territory, Liberia has room enough to accommodate the entire body of expatriated Africans.

The Liberians have counties, townships, chartered cities, mayors, aldermen, public libraries and librarians, churches and clergymen, coroners, colleges and schools, professors and teachers, lawyers and medical men, stores and merchants, warehouses, wharves, custom-houses, lighthouses, forts, a body of regular soldiers, militia, and police.

Among the important towns and ports of Liberia there are Monrovia, the capital, chief port and seat of government Harper, New Georgia, Caldwell, Kentucky, Millsburg, Marshall, Edina or Buchanan, Greenville, Robertsport, Grand Bassa, Cresson, Trade Town, Bexley, Readsville, Sesters River, Lexington, Cestos, Sasstown and Louisiana.

But are these the only evidences of Liberian civilization and progress? Far from it. Liberia produces and trades in cocoa, coffee, cotton, indigo, ivory, dye-woods (including cam-woods), gold, tortoiseshell, hides, iron, copper, rubber, the teeth of the sea-horse, palm-oil, cattle, goats, swine, fowls, ducks, sheep, the sugar-cane, rice, Indian corn, Guinea corn, millet, gums, wax, ground-nuts, ginger, pepper, arrowroot, palm-kernels, yams, bananas, cassava, pineapples, oranges, limes, cocoanuts, tamarinds, and other things.

The Liberian Constitution, we might have mentioned before, while it tolerates all religions and forms of worship, neither has, nor would allow, any Established Church; and this the Constitution of the United States also disallows. The Liberian Constitution, modelled, as it is, on the American, is better than the British Constitution for a newly-formed country.

In Liberia there is no such thing as an Ireland, or a Scotland, or a Wales, clamouring for Home Rule, as is the case in Britain.

The Chief Magistrate of the Liberians is not bound to belong to a particular branch of Christianity, as is the case with the British Sovereign.

There is no such thing as a politico-established religion in Liberia, as is the case with Britain. The Protestant Dissenters and the Catholics long to see the Anglican State Church and the Scottish Presbyterian State Church pulled to pieces and destroyed, as was the Irish State Church; and they are repeatedly assaulting these Churches, continually pecking at their crest. The Protestant Dissenters have formed the English Liberation Society with that as its object. The Liberian Constitution does not present such an incongruity or such an injustice as that, whilst a Protestant, or Orthodox Greek, or even a Jew, a Mussulman, an Agnostic, an idolater, or an unbeliever, may fill any post in Her Britannic Majesty's service, the British Catholic has two positions from which he is absolutely debarred; they are (1) the Viceroyalty of Ireland and (2) the Lord Chancellorship of England. But every post in the service of the Sovereign People of Liberia is open to all Christians alike, though to none but Christians.

Another weak point in the British Constitution is that every Member of Parliament, no matter of what religion he professes to be, no matter what denomination he belongs to, no matter whether he believes in any religion or in none, is allowed to legislate, if he can command a majority in some constituency, for the politico-established Episcopal Church of England. But such an absurdity does not exist in Liberia, the Liberians happily having no established church, and wishing for none.

It may not be amiss to add here that the days when Protestant Henry VIII. burnt, or beheaded, or otherwise persecuted, Catholics; the days when Catholic Mary I. burnt, or beheaded, or otherwise persecuted, Protestants; the days when the Atheistic Protestant Elizabeth burnt, or beheaded, or otherwise persecuted,

Catholics and Protestant Nonconformists or Dissenters; the days when James I., Charles I., and Charles II. persecuted those who differed from them in religious opinions, will never be known in Liberia.

The Puritans of New England, because they were persecuted in the Mother Country, fled to America, but when the Quakers, who were inferior to them in numbers, for the same reason followed the Puritans into the New England States of America, the Puritans burnt or otherwise persecuted the members of the Society of Friends. The Liberians are never likely to make so grave a mistake.

Liberia, as we said before, is in every way a fitting place for the Africo-American. It is the country to which the American Government ought to send its Africans ; and the Liberians would be only too happy to receive and welcome them. How Liberia is progressing, and how vastly superior she is to the Congo Free State, we have fully shown. And we add to all this that no *slavery* exists in Liberia, though it exists in a very virulent form in the Congo Free State.

This is the way in which we look at our Liberia ; but do others see our Liberia with the same eyes? Do the enemies, or rather (let us be generous) the opponents, of the Africans see our Liberia in the same light and with the same eyes as we do? Let us see how Laird Clowes looks at the Liberians.

Writing on pages 160 and 161 of his ' Black America,' this gentleman gives it as his opinion that 'Not only in St. Domingo has the experiment of Negro self-government been tried under pseudo-civilized conditions, it has been tried also in Liberia, and with almost equally bad results. To-day in Liberia whites are treated by the blacks much as blacks are treated by whites in the South. A Negro State has never yet shown itself worthy to rank on terms of equality with a white one, and there are no symptoms that it will ever reach that level. Diplomatic intercourse with such States cannot be carried on under ordinary conditions, neither can commercial transactions. Black rule means anarchy, and it invariably brings to the front the fact that the Negro hates the white as much as the white hates him, and is even more ready than the white is to play the tyrant and the oppressor. Life for a white in every existing Negro state is well-nigh unendurable.'

Laird Clowes's arguments are founded on his ignorance of facts. We have fairly shown that he has been contending against the African in his 'Black America' with the weapons of Ignorance and Prejudice. To take his statements piece by piece, Laird Clowes, in the first place, says that 'Not only in St. Domingo has the experiment of African self-government been tried under pseudo-civilized conditions.' But have we not proved that the Republic of Hayti or St. Domingo is flourishing? It would be needless to enter again on this discussion. At the same time, was Toussaint-L'Ouverture the Great, the Father of his Country and of the Haytian Constitution, a pseudo-civilized President and Commander-in-chief? Not the Royal Toussaint the Great, surely! Friends and enemies, countrymen and foreigners, and even James Anthony Froude and Sir Spencer St. John,* testify to the greatness of Toussaint-L'Ouverture. Laird Clowes would have us believe that the Liberator of St. Domingo was a pseudo-civilized man. A great Captain and Governor like Toussaint surely knew how to choose his ministers; and Dessalines and Christophe, his two first lieutenants and advisers, we all know were great men. Laird Clowes makes a great mistake when he imagines that his intelligent readers are gullible believers of what unfounded things he may be pleased to write. The statement

° Also see chap. vi., p. 227.

that 'the experiment of Negro self-government has been tried under pseudo-civilized conditions' is false from the beginning to the end.

In the second place, he says : ' It (*i.e.*, the experiment of African self-government) has been tried also in Liberia, and with almost equally bad results. To-day in Liberia whites are treated by the blacks much as blacks are treated by whites in the South.' Of course, Laird Clowes in this makes a mere unsupported statement. He does not attempt to support his statement by evidence, because there is none that can be offered. The first settlers who went to Liberia were great men. When the American Colonization Society generously called upon the African freedmen in the United States of North America (in 1822) to return to the land of their fathers, the liberated Americo-Africans did not shrink from the undertaking. No; they responded loyally and cheerfully to the generous call of the Africo-Americans. They (the first settlers) were a pious, God-fearing band ; they were few in number, a mere handful, but they had stout hearts, and every one of them was a host in himself. Their task in the land of their fathers, in Liberia, was not an easy one ; it was arduous and Herculean. But what will not stout hearts accomplish ? The founders of the Liberian nation, because they were brave, did not shirk their duty, but worked and fought like Trojans ; and because they were heroes they conquered.

Liberia is flourishing, is progressing. The American Colonization Society attest that Liberia is progressing, and keeping pace with nineteenth-century civilization. That society is not composed of one man, but of scores of intelligent white Americans. And can a mere assertion of Laird Clowes counterbalance the evidence of that society? Liberia has only had (1891) forty-four years of Independence, yet she is progressing. But what was the condition of England, Ireland, Scotland, Wales, France, Germany, Austro-Hungary, Russia, Spain, Norway and Sweden, Denmark, Holland, Portugal, Switzerland, when each of these countries had forty-four years of Independence or self-government? What that condition was the student of European History knows only too well.

But are the American Colonization Society the only persons who thus bear testimony to the progress of Liberia, and eulogize the Liberians? Brookes's 'General Gazetteer' also testifies to the capabilities of the Liberians for self-government, and to the condition of Liberia generally. It says:

'The greater part of the early settlers from America were men of decided piety, and their just, humane, and benevolent policy has given them an astonishing influence over the native tribes. In 1827 this sable community had risen completely above the pressure of urgent necessities. Monrovia was rapidly increasing in accommodation and increasing in magnitude, and several fresh towns were already springing up. The soil is extremely fertile; the natives of the country, without tools, without skill, and with little labour, raising more grain and vegetables than they can consume, and often more than they can sell. Cattle, swine, fowls, ducks, goats, and sheep thrive without feeding, and require no other care than to keep them from straying. Cotton, coffee, indigo, and sugar-cane are all the spontaneous growth of the forests, and may be cultivated at pleasure to any extent by such as are disposed. The same may be said of rice, Indian corn, Guinea corn, millet, and too many species of fruits and vegetables to be enumerated. Add to all this that winter is here unknown; the hills and plains are covered with perpetual verdure, and Nature is constantly pouring her treasures, all the year round, into the laps of the industrious. The trade and commerce extend to the coast, to the interior parts of the continent, and to foreign vessels, and are already valuable, and fast increasing. The chief exports are rice, palm-oil, ivory, tortoiseshell, dye-woods, gold, hides, wax, and a small (?) amount of coffee. The imports consist of the products and manufactures of the four quarters of the world. The harbour is seldom clear of European and American shipping, and the bustle and thronging of the streets show something already of the activity of the smaller seaports of the United States. Mechanics of nearly every trade are carrying on their various occupations, and not a child or youth in the colony but is provided with an appropriate school. The piety of the first settlers has continued to spread, and the standard of morals consequently remains high. The Sabbath is carefully regarded, and Sundayschools have been established for the benefit of the native children. The cheerful abodes of civilization and happiness; the flourishing settlements; the sound of Christian instruction, and scenes of Christian worship, which are heard and seen in this land of brooding pagan darkness; a thousand contented freemen united in founding a Christian Empire, happy themselves, and the instrument of happiness to others, while they refresh the hearts, cannot fail to encourage the brightest anticipations of Christian philanthropists.'

The Rev. W. Moister, a British clergyman of the Wesleyan persuasion, who has had a long residence among the African people of the west and south, and is, therefore, a competent and duly-qualified person to speak with some authority of Liberia and its people, also eulogizes the Liberians in this wise:

'The majority of the early settlers were men of steady, industrious habits and decided piety belonging to different Christian denominations, and they set about the cultivation of the ground, and the preparation of homes for themselves and their families in their adopted country, in a manner which augured well for the success of the enterprise. Their just, humane, and benevolent policy was, moreover, said to have given them astonishing influence over the native tribes, and the settlement was commenced under favourable and promising circumstances.

'Although thus commenced by emigrants from America, Liberia was not an American Colony, properly speaking, but a small Republic or Commonwealth, after the model of the United States, and entirely independent of the parent country politically, although receiving important moral and material aid from it in different ways when necessary.

'Accordingly, a Constitution and Laws were framed for the Government of the settlement, provision being made for the selection of a President, Members of the House of Representatives, and other public functionaries. Of course, the difficulties connected with the founding of this infant nation were neither few nor small, and some errors may have been made at an early period of the undertaking; but, notwithstanding every drawback, in all fairness it must be said that the enterprise succeeded better than could have been expected, all things being considered. As the number of settlers increased, townships were laid out, farms cultivated, towns and villages planned, and buildings erected in some of them which were very creditable to a rising community.

'The soil of Liberia is reported to be extremely fertile, and well adapted to the growth of all kinds of tropical produce. Cotton, coffee, indigo, and the sugar-cane thrive well, and rice, Indian corn, Guinea corn, millet, and various kinds of fruits and vegetables, are cultivated with ease and success. Cattle, sheep, goats, swine, fowls, and ducks are said to thrive with little feeding, and to require no other care than to keep them from straying.

'Much zeal and perseverance have been displayed in all these Christian agencies, and the result is seen in the parsonages, places of worship, colleges, and school buildings which have been erected in most of the towns and villages in the settlement, and in the improved morals of the people, which will compare favourably with those of many other Christian countries, and which augur well for the future prosperity of Liberia.'*

Yet Laird Clowes would have his readers believe that 'the experiment of Negro self-government has been tried in Liberia with *almost equally bad results.*' But the authorities just quoted evidently do not share Laird Clowes's opinions and sentiments. Nobler feelings and better passions towards their fellow-men actuate them; the truth of what they personally know guides them in their utterances. Like the good Mussulman, Abou ben Adhem, and the good Christian, the unfortunate American John Brown, they love their fellow-men.

But what can Laird Clowes mean when he says: 'To-day in Liberia whites are treated by the blacks much as blacks are treated by whites in the South'? Can he mean that whites in Liberia are lynched by Liberians? Can he mean that whites are refused a hearing, a fair hearing, in the Liberian Courts of Justice? Can he mean that the persons and property of whites are not protected by Liberian law? He cannot surely mean either of these things. Supposing it were even as Laird Clowes gives out, that the whites are maltreated in Liberia, have the European and American Ministers and Consuls-General in Liberia made any protest against the maltreatment of the whites by the Liberians?

---

* 'Africa: Past and Present,' by an Old Resident, pp. 222, 223, 225.

If Clowes were true in his accusation, would these officials not have lodged some protest with the Liberian Government? They have *not* done so; and we must therefore take it for granted that the whites are *not* maltreated by the Liberian citizens, or unprotected by the Liberian Government. Affairs are not in that strained relation, and we must again ask, What does Laird Clowes mean by saying that ' to-day, in Liberia, whites are treated by the blacks much as blacks are treated by whites in the South'? To that statement we attach one, and only one meaning. In plain words, Mr. Clowes would have his readers understand that the Liberian Constitutional Government absolutely refuses to confer citizenship on the white man in Liberia. That is how we take his words. We must admit —but it is familiar knowledge—that the Liberian Constitution confers citizenship on none save those of African descent; and for this policy the Liberians are certainly to be commended and congratulated. If citizenship were conferred on the white man, why, Liberia would simply be swamped by the white men, and this would endanger the safety and independence of the Liberian Republic. The Liberians protect the property and persons of the whites, and give them a fair and impartial hearing in their Courts of Justice. In Liberia white men are not lynched; but the Africans in the United States of North America, and particularly in the Sunny South, suffer all these maltreatments and are unprotected by the American law. The condition of the white in Liberia is far better than the condition of the black is in the United States. The African in the United States is regarded by the white man as an alien, and has no civic rights; and must the African in Liberia good-naturedly confer citizenship on the Caucasian? The British inhabitants of Cape Colony and Natal have a Constitution, but in neither of these do the African inhabitants possess civic rights. And must Liberia be the white man's milch cow and have citizenship conferred on him? The aboriginal inhabitants of Australia, though the natural owners of the soil, have no political rights, while the descendants of the convict-settlers lord it over them. Yet must Liberia, forsooth, bestow on the white man the rights of a Liberian citizen? The Liberians will be foolish indeed if they ever confer citizenship on the white man. Should they ever do so, they would be simply sharpening a sword for their own heads, and planting the seed of a Race Problem which would threaten the very existence of the Liberian Republic. But they have too much good sense to make such a fatal mistake.

In the third place, Laird Clowes gravely tells us that 'A Negro State has never yet shown itself worthy to rank on terms of equality with a white one, and there are no symptoms that it will ever reach that level.' Is Mr. Clowes aware, or is he forgetful of the fact, that such Hamitic or African States as Canaan, Phœnicia, Carthage, Assyria, Babylon, Ethiopia, Abyssinia, Morocco, Ashantee, Dahomey, Sokoto, Gandu, Bornu, Zululand and others, *have flourished*? Was not Canaan the equal of its white contemporaries? The Phœnician Empire was at least equal to its white contemporaries, when her ships, her navy, scoured every sea.

Did not Carthage, when in the height of her power, give laws to Spain and Portugal, and hold Sardinia, Sicily, Corsica, and the Balearic Islands in subjection? Were not the Carthaginians the equals of the Romans, and were they not the mightiest antagonists the Romans ever encountered? Was not the Assyrian or Babylonian Empire of the Nabuchadonosors one of the greatest that ever existed in the world? Yet Laird Clowes tells us that an African State has never yet shown itself worthy to rank on terms of equality with a white one ! Ethiopia (modern Nubia) and Abyssinia have been mighty Empires, and have not these in their prime, and in the summit of their glory, been each the equal of their white contemporaries?

Did not Morocco, when in the zenith of her power, dictate laws to the Spaniards and Portuguese? This State, when in its prime, equalled the best European States then in existence. Morocco, like Abyssinia, even now takes rank with many white States. Have not Ashantee, Dahomey, Madagascar, Sokoto, Gandu, Bornu, Zululand, and other African States, as we had occasion to point out, made their mark in this world's history? Liberia and Hayti, though they do not rank with Britain, France, Germany, Russia, Austro-Hungary, Italy, United States of North America, and Spain, and other Caucasian Countries, on terms of equality, are certainly on a level with Roumania, Greece, Bulgaria, Switzerland, Servia, Peru, Colombia, Venezuela, Ecuador, Bolivia, and Uruguay; while Paraguay, Montenegro, Honduras, San Salvador, Guatemala, Nicaragua, Costa Rica, Transvaal, Congo Free State of Belgian Leopold, Zulu Republic, Monaco, Andorra, San Marino, Liechtenstein, and Luxemburg are each immeasurably inferior to the respective allied kindred States of Liberia and Hayti.

In the fourth place, Mr. Clowes goes on to say that 'Diplomatic intercourse with such (African) States cannot be carried on under ordinary conditions; neither can commercial transactions.' This is, again, an *argumentum ad ignorantiam*.

Is Mr. Clowes aware that the principal countries of Europe and the Americas receive Ministers and Consuls-General and Consuls from Liberia and Hayti, while these latter receive in their turn diplomatic and commercial representatives from the Americas and Europe? It is common knowledge that whilst Britain is represented in Hayti in the person of Mr. James N. E. Zohrab, the Consul-General and Minister, Monsieur P. E. Latortue represents Hayti in like manner in Britain; Hannibal Price, Esq., does the same duty for her in the United States of North America, and Mr. Frederic Douglass is the Yankee Minister to Hayti. It is also common knowledge that whilst Liberia is represented by her Minister in the United States, the Yankees are represented in Liberia by the Rev. Mr. Ezekiel Ezra Smith, Consul-General and Minister-Resident. And while Sir James Shaw Hay represents British interests in Liberia, Mr. Henry Hayman discharges similar functions in Britain. That being so, is there anyone who will deny that the statement that 'Diplomatic intercourse with such (Negro) States cannot be carried on under ordinary conditions; neither can commercia transactions,' as made by Laird Clowes, is as foolish as it is untrue, and evidently based on ignorance and prejudice?

In the fifth place, Laird Clowes asserts that 'Black rule means anarchy, and it invariably brings to the front the fact that the Negro hates the white as much as the white hates him, and is even more ready than the white is to play the tyrant and the oppressor. Life for a white in every existing Negro State is well-nigh unendurable.' Does anarchy, then, reign in Liberia? Does anarchy reign, then, in Hayti? But has Europe never experienced anarchy? Have the Americas never experienced anarchy? Mr Clowes says that 'The Negro hates the white as much as the white hates him, and is even more ready than the white is to play the tyrant and the oppressor.' The opinion of an African is surely equal to that of a Caucasian; and, believing *our* say to be as good as *his*, we give an emphatic and entire denial to the allegations of Laird Clowes. Although he may hate the African, the African does not hate even the Commissioner of the *Times*. Though the Yankee plays the tyrant and the oppressor to the Africans in the United States, the Liberians and Haytians do not retaliate. How could our Liberians and Haytians retaliate? If the Liberians and Haytians did play the tyrant and oppressor, would the Europeans and American Powers take no action in the matter?

There are Britishers and other Caucasians in Liberia and Hayti, as all the world knows. Are they tyrannized over and oppressed, and do they remain passive? Surely Britain, the Power who is bullying small States like Portugal in South Africa, and Venezuela in South America on the Guianese Boundary Question, would not hesitate to bully, if not to bombard, the Liberians and Haytians if the Britishers in Liberia and Hayti were maltreated! But, as Britain takes no steps against the Liberians and Haytians, our knowledge of the world assures us that the ill-treatment of Caucasians in Liberia and Hayti is a dream of Laird Clowes. A more affable and hospitable people than the Liberian and the Haytian does not exist on this our earth. 'Life for a white in every existing Negro State is well-nigh unendurable' indeed! But would the British Indiarubber States Company (Limited) have been formed 'for the purpose of acquiring and working a concession from the Government of the Republic of Liberia, for the sole right of collecting and exporting indiarubber and guttapercha from the said Republic for the European and American markets,' if 'life for a white in every existing Negro State was well-nigh unendurable,' and 'black rule meant anarchy'? There are many Europeans and Americans both in Liberia and in Hayti who are happy and contented.

Laird Clowes wanted to show, but he did not show, that 'a fringe of Negro States on the southern and south-eastern borders of the (American) Union would be a perpetual danger to the whole Federation;' but he failed, we say. Instead of making that his business, he directed an angry tirade and rigmarole against the Liberians and Haytians and Africans' in general, and said that 'Not only in St. Domingo has the experiment of Negro self-Government been tried under pseudo-civilized conditions. It has been tried also in Liberia, and with almost equally bad results,' etc. But we have taken pains to refute every one of his calumnies. There must not be 'a fringe of Negro States on the southern and south-eastern borders of the (American) Union' is Laird Clowes's suggestion. And in that he has our support. The Africo-Americans ought on no account to remain; and in order to effectively solve the Race Problem, we counsel Repatriation to Africa and Independence in Liberia. Liberia is in every way a fitting Fatherland for the African in the United States. The founders of the Liberian Republic originally came from America, and returned to the land of their ancestors. Why should not the Africans in the United States of North America follow their example? Were the first President of the Liberians, Joseph Jenkins Roberts, to rise from his grave, he would express surprise at the progress the Liberians have made and are making.

Laird Clowes, after libelling the Liberians on pages 160 and 161 of his 'Black America,' thus writes on page 183 in the same book: 'Jefferson, who died nearly forty years before Emancipation became an accomplished fact, did not omit to prepare, so far as lay in his power, for the evil he saw approaching. With Henry Clay and others he founded the African Colonization Society, which established on the West Coast of Africa the Negro Republic of Liberia, and between 1820 and 1860 sent thither about 10,000 free coloured people. It may at once be admitted that the Colony has not been a conspicuous success, for the American immigrants and their descendants now hardly

number 5,000 souls, and according to Mr. Charles H. J.
Taylor, a late American Minister to the Republic, the place
is to-day "a land of snakes, centipedes, fever, miasma,
poverty, superstition, and death."'

The Colonization Society, which with philanthropic gene-
rosity sent the captive Africans from the land of the Yankees
to build up the Liberian Nation in Africa, was, and is,
not called the *African*, but the *American*, Society, inasmuch
as the society originated in America. It is a slight error
Laird Clowes makes, we admit, but it is still a mistake. A
more fitting name for that organization would, however, be
the *Liberian Repatriation and Colonization Society*. We
would humbly recommend it to the American Colonization
Society for adoption.

He gives us to understand that Jefferson, ' with Henry
Clay and others, founded the African (American) Colonization Society.' The real founder of the American Colonization Society was Henry Clay himself. He was *the* founder,
and not Jefferson. Clay did not merely support Jefferson,
but was the organizer of the American Colonization Society.
Henry Clay was not, however, a philanthropist and abolitionist of the William Wilberforce type. His philanthropy
and abolition were not of the right sort. While he was for
abolishing slavery in all the States of the American Union
lying to the north of latitude 36° 30', he advocated the cause
of slavery in Missouri and the Slave States. He was for
perpetuating slavery in California, if that State so desired,
while he was for abolishing slavery in Columbia, and for
leaving the States of New Mexico to their discretion.

Despite the eccentricity of Henry Clay, no one will deny
that he has rendered the Africans a service by helping to
send them to Liberia. Would that every white American
would contribute to send the American African to the land
of his forefathers—to Liberia! It is the debt every white

American owes the African in the United States, and one which he *must* some day discharge. The American Colonization Society, it is true, yearly sends expatriates to repatriation, Independence, and Liberia; but we think the American Government could easily spare a few millions of dollars for the American Africans, with which they might be sent in a body to Africa, to Liberia.

Laird Clowes tells us that 'it may at once be admitted that the Colony (of Liberia) has not been a conspicuous success, for the American immigrants and their descendants now hardly number 5,000 souls.' *Well, we do not 'at once admit' that Liberia has not been a conspicuous success, but we firmly declare that Liberia has been a conspicuous success.* The *African Repository* for April, 1891, the organ of the American Colonization Society, says with authority: 'Emigration to Liberia every year under the auspices of the American Colonization Society has been uninterrupted for the past seventy years. Those now reported make the number sent since the civil war to be 4,201, and a total from the beginning of 16,209, exclusive of 4,722 recaptured Africans, which it induced and enabled the Government of the United States to settle in Liberia, making a grand total of 21,921 persons to whom the Society has given homes in Africa,' thereby showing that Liberia is being gradually reinforced.

Mr. Clowes, again, says: 'According to Mr. Charles H. J. Taylor, a late American Minister to the Republic of Liberia, the place is to-day "a land of snakes, centipedes, fever, miasma, poverty, superstition, and death."' That was what Mr. Charles H. J. Taylor, said; but there are others who have spread even worse reports than that of Liberia.

The Hon. and Rev. Ezekiel Ezra Smith, who is not *the* late nor *a* late American Minister, but is the present (1891) Minister-Resident and Consul-General of the United States to Liberia, writing from Monrovia, April 1, 1891, thus bears witness to the condition or state of Liberia : 'Since I wrote . . . last I have seen much of Liberia. I have visited Cape Palmas, met with the different churches, and seen something of the operation of the institutions there. I had the pleasure to meet Bishops Ferguson and Taylor, and the leading men generally. I was much delighted while conversing with Bishop Ferguson to ascertain the high hopes he entertained for Liberia's future prosperity. The Bishop is doing effective work. The emigrants last settled at Cape Palmas are doing well. The bullock and cart are considerably employed at this point.

'From Cape Palmas I went to Sinoe, the home of Hon. Z. B. Roberts, Associate Justice of the Supreme Court, Hon. James J. Ross, ex-Attorney-General, ex-Senator Fuller, and other gentlemen of influence, who, notwithstanding their positions as officials of the Government, have farms. The emigrants located at Sinoe in 1888 are moving on more and more successfully.

'I next had the pleasure to spend a few days at Grand Bassa, which comprises Lower and Upper Buchanan and Edina. Grand Bassa surpasses either of the towns or settlements above mentioned in point of commercial transactions. While there I met some of the emigrants who came in May, 1889. They appear to be doing well, and seem contented.

'On the 15th ultimo, in company with Hon. C. T. O. King, Hon. H. A. Williams (Mayor of Monrovia), Colonel A. D. Williams, Judge Dennis, and a number of other gentlemen, I embarked for Grand Cape Mount on a small sailing craft. We encountered a most tempestuous voyage, arriving at Cape Mount on the morning of the 17th, being quite wet and much fatigued. Hon. C. T. O. King, myself, and others of the party called out to the settlement where the emigrants were located. After visiting each individual house and looking at their beautiful promising farms, a meeting of all the new-comers was held at the school-house. Oh yes; they have built themselves a school-house in the centre of the settlement. At the meeting short speeches were made by Mr. King and myself. Afterwards remarks by different persons of the emigrants were made. Each one expressed himself contented. Their farms, consisting of coffee, cassava, potatoes, yams, eddoes, cocoa, plantains, bananas, ginger, rice, etc., are as pretty as any I have seen in the country. They have evidently, considering the surroundings, done remarkably well. I also visited the Protestant Episcopal Mission at Cape Mount, and observed somewhat of its workings. I think it is doing a great, yea, a good work. Cape Mount is, indeed, a fine portion of this country.'

This is what the Hon. and Rev. Ezekiel Ezra Smith says. He is the present United States Minister-Resident and Consul-General to Liberia. He is on the spot, and writes on the spot. He does not say that Liberia is 'a land of snakes, centipedes, fever, miasma, poverty, superstition, and death,' as Mr. Charles H. J. Taylor does, but, on the contrary, he eulogizes it. We certainly prefer the statement of the present United States Minister in Liberia to that of the Minister of long ago. Yet we are sure that at no time was Liberia 'a land of snakes, centipedes, fever, miasma, poverty, superstition, and death' in the sense he means, not even at the time when he (Mr. Charles H. J. Taylor) was American Minister to Liberia. Liberia was never so unortunate as to be subjected to miasma. The sanitary regulations were always rigid, and as rigidly enforced. If there be snakes in Liberia, there are snakes all over the Americas, Australasia, and the West Indies. There are snakes in Asia, particularly in the East Indies, the home of the cobra di capello. If there be centipedes in Liberia, there are centipedes all the world over. If there be fever in Liberia, there is fever all the world over, and always will be. Liberia has never experienced such a fell disease as the 'Black Death,' which ravaged not only Asia, but the whole of Europe, laying low at least one-third of the population in every state it visited in the time of the Third Edward, the Prince who humbled the pride of France at Creçy.

Liberia has never experienced such a calamity as the Great Plague which made its appearance in Britain in the reign of the Merry Monarch, carrying away between 300,000 and 500,000 Britishers to the mansion-house of Hades. But a few years ago cholera, a fell disease, struck down Frenchmen, Spaniards, and Italians, and they perished by the hundred. Thousands of Trinidadians perished by the cholera of 1854; but Liberia has never experienced cholera—never has had a miasma of any sort. If there be poverty in Liberia, there is poverty all the world over, and always will be. London, the largest, most populous, and richest City and Metropolis in the world, contains the greatest number of poor persons that ever congregated in any one country in proportion to its population. Liberia cannot be poor, for Liberia is one of the chosen spots—perhaps the best and richest spot—in Africa. And was not Africa always rich? Is it not rich now? Are not the Europeans vying with one another as to whom the greatest part of Africa should fall? Why? Because Africa is rich.' When H. M. Stanley and his band of buccaneering freebooters rushed into the heart of Africa, was it not to plunder the Africans, and obtain the wealth of the African natives? They were seeking for wealth, for ivory. for gold. Africa is a rich country, and Liberia is one of the richest countries in Africa. Who are the Anarchists and

Socialists? Are they not an organization of poor, hard-up men who wish to wring out money from the tenacious grasp of the wealthy? Where in Europe or in America are there not Socialists? There are Anarchists and Socialists in Britain, Anarchists and Socialists in France,* Anarchists and Socialists in Germany, Nihilists in Russia, Socialists and Anarchists in Austro-Hungary, Socialists and Anarchists in Italy, and, indeed, all Europe over; there are Socialists and Anarchists in the United States of North America. But there are no; Socialists, no Nihilists, no Anarchists, in Liberia? And why? Because Liberia is a rich country, and has wonderful resources. There wealth is more proportionately divided than it is in any other country. Liberia has gold, ivory, copper, iron, and what not.

We are, again, informed by Mr. Charles H. J. Taylor, through Laird Clowes, that Liberia is 'a land of superstition and death.' No comments from us are necessary here in relation to superstition, for we have dealt with the subject at length. But the Liberians as a nation are not superstitious. In the fourth Chapter we prove that not only the Europeans and the Americans, but also the Asiatics, are superstitious.

Mr. Taylor alleges that there is death in Liberia; but does he forget the fact that death is everywhere, and that all men must die? Liberia, far from being 'a land of snakes, centipedes, fever, miasma, poverty, superstition, and death,' we assert and maintain, is one of the loveliest and grandest spots in God's earth.

Liberia is the Fatherland which the American Africans must seek. Can it be possible that there are not more than 1,000,000 of them who wish to move away from the land of oppression, and repatriate themselves in the land

* The French Anarchists are at this moment keeping the Minister of the Interior and Prefect of Police fully employed.

of their fathers—in dear Liberia? The Africans are oppressed in the United States, and cannot the 10,500,000 of them agitate for Repatriation and Liberia? March some day they must; and they must march from the Land of Goshen—from Babylon. But it must be to Africa—it must be to Liberia.

Laird Clowes advocates emigration to the Congo Free State by the American Africans; but we point out that Liberia is altogether more desirable, and a more fitting Fatherland. Laird Clowes, again, suggests that 'for the half-breed of the South another haven must be sought' (than the Congo Free State). 'He is no more the friend of the black than he is of the white. Neither desires his company. But in the West Indies, or in some parts of South and Central America, he might, no doubt, discover a land in which his existence would be a not unpleasant one.' How comes Laird Clowes to know that the mixed-blooded African 'is no more the friend of the black than he is of the white'? We say that he is 'the friend of the black,' and in many instances even of the American white. The half-blooded African 'is not the friend of the black'!

Is Mr. Clowes aware that there are half-blooded Africans in Liberia as there are in Hayti? Is Mr. Clowes aware that the mixed-blooded Africans in Liberia and in Hayti enjoy not only full citizenship and live on terms of friendship and brotherly love with their full-blooded African countrymen, but that they have, in many instances, risen to the Presidential Chair, both of Liberia and Hayti? Is Laird Clowes aware that the great Pétion, the Haytian, was not a full, but a mixed-blooded African? We say that the full-blooded and half-blooded Africans must move and march together, for they are one people, and have one common destiny. They must live together. When Toussaint the Great was bravely battling for the Independence of his Haytian Fatherland, he had half-blooded Haytians, his countrymen, in his Army. So had Dessalines and others. And must the half-blooded Africans betake themselves to the West Indies? If so, to what part? Every part of the West Indies is unsuited to the African, whether he be full-blooded or half-blooded. Or must the half-blooded African go to South or Central America, as Laird Clowes suggests? Neither South nor Central America, no matter what part, is a fitting place for the African. We should suggest Liberia as a fitting and the only Fatherland for the half-blooded African. There he will enjoy peace and happiness. There he will be a citizen, and not a semi-slave, as he almost always is in the United States. Every office will be open to him. His progress cannot be retarded in Liberia. All Africans, whether they be half or whole blooded, are to march to Liberia, the Land of the Free, the Light of Africa, in preference to the Congo Free State, or any other State.

The Puritans, because they were persecuted at home by the Second Stuart, and despaired of their country, directed their steps to America, and founded the United States; and will the persecuted Africans of the United States remain therein? Charles I. prevented John Hampden and Oliver Cromwell, Independents or Puritans, from migrating to America; but the former remained to perish fighting valiantly against the King at Chalgrove Field; while the latter, Oliver Cromwell, lived to sign the death-warrant of the King, who was beheaded at Whitehall. We believe, like the Rev. Mr. Lee, that the Africans must march out of the United States. We believe it must be to Africa. We believe they must be independent. And we indulge in the dream that they will betake themselves to the Independent Republic of Liberia.

The Turks, because they were persecuted at home in Central Asia, and were unwilling to live as the subjects of the Mongols, fled from Central Asia, with their wives and children and whatever they possessed, and marched into Europe, conquered a part of it, and are still there. And will the Africans in the United States of North America, oppressed and lynched as they are, and deprived of their rights by the Yankees, continue to live in America?

In 1840 the Boers, because they were dissatisfied with the British Colonial Government at the Cape Colony, quitted that Colony, and entrenched themselves in Natal, where the jealous Britishers followed them. Nothing daunted by the annexation of their new home, Natal, by the Britishers, they quitted Natal and founded the Transvaal. Britishers again followed them there in 1877. For three years the Boers bore the uninviting attentions of Britishers, but in 1880 they rose in rebellion, took the field, and the Britishers, though they were always better armed and numerically at least equal to the Boers, suffered signal defeats. But it was the decisive battle of Amajuba that shed the greatest lustre on the arms of the Boers, and secured to them Independence and the possession of the Transvaal, while the beaten Britishers returned home crestfallen from Amajuba, leaving their commander-in-chief, and the flower of the youth of England, Ireland, and Scotland on the field of battle. -The courage of the Boers was a noble one. They disliked British rule; they preferred freedom and independence.

The Africans in the United States are not citizens, but subjects. Formerly they were a nation of slaves, now they are a nation of servants. They are not protected by the American law. Will they remain in that land? Time, no doubt, will show. There are those who say that we are preaching removal from the United States to a people who have no money. We say that there are two things that the African in the United States must do or have. First, he must have the will to quit the United States ; and surely the Africans, who are ill-treated, unprotected, and enjoy no rights whatever, ought to be only too willing to quit the United States. If he has the will, then, secondly, the African must organize his ranks, agitate for removal, and bring the Yankee to his senses. Then only, we are sure, but only then, will he receive the money that the American owes him. We are afraid the Africans in America are too apathetic and indifferent to their birthright in Africa, in Liberia. The apathy and indifference of the expatriated African are construed by the whites as laziness; but we think they are the reactions from slavery, and not laziness. So long as they continue apathetic and indifferent, so long will their conduct be construed into laziness. Sir Edwin Arnold gives it as his opinion that 'the Africo-Americans are as merry as crickets, lazy as pigs.'*

The apathy and indifference of the Africans are also construed into inferiority by the whites. Africa is fast being partitioned by the European Powers. And the Africans of the United States, who are as a rule poor, thanks to slavery, dare not go and claim the land of their ancestors. In Africa they can become rich with rapid strides. But it must be to Liberia that they go. In the words of the Hon. Henry W. Grimes, ex-Attorney-General of Liberia, who writes in the earlier part of this year (1891), 'Liberia has in her all the elements of progress. I will go further, and say that I believe she will progress; but just at present I must confess that those on whom she should be able to depend for aid in her work are strangely indifferent to her needs. The cry has been sent out across the water to the sons of Ham, who are "learned in the wisdom of the Egyptians," "Come over and help us !" but they heed it not. Here and there one comes; some fear to get sick

* Letter to the *Daily Telegraph*, 1889.

and die, as if disease and death were not everywhere; others say, " How can we leave the good things of this land to go to savage Africa?" And so,' continues Mr. Grimes, 'we stand on the threshold, waiting and watching for help to go up and possess the land. Thank God, the help is coming ! Every year one or two more are drawn to us from the mass around, and they are useful allies. With their help we will yet go forward, triumphing and to triumph, for the promise is sure: Ethiopia *must* stretch forth her hands to God. Africa must be won for Christ; and if our brethren here in the United States are as careless of their birthright as was Esau, then the blessing will go with it to him who appreciates it, and he, in the long, dark night, will wrestle with God, and, prevailing, will get the blessing at dawn.'

Suppose that all the 10,500,000 of Africo-Americans, being intent on returning to the land of their ancestors, had marshalled their ranks and petitioned the Yankee Government for a subsidy to enable them to do so, and had the prayer of their petition refused, we do not doubt that the money could be raised otherwise.

The Independents, in the time of the First Charles, left England for America in ship after ship. They did so because life was too hard for them to bear under the iron rule, or, rather, the misrule, of the despotic Charles. Charles's Government did not aid them in any way. It did not pay their passage, or allow them money for their use, and to start with in America. On the contrary, wrathful that its opponents should escape from its power, the Government of the First Charles prohibited eight ships of the Puritan Iconoclasts from quitting the Thames. But it is not likely that the American Government would stop and detain any ship laden with expatriated Africans who were homeward bound to their Africa. On the contrary, the American Government would feel it a relief if the Africans were to suddenly leave. For there would be no more Race Problems to confront. No doubt the American Government would like to see the Race Problem settled. But they cannot make up their minds to grant the Africans a subsidy to enable them to return to Africa. The Democrats of the United States indulge in tall talk about sending the Africans from the United States to the land of their ancestors when they are out of office, but they shirk the work when they are in office. It is not likely that a Republican Government, like the present American Administration, will ever send the Africo-Americans to Africa, and solve the burning Race Question in the United States.

The Independents, we were saying, betook themselves to America merely as British Colonists, and proposed to remain British subjects. But, were the American Africans to leave the United States for Africa, it would not be to be as mere colonists, and to remain subject to the Caucasian, and to live under the ægis of the Second Belgian Leopold and his successors in the Congo Free State, as Laird Clowes with unpardonable simplicity suggests, where they or their descendants might have to do battle with the Belgians for the exclusive Independence of their Congro Free State, as the descendants of the Puritans or Independents did with the Britishers; but they would simply be leaving America and oppression behind them once and for ever, and marching into Africa, into Liberia, not as mere colonists, not as subjects, we say, but as fully-qualified, independent citizens.

The Africo-Americans should be able to raise money by the same means as the English Puritans who settled in America did more than two hundred years ago.

Where did the Turks, who fled before the Mongols and oppression from Central Asia, into Europe, find capital to facilitate their passage to the European Continent? The

Turks were practically as poor as the Puritans were, and as the Africans in the United States are now. But the Turks, like the Puritans, though poor, preferred liberty to oppression; and their thirst for liberty sustained them on their journey. The Turks had to fight with the Byzantine Greeks for a shelter and a home; but were the expatriated Africans in the United States to quit America, it would not be to contend with anyone for a home and shelter. Their task would be easier and their path smoother than were those of the Turks. They need only sail to Africa, and there find a shelter ; they need only march to Liberia, and there find not only a home, but Liberty, Independence, and her daughter, Citizenship.

Dare not the Africo-Americans, with more opportunities and greater facilities, try to do what the Caucasians, in the persons of the New England Independents, and what the Asiatics, in the persons of the Turks, achieved? Is it possible that our oppressed brethren and countrymen in the United States cannot find means wherewith to quit America and find a home in Africa, the land of our ancestors ?

'Where there is a will there is a way,' they say. The countrymen of Moses and descendants of Jacob, the Israelites, because their brethren and co-religionists in Russia and Poland are being persecuted and oppressed by the Gentiles, have formed the Anglo-Jewish Association, the Syrian Colonization Society, and other organizations, to enable those of their Russian and Polish brethren who wish it to return to the Holy Land. Toiling Hebrews of the East-End, poor though they be, are contributing a penny a week per man to the fund of one of the Jewish Colonization Societies.*

A penny a week seems next to nothing. But something

* *Lloyd's News*, 1891.

is surely bettter than nothing; and do not little things grow into mighty mountains? But have the Africans in the United States any similar organizations to enable them to return to their Africa? Have they even one organization for such a purpose? It is the boast of every African that he is the Caucasian's equal, if not his superior, while the Asiatic and the Red Man, being immensely his inferiors, bow down before the African in token of their inferiority. And dare not the African act as he ought?

The fire which burnt, and continues burning, in the breasts of the Haytians; the fire which burnt, and continues burning, in the breasts of the Liberians; and the fire which burnt in the breasts of our African forefathers generally, the Americo-African, we fear, is very low just at present. The Haytians wanted Liberty and Independence. They fought for and got both. Their enemies were as implacable as they were indefatigable. The Haytians had *the will*, and they found out *the way*. They wrung both Liberty and Independence from the feeble grasp of the Gaul, driving the defeated Frenchman into the sea.

The founders of Liberia, preferring Liberty and Independence in 'savage Africa' to Oppression and Non-Possession of Civil Rights in the 'civilized' United States, quitted America, sailed to the land of their forefathers, and founded the Republic of Liberia, the Land of the Free. What do we Africans not owe to these first settlers, the colonizers, the founders of Liberia? They did not wait for the American Government to help them, to furnish them with fabulous sums. When the 'American Colonization Society,' with characteristic benevolence, offered them a home on the West Coast of Africa, they (the then American, and future Liberian Africans) cheerfully, gladly, and readily answered to the call, and went to Africa. Their task in the land of their ancestors was not an easy one; it was uphill work for them. Did not the encounters they had in 1835, 1857, 1875, 1876, and other periods during their colonizing march, with the native Africans, make their task arduous? But they surmounted all difficulties; having *the will*, they found out *the way*. The descendants of those stout and stubborn men are enjoying the legacy their fathers left them.

The names of such men as Joseph Jenkin Roberts, Hilary Leage, Stephen Allen Benson, Daniel B. Warner, James Spriggs Payne, Charles H. Hanlon, A. W. Gardner, G. W. Gibson, A. J. Russell, who were Liberians of distinction, must be handed down to posterity as a band of heroes. What debt do we Africans, who hunger after Independence, not owe that sturdy band of heroes? We must follow in the path which they have made.

Cannot the leading Africans in the United States see the false position in which they stand?

The American Government, not wishing to send Americans to Liberia and Hayti to represent them diplomatically and commercially, send two Republican Africo-Americans —as much as to say that the Liberians and Haytians are not fit persons to have white American Ministers, Consuls-General, and Consuls amongst them.

Comment by us is unnecessary. The leaders of the Africans in the United States, however, should see the false position they stand in. No American Government, be it Republican or be it Democrat, will send black men to represent the American people in Britain, in France, in Germany, in Russia, in Austro-Hungary, in Italy, or in other Caucasian country, either diplomatically or commercially. The black Ministers and Consuls-General of the United States to Liberia have never been transferred to any Caucasian countries. The American Africans, Messrs. E. D. Bassett, J. U. Langston, J. E. W. Thompson, who have been Ministers of the United States in Hayti, have not been promoted or sent to Europe to represent the United States there. It is a useless thing for any leading Africo-American to hope that he will ever be sent to Europe as United States Minister.

It is foolish for any Africo-American to hope that some day he will be elected to the Presidentship of the United States. He shall never sit in the chair of Washington, Jefferson and Madison. It is foolish for any African in the United States of North America to cherish the delusion that some day he will be given a seat in President Harrison's Cabinet, or in President Cleveland's Cabinet, or in the Cabinet of any other and future American President.

It is foolish for any African in the United States to cherish the delusion that he will be made the Chief Justice or a Judge of the United States. And the Africans persist in remaining in the United States. We doubt not that if the leading men of the African race in the United States were in Liberia, they would now be filling posts of distinction in that African Republic. But they prefer remaining in America, hoping against hope that one day they will be called to the chief offices of the American Republic. If this is not infatuation, what is?

But the Africo-Americans are not the only Africans we should earnestly counsel to join the Liberian Republic; we should also advise the British Africans to join Liberia. We should like to see the British Africans of Africa, and the British Africans of the West Indies, Canada, and elsewhere on the American Continent, and throughout the British world, members and citizens of the Liberian Republic.

But our reasons for counselling Emigration from the British Colonies are sufficiently set forth in our fifth Chapter, and consequently we do not propose to recapitulate them here. The British Africans, as a race, enjoy no civil rights in the British Possessions.

Where could the Africo-British go so well as to Liberia? and go those must who are patriotic, and have the welfare of their race at heart.

The British Colonies in Africa, America, and the West Indies send forth yearly their hundreds of white and black young men to Europe to study medicine. The moment these get duly qualified to practise as medical men, they, of course, make it their business to return to the Colonies from which they came; and when there they immediately apply for Government appointments in the medical department. Would anyone believe that every *white* medical man, the moment he applies, is invariably appointed to the post applied for, while the *black* medical man who also applies has his application refused? Even if the black medical man be received in the service of Colonial Governments at all, it can only be as a supernumerary. But in Liberia things are done otherwise. In Liberia there can be no jealousies, no heart-burning. And why? For the simple reason that the black man, not the white, rules there. Almost every Government office in Liberia is elective. Liberia, we say, is the Mother of the African Race. She is the Hope of Africans. She is the nucleus, the centre Country, the rallying standard, round which all Africans *must* gather, her Lone-Star serving as a beacon.

The British Government does not reward merit. Mr. Mitchell Maxwell Phillip, now deceased, found himself Solicitor-General of the British Colony of Trinidad. He served the Colony long and usefully. He hoped against hope that his services would have been rewarded by promotion to the Attorney-Generalship, or some other post in or out of the Colony. But he died in 1888 only a Solicitor-General. The post of Attorney-General of Trinidad before his death was vacant, but Downing Street sent a British gentleman to occupy the post instead. And when Mr. Maxwell Phillip died in 1888, it was hoped that some talented Trinidadian African barrister (and there are many such in Trinidad) would have succeeded him in the Solicitor-Generalship. But Downing Street gave it to a white man instead. It would be useless for us to relate how the authorities at Downing Street treat the British subjects of African Race. There are a few judges, magistrates, medical and law officers of the British Crown of African Race, we do admit, but these *never meet with promotion.* Does there live the judge, or magistrate, or any other functionary of the British Colonial Government of the African Race who indulges in the fond delusion that he will be appointed the Governor of any British Colony, or be appointed to any similar function? Does the British African live who cherishes the fond delusion that he will be made a Chief Justice of one of the Colonies of the Dominion of Canada or Australia? We may mention here that one, and only one, British African has ever been knighted by the British Sovereign, and that one African is the Chief Justice of Barbadoes, and he is only a Knight Bachelor. He is the first British subject of African blood who has ever been knighted; but we fear much that he will be the last.

Does the African subject of the British Empire desire Home Rule? There is Liberia; she enjoys *Independence.*

The British African does not live who dreams that he will be admitted a Member of the House of Lords or the House of Commons; but in Liberia he can be a Senator or a Member of the House of Representatives.

The British African does not live who imagines that he will be made a Member of Her Britannic Majesty's Government; but in Liberia he can be appointed a Member of the President's Government. No British African can be so infatuated as even to dream that he will be made King of Great Britain and Ireland and Emperor of India; but he can be elected Liberian President.

Of course we expect much opposition, not only from our British Africans, but from our American Africans as well, for proposing that both the British and the American Africans should go to Liberia. We are confident, however, that time and posterity will justify us in advising that all Africans living under Caucasian rule should throw in their lot with the Liberian Republic. If the British and American Africans dislike the idea of going to Liberia, it remains to be seen whether their descendants will dislike it. They will certainly not thank their fathers for failing to leave them a mighty country as a legacy.

There are many briefless but talented African lawyers in the over-lawyered British Colonies who are almost on the point of starvation; but Liberia is a fine field for them, and would prove a land of plenty. Liberia needs talent; and why should not the British as well as the American Africans go to Liberia? Surely half a loaf is better than no bread, and there is more than sufficient for all in Liberia.

The African doctors in the British Colonies should do the same, or if they are supernumeraries in Hospitals, we express the opinion that it is better to practise on one's own account in Liberia than be a supernumerary in the Hospital of a British Colony. The British Colonies, generally where the Africans preponderate, are not only over-lawyered, but over-doctored as well, while Liberia needs the services of all these talented Africans.

The British Crown does not offer any incentive to its African subjects' ambition. Not in the least. To use the words of a man in close touch with Lord Salisbury's present Government (Sir John Gorst, Under-Secretary of

State for India) : 'Governments' (*i.e.*, Caucasian Governments, British particularly) 'had always discouraged independent and original talent, and had always preferred docile mediocrity. This was not a new policy. It was as old as the days of Tarquinius Superbus, and examples of its practice were to be found in the more recent times of Cetewayo, Arabi, and Zebehr. In this he' (Sir John Gorst) 'thought Governments were very likely right.'*

We see no reason, then, why the British African should hesitate in joining Liberia. Perhaps he will urge as a reason for his hesitancy the fact that the Liberian is based on the American Constitution, and that he is no admirer of Yankee institutions. Let us once and for all dispel all such prejudices, and try to convince him who would be convinced.

We shall endeavour to do so in this way. Is it not a well-known, though hard-to-be-admitted, fact that the United Kingdom and her dependencies, if not the rest of the world, are slowly but surely being Yankeeized—socially, politically, and in a literary point of view? Words such as *centre, labour, honour, tenour, civilise, programme, favour,* etc., and those derived from them, are now being spelt by many of the British people, their colonists and subjects, particularly those with Liberal and Radical tendencies, as *center, labor, honor, tenor, favor, civilize, program,* etc.—all Americanisms.

Because America has never had any and has no Established Church, the British Parliament, under the able leadership of Liberal Mr. Gladstone, disestablished and disendowed the Irish State Church in 1869; and for the same reason the State Church in England, Scotland, and Wales is being threatened with extinction.

Because the American Supreme Court claims and exercises, and has always claimed and exercised, the right to

* Sir John Gorst's speech in the House of Commons on the Manipur Question, 1891.

determine questions of disputed elections, the British Parliament assigned and transferred that right (which the House of Commons had claimed and exercised from 1604 to 1868) by 31 and 32 Vict., chap. 125, the Parliamentary Elections Act, to the Court of Common Pleas, which is now exercised by the Queen's Bench Division of the High Court.*

Because America has a Federal Constitution, and every State composing the American Union is autonomous, Liberals, Radicals, and Nationalists would federate the United Kingdom by giving first Ireland, secondly Scotland, and thirdly Wales, a measure of Home Rule or autonomy. Is not the Constitution of all the Spanish American Republics, with Germany, Austro-Hungary, Norway and Sweden, and Switzerland, more or less based on the Yankee? Is not the British Dominion of Canada federated? In other words, is not its Constitution or Government modelled on the American? And what, we ask, would Australasian Federation be like?

Because the Yankees pay, and have always paid, their Senators and Representatives, the Canadians are now paying their Senators and Commons, the Australasians and others of the British race pay the members of their Legislative Council and Assembly. And do not the states of the earth, as a rule, after the Yankee fashion, pay their legislators? And will not the honourable member for the Wansbeck Division of Northumberland, Liberal Mr. Charles Fenwick, bring in a Bill for the Payment of Members of Parliament in the House of Commons in the seventh Session of the twelfth Parliament of the British Victoria?

Because American women more or less enjoy the fran-

* Taswell-Langmead's 'English Constitutional History,' p. 356, fourth edition; Anson's 'Law and Custom of the Constitution,' Part I., p. 149.

chise, Conservative Lord Denman will in the House of Lords, in the present (seventh) Session of British Victoria's twelfth Parliament, bring in his Women's Franchise Bill.

Because the legal professions are amalgamated in America a movement is on foot in the United Kingdom to amalgamate the British legal professions. And are not the legal professions in British North America, Australasia, British Africa, and other British dependencies amalgamated after the Yankee fashion?*

Because America is Protectionist, all the British dependencies, and the rest of the world more or less, glory in Protection. And are not the Right Honourable J. Lowther and the honourable and gallant Colonel Howard Vincent, M.P.s who command a respectable following, now doing their very best to convert stolid, stiff-necked Free-Trading Britishers to the principles of Fair Trade, which designation has only to be scratched, and Protection would be found in its place?

Though British coin is the money chiefly in circulation, yet because America uses the dollars and cents currency nearly all the British possessions keep their accounts in United States dollars and cents, while in many of those dependencies there are actually dollar-notes framed after the Yankee pattern.

Take the railway. *Lloyd's News* for Sunday, February 28, 1892, says: ' Railway outrages having considerably increased in number of late years, obvious interest is attached to the forthcoming introduction into this [British] country *of a new train, constructed upon the American principle, the distinguishing feature of which is a gangway right through the carriages from end to end. The South-Eastern Railway Company takes the first step in this direction. On Wednesday next Sir Miles Fenton will despatch a special train, built in*

* 'Professional Handbook,' pp. 3-5, 11-14, 20, 21.

New York for the S.E.R., on a trial trip from London to Hastings,' etc., etc.; the Yankees thereby teaching the countrymen of George and Robert Stephenson and Isambard Brunel literally and truly 'to suck eggs.'

When their British governors are being Americanized, must the African subjects of the United Kingdom hang back and hesitate and say that they are not enamoured of Liberia because its Constitution is based on the American ?*

We are glad, however, to learn that the Sierra Leoneans are surely, if slowly, beginning to see the necessity and importance of joining Liberia. Liberian Dr. Edward Wilmot Blyden, in his 'Christianity, Islam, and the Ethiopian Race,' page 230, assures us that 'the progress of events—the growth of the two countries—has shown that not only has Liberia not interfered prejudicially with Sierra Leone, but it has presented a field for the energies, industrial and commercial, of many a native of the settlement. An interesting fact in the present history of Liberia, which Sir Charles McCarthy could not have foreseen, is this—that a native of Sierra Leone, brought up amid the institutions of the colony, is a successor of Messrs. Mills and Burgess as agent of the American Colonization Society, having charge of the location and rationing of all emigrants arriving in Liberia from America. This native of Sierra Leone is also the Mayor of the city of Monrovia, the capital of the republic.' The late Liberian Consul in, and a native of, Sierra Leone is now a leading citizen of the West African Republic.

* We do not mean to convey the idea, by our comments in the text, that we warmly admire *all* Yankee institutions, or are in any way suffering from Yankeemania. Quite the contrary. We only tell the truth, the whole truth, and nothing but the truth. We are of opinion, also, that the Chicago Exhibition or World's Fair will tend to further Americanize the world—at least, the Caucasian world.

We return to Laird Clowes for a moment. Writing on page 189 of his 'Black America,' amongst other matters, Laird Clowes says : 'Professor Edward Wilmot Blyden, formerly of the West Indies, and more recently of Sierra Leone, is another distinguished Negro who advocates Negro Emigration from the States.'

As the purport of the present work is to refute Laird Clowes's libels and to disprove his allegations, the reader may not see at once our reasons for extracting the above passage. We have, however, our reasons for so doing. And we must be allowed to point out here, in the first place, that though the Honourable Professor advocates African Emigration from the United States of North America, he does *not* advocate, and has never advocated, African Emigration to the Congo Free State, or to any other such State in Africa, or anywhere else. Dr. Blyden sees the situation clearly, and being both patriotic and having the welfare of his race at heart, he advocates African Emigration to the Independent Republic of Liberia, just as we do.

But that is not our only reason for extracting this passage. We wish also to point out that Dr. Blyden does not belong, and never has belonged, to Sierra Leone, as Laird Clowes would have us believe. He was born a European subject and a West Indo-African; but the Liberian Professor, preferring Independence to living as a subject under British or any other Caucasian rule in the West Indies, Africa, America, or elsewhere, in his youth sailed for Africa and joined the Republic of Liberia, and there found Independence and citizenship. He is a patriot, loves his Africa and his Liberia. By becoming a Liberian Dr. Blyden followed the patriotic and commendable examples set him by Joseph Jenkin Roberts, Hilary Teague, Stephen Allen Benson, Daniel B. Warner, James Spriggs Payne, Charles H.

Hanlon, A. W. Gardner, G. W. Gibson, A. J. Russell, Lot Cary, Elijah Johnson, and other illustrious Liberians.

Had he remained a European, or any other Caucasian subject, Dr. Blyden's brilliant talents would never have come to the fore. But what will not Independence produce, encourage, and reward? He is not only a Professor, but he is also an Author of great celebrity and eminence. By going in his youth to Liberia he may be said to have been bred in Liberia.

We believe—ay, we are confident—that even in this our generation many other Africans will follow the examples set them by the Liberian first settlers, by Blyden and others, and become free and independent citizens of the Liberian Republic.

Blyden is known throughout the English-speaking world because he is an independent free Liberian. His talents shine out as a Liberian, but they would not have shone if he had remained a European subject. Even Laird Clowes—not the African's friend by any means—is bound to recognise Blyden's sterling worth, applying, as he does, the epithet 'distinguished' to him. The *New York Evangelist* also eulogizes him thus: 'Dr. Blyden is a Negro of pure blood. Born on one of the West India Islands, he has been a Liberian African from his youth, and has won a high rank among the ripest and foremost scholars of the age.' Last, not least, British Sir Alfred Moloney, K.C.M.G., did the same in public.

Arriving in Liberia as an ordinary immigrant, Blyden worked his way up to be one of the highest servants in the service of the Liberian Republic. He was Liberian Minister to the Court of St. James from 1878 to 1883. Here was a man representing the might and dignity of the Liberian Nation in the British Isles. Does there live the Americo-African who imagines, even for a moment, that he will some day be sent to the Court of St. James as Minister representing the might and dignity of the United States of North America ? Again, Does there live the British African, whether in British Africa, in British America, British West Indies, or elsewhere, who imagines that he will some day be sent to the White House as Minister representing the might and dignity of the United Kingdom ?

Let the reader only imagine a Caucasian Country sending a 'Nigger' as Ambassador or Minister to represent it in another Caucasian Country !

But the Liberian-African lives who can with good reason hope that he will some day be sent to represent the might and dignity of the Independent Republic of Liberia either at the Court of St. James, or, it may be, in France at the Elysée, at the German Court, at the Russian Court, at the Austro-Hungarian Court, in Italy at the Quirinal, at the White House of the United States of North America, at the Court of Madrid, or at any other Caucasian Court.

The African native can join the Liberian Republic with greater facility than either the expatriated African in the United States or the expatriated African in the British Possessions out of Africa can ; but though near at hand, he may yet be far off if he has no wish to become an independent citizen of the Liberian Republic ; and the expatriated African, if he has only the wish to become a Liberian, no matter how far distant he is from the republic, can always surmount his difficulties and obstacles, and find out the way to betake himself to Liberia and Independence.

Are the Africans living as subjects of the Caucasians, the kinsmen of the Assyrians, Carthaginians, and Phœnicians, and other glorious Nations of the African Race, and do they not love Independence and Self-government ? Can they be the kinsmen of Hannibal the Great, the kinsmen of Toussaint the Great, the kinsmen of the Great African

National Poetess, the gentle Phyllis Wheatley (who, besides writing many works, wrote 'The Negro is equalled by Few Europeans'); and do we, the descendants of Ham, disregard and ignore the appeal and the cry, 'Come over and help us,' of our kinsmen the Liberian People? Liberia is moving and progressing, but the Liberians would move faster and their progress would be quickened by the Immigration of Africans who are now living under Caucasian rule. Why, we ask, is the rapid growth of the United States the marvel of the world? We answer that the only reason is that Immigration has set in from Europe. Let Africans who are living under the ægis of the Caucasian migrate to Liberia and cause her to grow faster and to quicken her pace and hasten her progress.

The starving barristers and solicitors, the starving doctors, teachers who can hardly earn a pittance, and others who are not blessed with this world's goods, should quit the over-doctored and over-lawyered, etc., countries, and join the Liberian Republic, where every man's condition can be bettered, for Liberia needs talent, and we are happy to say the African Race is a talented and progressive one.

Liberia, we assert, is in every way a fitting Fatherland for all Africans. We say that she is progressing, but let us assume that Liberia is *not* progressing, the Africans who are non-Liberians ought surely to be patriotic enough to go to the rescue of Liberia and make her progress. But Liberia is progressing, and that we have proved, only she can be made to hasten her progressive steps by Immigration on the part of Africans who are non-Liberians.

Let the village schoolmaster of the African Race, who may be on the point of starvation, seek his home and country in Liberia; let the briefless lawyer of the African Race who may be on the point of starvation seek a home and country in Liberia; let the impecunious doctor of the

African Race find a home and country and better his condition in Liberia.

Liberia is rich, fertile, and is a happy hunting-ground for us, the descendants of Ham, who must become as mighty on the earth as our kinsman Nimrod was of yore.

Let the non-Liberian-African cease to be a backwoodsman, it may be, in Carapichaima, in Guayaguayare, in Toco, in Couva, or, it may be, in Chaguaramas or elsewhere, and go and better his position in Liberia.

Must those of us Africans who are non-Liberians wait until our Maker calls us unto Him, and sink into our Mother-Earth 'unwept, unhonoured, and unsung,' and 'with none so poor as to do us reverence'? Or must we instead go to our Liberia which is ready to welcome us with outstretched arms, and help to build up the already-growing Liberian Empire?

Instead of the Trinidadian Africans striving as to who should be Solicitor or Attorney General, or a Trinidadian Government Medical Officer, or a San Fernando Town Clerk, is it not better, we ask, that these Trinidadian Africans should be Liberians, since the Liberians as a Nation are happy and contented. Better to have a cot in one's own country than a palace in the land of the stranger. That was the patriotism of the great Sir Walter Scott, and that is how he thought. Throughout all his writings—amongst others, 'The Lay of the Last Minstrel'—he breathes nothing but patriotism. And it is familiar history that when Sir Walter, who was cruising about in a British man-of-war in the Mediterranean for the benefit of his health, began to perceive that his life was approaching its crisis, and that he was about to pay the debt due to nature, made it a point, he even insisted, that he should be taken from the Mediterranean, and carried across Europe to his beloved Caledonia, that he might have the pleasure of dying in his own country and in the land of his forefathers. He expired at Tweedside late in 1832.

The patriotism of the English Nelson and of the Irish Wellington, sturdy and mighty Britishers both of them, made them heroes in their duty.

The patriotism of the Africans who are subject to, and living under, Caucasian rule, we must assert, falls far short of that of those Africans who enjoy independence.

The Haytians, because they were patriotic, extorted Independence from the Frenchmen, and their descendants continue to cherish affection for their Fatherland.

The patriotism of the first settlers caused them to quit America and return to their Africa and found Liberia ; and the Liberian of to-day is as fond of his Fatherland as the Scotsman is of Caledonia.

The patriotism of the Ashantees, the patriotism of the Dahomans, etc., enables them to keep their respective Fatherlands intact, independent, and free from foreign aggression.

We cannot too often urge on the African who is subject to white rule the importance of having a mighty Liberian Empire. It is essential that Liberia should be reinforced, consolidated, and extended, for Africans throughout the world must be protected by Africans. Does there live the African subject of the United Kingdom or of the United States who will look us in the face and maintain that if a British or American subject of his (Ethiopian) race were to be murdered in Germany, France, Russia, Austro-Hungary, or Italy, the British or American Government would in any way trouble themselves concerning the murdered African and demand compensation? We are sure they would not stir a finger in such a matter, and as for asking for compensation, such a thing is out of the question altogether.

We assert that an African subject of the British Crown or of the American Republic may be murdered or ill-treated by any person or persons out of the territories of the American Republic or the dominions of the British Crown with impunity. In the British dominions, as well as in the territories of the American Republic, an African can be murdered or maltreated, but the villain who maltreats him escapes justice; and such outrages occur only too frequently in the United States. Our remarks apply equally to the case of the African living under the rule of, and subject to, other whites.

With Liberia, a strong Nation, these outrages would never occur; or if they did occur, they would be swiftly avenged, and pressure brought to bear on the defaulting State. Were the American Africans of the United States to leave America for Liberia, the Yankee rulers of the United States would have no Africans to 'lynch,' and otherwise ill-treat, and would fall to 'lynching' one another, or otherwise ill-treat one another in order to keep their hands going, or would fall to 'lynching' or otherwise outraging foreigners: witness how some Italians a little while ago were 'lynched' by an avenging American mob!

Were Liberia a mighty country, would slavery and the slave trade prevail in Africa, Turkey, and her dependencies? The Arab slave-hunters would have been extirpated long ago. As it is, they (the Arab man-hunters) still flourish and prowl about in Africa. Slavery, like its ally polygamy, exists in Mahommedan countries; and we are sanguine that the Koran, the Mahommedan Bible, contains passages in which slavery is both commanded and sanctioned. Therefore we are not surprised that slavery should exist in European Turkey, in Asiatic Turkey, in Egypt, in Tripoli, in Persia, and throughout the Mahommedan world. But Liberia, with a powerful Navy and an efficient Army, would check the execrable traffic in human flesh, and would blockade the Mahommedan ports if necessary. Does the Caucasian bring pressure to bear on the Mussulman Turk, and cause him to manumit the slaves who guard his harem, and otherwise do his dirty work? Does Britain, who has the copyhold and paramount authority in Egypt, exterminate the Slavery which exists in the Land of the Pharaohs? She does nothing. African Slavery by the Semitic Egyptian may be mild and of a domestic nature, but Slavery is *Slavery*, no matter what are its peculiarities, and it ought in no way to be tolerated in Egypt by the British authorities.

Were the Liberians a mighty People, and if they had a great Empire, would the Massowah Massacres have been perpetrated by the Italians? Perhaps they would; but would Liberia have suffered Italian Lieutenant Livraghi and his associates in crime to wander at large unpunished? The Liberian Elephant, gentle and docile though it be, would have fallen like an avenging Nemesis on Italian Livraghi and his fellow-felons, and meted out swift but 'even-handed justice' to these bloodthirsty Italians. But unfortunately, Liberia is not a powerful country, or she would have brought the Italians to their senses.

Livraghi and his subordinates massacred perhaps a thousand of the African Natives of Massowah; but did Mr. Gladstone write a pamphlet on the Massowah Massacres, as he did on the Bulgarian Horrors a few years ago? And what could be the presumed reason or reasons? We answer by asking, Is not the Massowah Native *black*, while the Bulgarian Native is *white*? It was Turkey which butchered the Bulgarians, but it was Italy which butchered the Massowans. Mr. Gladstone knew that Turkey could be crushed; but Italy is of greater importance than Turkey, and the prudent man held his tongue. Besides, are not the Massowans, in the opinion of the white man, of far less importance than the Bulgarians? and, for all we know, the Liberal Chief might not have heard of the Massowah Horrors, the Massowan being too small a fry for the British Press to take much cognizance of.

Did we see in large type in the British Press, 'Persecution of the Massowans by the Italians,' or, better still, the 'Massowah Horrors'? Let the Jews and the Poles be persecuted and slaughtered by the Russians; let the Jews be slaughtered by the Greeks in Corfu, or other places, and we should have a plentiful supply of these large-type headings. The Massowah Natives were not favoured with leading articles, which are the especial property of the Poles and Jews; they were relegated to an obscure corner in the newspapers which referred to the matter. Did the British Foreign Anti-Slavery Society* take any action when the Massowah Massacres became known? Did the Aborigines Protection Society take any steps in the matter? Were there any Mansion House and Guildhall indignation meetings held to protest against the cruel and heartless treatment of the People of Massowah by the Italians? Did they send a Memorial to the King of Italy requesting him to punish the malefactors, and to use his influence to prevent his Italian subjects from ill-treating the Natives of Massowah? Did the Five Great European Powers—Britain, France, Russia, Germany, Austro-Hungary—address a Collective Note to the Sixth Great European Power, Italy, commanding it not only to punish the perpetrators of the Massacre, but to take steps that no more Massacres should occur at

---

* We absolutely decline with thanks the 'protection' of these two 'philanthropic' societies. We shall have none of their 'protection.' We should not be sorry if they were to come to grief.

Massowah? They did nothing of the kind; but were some petty Balkan State in question, the Great European Powers would not have hesitated to address such a Collective Note to the Sick Man at the Ottoman Porte.

We agree with Laird Clowes when he suggests that the European Nations should help the American Government pecuniarily in effecting the removal of the African from the United States to Africa; but we are not in agreement with the same gentleman when he suggests that the Americo-African should be sent to the Congo Free State. We are convinced that Liberia is the only fitting place for the Africo-American.

The American whites owe the Americo-Africans a heavy debt. And should they wish to discharge that debt, they should by all means do it quickly. We are confident in asserting that even if the American Government should be actuated by the desire of assisting African Emigration from America to Africa, there would be those of the Africans who would wish to remain in the United States; but these by no means should have pressure brought to bear on them. Emigration from the United States should be *free* in every way, because the Americo-Africans are now a free people. Come what may, however, it is the generally received opinion that some day, it may not be in this our generation, the Americo-Africans, one and all, *must* leave the United States.

There is one point on which Laird Clowes and the Africo-American, opposites and extremes though they be, are singularly yet worthily in agreement. And that one point is this, they both cherish the hope, the vain hope and fond delusion, that the white man will, of his own will, come to the rescue of the African; and the Americo-African actually waits expecting that help from the White Man's Government. We call that hope a vain hope, a fond delusion. If it is not, what is it? That we are justified in calling this a vain hope we shall attempt to prove in the following pages.

Before we show the relations of the white man with the black man, we must cast a glance backward at the ancient period of the world, and observe how the rich white has treated the poor white.

It is familiar history that there was Grecian Slavery; that in days long ago Greek enslaved Greek, and Greek enslaved Barbarian. We know that the stern Spartans, after taking Helos by storm, reduced her inhabitants to a state of bondage; and we know that even Athens, the Mother of the Arts and European Civilization, like the rest of Greece generally, had slaves.

It is familiar history that there was Roman Slavery, when Latin deprived Latin and non-Latin of their liberty. The rich and powerful Italian, like the Greek, enslaved his poor countrymen, and the conquered stranger, with an avowed reason, however unjustifiable that reason may have been.

It is familiar history also that there was Hindoo Slavery, when the Hindoo owned his fellow-man. As it is also familiar history that there was Russian Serfdom in our own time, the poor and lowly Muscovite owning the haughty and opulent Muscovite, his countryman, as his lord and master.

It is also a matter of common knowledge that there was Anglo-Saxon Slavery, from time immemorial to so late as the Plantagenet period. But what were Grecian, Roman, Hindoo, and Anglo-Saxon Slavery and Russian Serfdom in comparison with African Slavery by the Caucasian, particularly by the Britisher, the Yankee, and the Frenchman? Were they not of far less importance and gravity than African Slavery? The Grecian, Roman, Hindoo, Russian, and Anglo-Saxon Slaves were generally of the same colour as their masters, and often of the same race. These slaves were, as a rule, not uneducated. They were not, as a class and corporate whole, kept in ignorance. They lived in the midst of their masters' families, and not rarely filled positions of trust and honour.

We have not heard of the Hindoo slave rising in insurrection against his Hindoo master. We have not heard of the Anglo-Saxon slave rising in insurrection against his Anglo-Saxon or Norman master. We have not heard of the Russian slave rising in arms against his Russian master.

History tells us that only in very few instances have the helots taken to arms against their masters of Greece; while history also teaches us that only in very few instances have the Roman slaves been compelled to fly to arms, and levy war on their Roman lords and masters, the most notable instance being the uprising of Thracian Spartacus and his heroic band of fellow-captives. But, after all, 'Roman slavery at its worst was a humane institution compared with the slavery of the Negroes.'*

What was the slavery of the Africans by the whites, particularly by the Yankee, Frenchman, and Britisher, like?

The slavery instituted in 1442 by Portuguese Prince Henry the Navigator; in 1517 by Bartolomé de las Casas, Bishop of Mexican Chiapa, who gave out that one African was worth four Red Indians; and in 1562 by Captain Sir John Hawkins, all three of infamous and execrable memory, was a 'compound of everything that was vile.' African slavery by the white man was of such a type that the African slave often flew to arms. Martial law was paramount in every locality where there was slavery. Yet that did not deter the Africans from repeatedly flying to such arms as they could obtain. But the European and American troops, efficiently armed as they were, did not find it an uphill work to subdue inadequately-armed men.

* Hunter's 'Introduction to Roman Law,' chap. ii., p. 18.

The Africans rose in Jamaica; the Africans rose in Barbadoes; the Africans rose in Dominica; the Africans rose in Martinique, and sundry other places in the West Indies and the Americas; but every attempt of theirs was fruitless—it was nipped in the bud by the white man's power. The African rose in Hayti; he rose in his might in August, 1791, under the leaderships of Jean François and Biassou, and continued to struggle for freedom until the Liberator of San Domingo, Toussaint-L'Ouverture, came upon the scene, when that great master of war, in a comparatively short space of time, gave his Haytians both Liberty and Independence.

The African slave, unlike the white and Asiatic slaves, was kept in ignorance. White law, white public opinion, and white custom, imposed ignorance on the African slave. He did not, like the white or Asiatic slaves, fill posts of trust and honour. The drudging work of the cane-fields was his, with hardly a shirt to his back, and even then he was half starved.

The white or Asiatic debtor who was unable to discharge his debt became, according to law, the slave of his creditor. The white or Asiatic was reduced to bondage also in another way. If he was conquered in war, he became the slave of his conqueror, according to the former law of nations. Neither of these cases applies to the African. The African was not the white man's debtor, while the laws which decreed that the conquered must be his conqueror's slave had long since been obsolete. But the African was unsuspectingly kidnapped, and by main force, by those to whom he had given hospitality. We do not propose to enter on a discussion here as to how many Africans perished in the Middle Passage and during slavery, and their sufferings generally during that period, for they are sufficiently known to the world. Suffice it to add here that the

Christian Church was the 'bulwark of slavery,' for the *Reverend* Slaveholders were legion. And when the British Government emancipated the British African in ever-memorable August, 1838, instead of compensating the African for his losses and sufferings, it indemnified the *Reverend* Slaveholders, with the Planters and others, for their supposed losses through African emancipation.

The British and other nations are now engaged in Africa in endeavouring to Christianize and civilize the aboriginal African. The British, French, Italians, Germans, Spaniards, Portuguese and Belgians ought surely to be aware that their efforts are not only vain and fruitless, but also that they are not genuine philanthropy. If Africa is to be civilized and won for Christ, the only true way for effecting this twofold object is to bring back the captive tribes of Africans from America and the West Indies. Only Africans can civilize Africa; they only can Christianize Africa; they only can put down slavery and the slave trade. Were the European nations in Africa actuated by genuine philanthropic motives, that is what they would do. They would assist the African of the American Continent and Islands to migrate to Africa, his Fatherland.

John Brown, who fought for, and suffered martyrdom on behalf of, the American African, was a genuine philanthropist. Elijah P. Lovejoy, the Martyr, earned the Martyr's Crown for the sake of the African because he loved him. Gerrit Smith, who gave 120,000 acres of land to the Africans in the United States, was a genuine philanthropist. Miss Kate Drexell (Sister Catherine, Catholic Superior of the Convent of the Holy Sacrament), who gave over £1,000,000 to the Africans and Indians of the United States, is, without the shadow of a doubt, a genuine philanthropist.* The American Colonization

* We, in the name of the Ethiopian race, sincerely thank Miss Kate Drexell for her munificent gift.

Society, which has done and is doing such priceless yeoman service to the Ethiopian race, is genuinely philanthropic. But what philanthropy does the European in Africa possess? The European has as much philanthropy as Stanley. The European has gone to Africa, not to civilize and Christianize the African, but to impoverish him and ruin him. He has gone to ease the African of his territories, his gold, his silver, his ivory, and for profit and riches generally.

The European brought in the train of *his* Civilization and Christianity the Liquor Traffic into Africa, which is doing woeful harm to the African Aborigines, especially to those who come across the fire-water for the first time.

German Arminius, fighting for Independence, surrounded and annihilated the Roman legions of Varus, and secured Independence. When the Roman Emperor Augustus heard that Varus and his soldiers had experienced not only defeat, but extermination, at the hands of German Arminius, he exclaimed: 'Varus, Varus, give me back my legions!' He said very little, and never contemplated sending another expedition into Germany to subdue German Arminius and his countrymen. He never entertained the thought for a moment of taking the Liberator of Germany captive, and bringing him to Italy. Arminius, Augustus knew, was a white man like himself, though he did not belong to the same race as he did.

American George Washington, with the active co-operation and assistance of the French, Spaniards, and Dutch, and with the countenance of Russia, Sweden, and Denmark, fought for and won Independence for his Fatherland, the United States; and this he might not have gained had the above-named powers not assisted him both with men and money and munition of war. The British, much as they disliked parting with the American Colonies, had to concede Independence to the United States. They did not, after the War of American Independence, send an expedition to reconquer the United States, and seize George Washington, treacherously or not treacherously, and convey him a prisoner to Britain. They took no such steps as these; for American Washington was their kinsman, and a white man.

Venezuelan Simon Bolivar liberated Venezuela, Peru, Columbia, Ecuador, and Bolivia from the yoke of the Castilian; but the Spaniard did not, after the Independence of the five named States was acknowledged, send an expedition to reconquer these, and treacherously seize their Liberator, Simon Bolivar. Venezuelan Bolivar had white blood in his veins and was related to the Castilian.

Chilian San Martin de José, with the active co-operation of British Cochrane, the first Earl of Dundonald (and, next to Nelson, the greatest Admiral Britain has ever produced), and sundry other Britishers, and supported by American public opinion, gave Independence to Chili and Argentina, and other Countries on the American Continent, and freed them from the yoke of the Spaniard. But the Spaniard did not in revenge send another expedition to reconquer those countries. The Castilian did not attempt to treacherously seize San Martin de José. For De José had not only white blood, but he claimed consanguinity with the Castilian, with the Spaniard.

Mexican Iturbide is reputed to be the Liberator of Mexico. After that personage gave Independence to his country the Spaniards did not try to reconquer Mexico; they did not send an expedition into Mexico with orders to take Iturbide prisoner in a faithless manner, for Mexican Iturbide was a white man, and claimed a Spanish ancestry.

Boer Joubert is the Liberator of the Transvaal; for he it

was who defeated Britain at Amajuba in 1881, and extorted Independence from the reluctant Britishers. But the British did not, on account of their disasters, seize Joubert, Krüger, and Smit. Far from it; and why? Because Joubert and his Boers of the Transvaal, being the descendants of Dutchmen, are white, and the Britisher is of the same Low German Family as the Dutchman. Therefore, the Boers of the Transvaal were left unmolested after Amajuba Hill.

But when the Haytians were bravely battling for Liberty and Independence against the Frenchmen, what European Country, what European nation, was there that stirred a finger on their behalf? No nation thought for an instant of marching to the assistance of San Domingo; the Haytians, unlike the Americans, who received the active assistance of the French, Spaniards, and Dutchmen, while Russia, Denmark, and Sweden countenanced them—the Haytians, unlike the Spanish-American Colonists,* who received the countenance of many civilized nations of the earth, while British soldiers and sailors fought by their side —the Haytians, unlike the Greeks, who had the might of the British, French, and Russians fighting on their behalf, when they were struggling for Independence, were left to fight out their battles singlehanded and alone, as best they could. They received no sympathy and no countenance from the white man, as did the Germans, the Belgians, and the Boers of the Transvaal when they were fighting for Independence.

The Haytians, unlike the British-American and Spanish-American Colonists, the Greeks, the Germans, Belgians,

* President Pétion, of Hayti, supplied Venezuelan Simon Bolivar with four Haytian battalions, who in 1816 covered themselves with imperishable renown when fighting against the Spanish Royalists on the plain of Savannah.

and Transvaal Boers and Swiss, fought not only for Independence, but also for Liberty.

The Haytians of François Dominique were few in number, but they were mighty, stalwart, and plucky men. They were a devoted, fearless band of heroes. But what will not heroic souls undertake, what will they not achieve, with a Toussaint the Great at their head to lead them? Toussaint the Great and his Haytians not only resolved to fight for, but to win, their Liberty and Independence. The struggle which Biassou and Jean François began in August, 1791, was continued under Toussaint the Great in 1793. Toussaint not only took the field, but he joined battle with the Frenchmen. He did not merely grapple with and fight, but he defeated the Frenchmen. To defeat them in battle was of great moment; but the Haytian soldiers of L'Ouverture did more than that: they subdued the Frenchmen, and almost annihilated them. The Frenchmen who were left were expelled from San Domingo or took to flight of their own accord, putting a long space between themselves and the Haytian bayonets.

Far from helping the Haytians, the white men, in the persons of the British and Spaniards, tried to wrest Independence from the Haytians. General Maitland and his British countrymen came to grapple with Toussaint the Great, but Maitland was no match for the Haytian Liberator; he was compelled to return home disappointed. The arrogant Castilian tried his hand also, but Toussaint the Great easily drove the Spaniard into the sea. The history of the Haytian struggles for Liberty and Independence is unique; it is without a parallel. Here were the Haytians, enjoying practical Independence from the Frenchmen. Yet, because the Haytians are Africans, they must needs be attacked by the British and Spaniards. The Americans, after they had achieved Independence, were not attacked by any nation. Mexico, Central America, Chili, Argentina, Peru, Bolivia, Venezuela, Ecuador, Columbia, after they gained their Independence from the Spaniards, and like the Belgians, after they extorted Independence from the Dutch, and like the Greeks, after they won their Independence from the turbaned Turk, were not molested by any individual or united States. But the Haytians were molested by the British and by the Spaniards. Said they: 'What right under Heaven have the Ethiopians of Hayti—men who were the slaves of yesterday—to be independent?' They tried with might and main to retake Hayti and wrest Independence from the Haytians; but Toussaint-L'Ouverture, few though his Haytian soldiery were, prevailed everywhere, an unconditional surrender alone saving the crestfallen Britishers and Spaniards from destruction by the Haytian bayonets.

Toussaint the Great won Liberty for his countrymen in 1794, but it was nearly 1800 before he gained absolute and unqualified Independence.

Unfortunately, Corsican Bonaparte was bent, for sundry reasons, on re-conquering San Domingo, and for this purpose the French First Consul organized and despatched a squadron of fifty-four sail of the line, under his brother-in-law, General Leclerc, and Admiral Villaret Joyeuse, to San Domingo, with orders to re-establish slavery in San Domingo on its reduction beneath French sway. Such proceedings on the part of the French were unprecedented and unsurpassed, as they have never been followed.

The Americans extorted Independence from stubborn Britishers, but the British, to their credit, did not try to retake the United States when their arms were free to be directed in any direction, particularly in a weak direction.

The Spanish-American Colonists, after they had become Independent Nations, were not molested by the Castilian.

The Belgian, after he had driven the slow-moving Dutchman from his country and wrested Independence from him, was not subjected to annoyances from the Hollanders.

The Transvaal Boers, after they had been given Independence consequent on Amajuba, a decisive battle and well-fought field, were not subjected to annoyances at the hands of the Britishers. But the Haytians were more than annoyed by the French.

We say that Napoleon sent a formidable expedition against San Domingo; but the conquering Toussaint the Great, though a price was set upon his head and he was declared an outlaw by the French, was equal to the occasion. He was the most active man in Hayti, in addition to being the most capable and the most indefatigable. He gathered the 'thin red lines' of his Haytians around him, and issued (on December 18, 1801) a counter-proclamation against Napoleon's insolent and arrogant edict for the re-establishment of slavery in San Domingo.

There were sieges; there were burnings; there were marches and counter-marches; there were bivouacs, and whole nights under arms; there were laying wastes; there were skirmishes; there were battles stout and long and hotly contested.

Still Toussaint the Great fought on and on. Was he not a hero and a master of the art of war as well as that of diplomacy? And he continued to harass them so that the Frenchmen got sick and tired of the war, and were fain to cry 'Enough!' They offered him, and Toussaint the Great accepted, peace on his own terms.

The Treaty, following in the wake of the Peace, of course, could only have been an honourable one to L'Ouverture the Liberator; for what Treaty or what Peace other than an honourable one has the Great Toussaint ever concluded?

The principal Terms of the Treaty provided that (1) Toussaint the Great was to be Governor and Commander-in-Chief of San Domingo or Hayti for life, with power to name his successor; that (2) the French General Leclerc was to reside in San Domingo as Agent representing the First Republic; that (3) all Toussaint the Great's Haytian officers were to retain their rank and command in the French Army of San Domingo; that (4) slavery was to be perpetually abolished in San Domingo.

The Treaty concluded between Leclerc and Toussaint L'Ouverture the Great was, however, only a cloak for French perfidy of the deepest dye. The First Consul, Bonaparte, had given his brother-in-law, Leclerc, orders to seize Toussaint L'Ouverture alive where he could. Said the Frenchman, Napoleon: H ares he try to act the part of Liberator of San Domingo, as German Arminius did thousands of years before him for his Germany, and as American George Washington did for the United States a score of years before? We, said Napoleon, must 'suppress' him. And do you, Leclerc, bring the First of the Blacks to France alive or dead; it is your duty—is our commission.

And Leclerc, to his shame, and to the shame of the Corsican, if either could be said to have had any shame, carried out to the letter his commission. It was early in the year (1802) when General Leclerc selected General Brunet, one of his chief officers, to carry out his unworthy commission. The seizure by the Frenchman was effected in this way: Brunet invited Toussaint to a friendly conference midway between Sancey and Gonaïves on the 10th of June, 1802. The unsuspecting L'Ouverture, relying on the honour and good faith of the Frenchman, with his noble, fearless and soldierly mind, for was he not a preux chevalier, the Bayard *sans peur et sans reproche* of Hayti? entertained no mistrust, and accepted the invitation and attended the conference at the rendezvous on the day named. But while he was thus engaged, Brunet, with true Gallic perfidy, disarmed L'Ouverture's handful of bodyguard, and seized the First and Greatest of the Haytians, the Liberator of San Domingo. So he whom they could not crush or subdue, was treacherously seized by pledgebreaking Frenchmen, and conveyed as a close prisoner to France, which was the implacable enemy of him and his country. They had caught the lion in their snare, but the Frenchmen never succeeded in turning L'Ouverture's proud and lofty spirit. The Corsican incarcerated the Haytian in an Alpine dungeon in the Castle of Joux, near Besançon, where Toussaint. ̄ ̇ nd more than ordinary conqueror, and more th. artyr, perished of cold and starvation, if not of u.., and more sinister agencies, at the hands of the Frenchman, the then First Consul Bonaparte, on April 27, 1803.

Toussaint's treacherous seizure, imprisonment in a cold Alpine dungeon and death from starvation, are foul blots on the reputation of Napoleon. His fate is unparalleled in history so f deals with Liberators. None save a bl(frican could have experienced the fate which the ι. Liberator met at the hands of the French. Only black—an *African*—Liberator could have met with such a ate. And are we not justified in saying this? In the first place, did Arminius, the Liberator of Germany, experience maltreatment at the hands of the Romans for freeing Germany from their yoke? But the Haytian Liberator did at the hands of the French.

In the second place, did George Washington suffer illtreatment at the hands of the British because he freed his country from their rule? On the contrary, no American, we shall say, no foreigner, is held in greater honour amongst Britishers than George Washington.

In the third, fourth and fifth places, Simon Bolivar, San Martin de José, Iturbide, the Liberators of Spanish America, as we before pointed out, were not in revenge treacherously seized and ill-treated by the Spaniards, though the Castilians were strong enough to do it, just as the British were strong enough to entrap Washington and convey him to Britain if they had wished it.

In the sixth place, we hear that the Belgians have had their Liberator, but it is not recorded in history that the Dutchmen treacherously seized and ill-treated the Belgian Liberator. Nor does history tell us, in the seventh place, that the Liberator of the Greeks, for taking up arms against the Turkish Crescent, was ensnared and put to death by slow or quick methods. While we have pointed out that, in the eighth place, the Liberator of the Transvaal, Boer Joubert, who inflicted a defeat on the British Lion at Amajuba Hill, did not experience any calamitous fate. He did not experience at the hands of the British the fate which Toussaint the Great, Liberator of San Domingo or Hayti, met with at the hands of the French. And the British, so far from entertaining any animosity against Joubert, who gave Independence to the Transvaal, went to the length of giving a dinner in his honour on December 11, 1890, when the gallant Boer gentleman, the Transvaal Liberator and General, was paying a visit to the British Metropolis.

But the Frenchmen did not wreak their vengeance on Toussaint L'Ouverture the Great alone : for after the demise of the Haytian Liberator L'Ouverture's family were also confined to prison at Brienne-en-Agen, where one of his sons died, while his widow in 1816 expired there in the arms of her two remaining sons, Isaac and Placide Toussaint L'Ouverture, as a state prisoner of perfidious France. But the awful and mysterious Adrastea, retributive Nemesis, avenged the cruel, brutal and disgraceful wrongs heaped upon the

Great Toussaint, and the Toussaint Family, not only in the persons of the Bonaparte Family, but in the persons of Frenchmen in general. For though First Consul Bonaparte mounted the Imperial Throne of the French, he found himself at Leipsic, and in the year of Leipsic, not only deprived of all his conquests, and his brothers, other kinsmen and intimate friends, driven from thrones and power, but he was, after being driven from burning Moscow with humiliating loss, pursued by the aggressive and harassing Muscovite hordes of the White Czar, humbled at Leipsic, and imprisoned at Elba. He returned from Elba not only to fight, but to be defeated ; not only to be defeated, but to have his Frenchmen almost annihilated at Waterloo by the omnipotent allies. Waterloo, for Napoleon's Frenchmen, was not a battle, but a massacre—at least, from the time when the Prussian Blücher reinforced the British Wellington. He was crushed at Waterloo only to abdicate the French Imperial Throne at Fontainebleau. He by compulsion laid aside the Imperial Diadem, but it was only to be conveyed a prisoner for the term of his natural life to St. Helena, an African island, where the executioner and oppressor of Toussaint the Great died in 1821.

Nemesis the Avenger punished Frenchmen and the Napoleons in other ways also. For the son and heir of the First Napoleon, the King of Rome and Duke of Reichstadt, never reigned over France. He died in the land of his grandfather more or less an Austrian state prisoner.

Retribution also overtook the Frenchmen in 1870-71. For Napoleon III., 'the nephew of his uncle,' was conveyed a prisoner to Prussia and incarcerated in a castle of the Teuton after Sedan. Frenchmen lost not only men, and not only met with humiliating defeats and experienced disgraceful surrenders by their soldiers, but they were also compelled to hand over the whole of Alsace, and a great part of Lorraine, to their German conquerors; while the victorious Teutons, in the pride of victory, also extorted a heavy war indemnity from the crest-fallen Gauls. Did not 'the grand-nephew of his grand-uncle,' the French Prince Imperial, meet with his death at the hands of the Zulus—men of the same Ethiopian race as Toussaint L'Ouverture—at Isandhwlana in 1879? And may we add here, that the power of the Bonapartes in France at present is not by any means of importance, and that the heir of the First Napoleon is an uncrowned Emperor living in constrained exile?

The Frenchmen evidently under-estimated the capacities of the Haytians for organization. They found out their mistake to their cost when it was too late; and bitterly did they repent of their blunder. And the blunder of the Frenchmen was this: They treacherously seized, wrongfully incarcerated, and feloniously brought about the death of the Haytian Chief, thinking thus to crush the spirit of the Haytians in their struggles for Independence. For, said the Frenchmen, if we only take their Chief out of the way, affairs will proceed smoothly with us, and our work will be downhill and easy; only remove their idolized Chieftain from off the scene, and there will not be found the Leader who will have the courage or the capacity to lead the Haytians on any further struggle for Independence. But the Frenchmen reckoned without their host. And, fortunately for the Haytians and the African Race in general, they blundered when they left the swift, the agile, the indefatigable, the talented, and fearless Jacques Dessalines in San Domingo alive and at large, and occupying one of the chief commands in the French Army of Hayti. For the distinguished and fearless Dessalines rose and flew to arms with his Haytians only six months after the demise of their beloved Chief. They rose in their might in October, 1803, fought the Gauls, won battle after battle, captured town after town, fort after fort, from the Frenchmen. But the ever-memorable battle of St. Mark, the Amajuba of Frenchmen, brought untold and humiliating disasters on the French arms. It was fought in November, 1803. Dessalines commanded in person. There the European and the Africo-West Indian, the Caucasian and the Ethiopian, the Gaul and the Haytian, met face to face on equal terms and on a well-planned field. The veterans of Napoleon were pitted against the veterans of Toussaint; but the former were eclipsed by the latter. That battle, which tested the superiority of the black man over the white man, freed the Haytians, for the victorious troops of Dessalines compelled the Frenchmen to evacuate San Domingo in November of the same year (1803). Is it not hard to believe that the Spaniards tried their hand in recovering the western portion from the grasp of Dessalines, though the Haytians had proclaimed their Independence? Is it not hard also to believe that France never recognised the Independence of Hayti till the year 1825, though they were driven finally from San Domingo in 1803? Frenchmen recognised the Independence of San Domingo only so late as 1825, but on what condition? On the condition that the Haytians should engage to pay 150,000,000 francs, or £6,000,000, to the avaricious and insatiable Frenchmen.

Britain did not take so long a time to recognise the Independence of the United States of North America. Spain did not take so long a time to recognise the Independence of Spanish America. Holland did not take so long a time to recognise the Independence of Belgium. Turkey did take so long a time to recognise the Independence of Greece. Britain did not take so long a time to recognise the Independence of the Transvaal as the Frenchmen took to recognise the Independence of Hayti. And why was it so? The Haytians were, and are, *Ethiopians;* but the Americans, the Greeks, the Belgians, the Transvaal Boers, the Spanish Americans (partly) were, as they are, *white.* At the same time the Yankees had to pay no indemnity to Britain; the Spanish Americans had to pay no indemnity to Spain; the Belgians had to pay no indemnity to the Hollanders; the Greeks had to pay no indemnity to the turbaned Turks; the Transvaal Boers had to pay no indemnity to Britishers as the price of their Independence. But the Haytians (alack-a-day for the Haytians! alack-a-day for the African—the African Race in general!) had to pay 150,000,000 francs, and no less, to the Frenchmen as the price of their Independence. As white rule over the black means injustice and cruelty, we cannot help reflecting that it was better for them to have paid 150,000,000 francs, or even more, to the Frenchmen rather than have allowed them (the Frenchmen) to reinstate their rule over the Haytians again. Is it not hard to believe that Britain did not acknowledge the Independence of the Haytian People until 1850? But the fact is so. When Belgium proclaimed her Independence of Holland, Britain immediately acknowledged it. Britain not only acknowledged the Independence of Greece, but even sent British men, British money, British ships with British munitions of war to the help of the Hellenes. While the Independence of Spanish America and the Transvaal were acknowledged almost immediately by the Britishers, and we know that they sent men, money, ships and arms to the assistance of the former when she was bravely battling with Spain.

 The present attitude of the white towards the black, where the former rules, is treated in the First, Second, and Fifth Chapters of this work. From one white Anglo-Saxon race we can form an estimate of the whole white race. And is it reasonable for the African to dream, and for Laird Clowes to suppose, that the white man's Government will some day

REPATRIATION AND LIBERIA. 323

(say in the near future) spontaneously, and in a philanthropic spirit, offer to take the African expatriates from America to their Fatherland Africa?

Because Cetewayo, the renowned King of the Zulus, was fearless and patriotic enough to take up arms in 1879 to assert his rights and maintain the integrity of his Kingdom, and repel the British invaders of his dominions; and because he inflicted humiliating and disastrous defeats on the British arms at Isandhwlana, Inyezane, Intombi River, and Hloblane Mountain and elsewhere, he was, after Ulundi, treacherously seized at durbar, conveyed a close prisoner of state to Britain, had his Kingdom taken away from him and divided, and his son, Prince Dinizulu, was deprived of the Royal Heritage of Zululand.

Because Dinizuli, King Cetewayo's son and heir, rose in arms to vindicate his rights in Zululand he was taken prisoner, and after undergoing a mock trial was, together with many of his vassal Chieftains, transported to the Island of St. Helena by the British to go through a long term of imprisonment.

The conduct of the British towards His Opoban Majesty King Ja Ja is one of the worst on record. Ja Ja of Opobo, after he was treacherously seized at durbar by Consul Johnston, for no just cause, on the West Coast of Africa, was banished to the British West Indian Island of St. Vincent, and thence to Barbadoes, another British West Indian Island. In an article on 'England's Honour,' in a widely-read and influential British journal, the dishonourable action of British Consul Johnston towards Opoban Ja Ja is thus dealt with:

'It is now' (May 1, 1891) 'nearly three years since we deemed it our duty to direct attention to the action of Mr. Consul Johnston in seizing and deporting an African Chief, Ja Ja. At that time Mr. Johnston was Consul on the West

Coast, and he was called upon to settle a quarrel between the traders and the Chief. It is not necessary for our purpose to enter into the merits of the dispute. It is sufficient to say that Ja Ja claimed rights over the oil districts, which were scouted by the traders, ridiculed by Mr. Johnston, but partly admitted by Lord Salisbury, then, as now, Foreign Minister. Right was on the side of the Chief, and Mr. Johnston knew it. But the Consul is a man of resource, untrammelled by scruples. Beaten in argument, he summoned a man-of-war; but a warship cannot do much injury to a Chief who has no towns to destroy, and can paddle into the interior of a country known only to his own people. And this is what Ja Ja was about to do when Mr. Johnston summoned treachery to his aid. He invited the Chief to a conference. "We have been quarrelling long enough," said the Consul. "I have written despatches innumerable; you have replied; the traders have rejoined; Lord Salisbury has had his say, and we are—as we were. Meet me in my tent, and we will settle our differences as becomes friends." But Ja Ja was suspicious. He would come, he said, but not without a safe-conduct. The safe-conduct was given, and Ja Ja came to the conference unarmed, and almost unattended. No sooner there than Mr. Johnston presented his ultimatum. He told Ja Ja that he was a pestilent knave, who had given an infinity of trouble, and must go on board the man-of-war in the offing, and be taken to Accra, a thousand miles away, there to stand his trial. Ja Ja protested. He was present to negotiate on equal terms, not to be seized and sent abroad. Mr. Johnston was obdurate. Ja Ja then reminded him of his safe-conduct. And what was Mr. Johnston's answer? "True; you have a safe-conduct, and I will respect it. You are free to leave. But what can you do? My boats have blocked your escape by the river; you

REPATRIATION AND LIBERIA. 325

cannot escape by land. I will offer such a heavy reward for your head that your life will not be worth an hour's purchase. Go if you will, but if you go, you go to certain death." Ja Ja saw he was trapped. Sullenly he submitted, and was taken to Accra, where even the judges who tried him spoke well of him. He is now an exile in St. Vincent* 'Mr. Johnston won the game, but it was with loaded dice. He sullied England's honour by violating a safe-conduct, by doing that to a savage which, if done to a civilized foe, would have branded him with an indelible stigma.'

Again, as indicating the far from friendly attitude of the white towards the African, no European sovereign would for a moment think of conferring a distinction and an honour on African crowned heads, though half-civilized and half-wild Asiatics, with the Sultan of Turkey and the Khedive of Egypt, have had such honours and such distinctions conferred on them.

There are exceptions, however, to the rule embodied in the former part of the above statement. For the present Sultan of Zanzibar, His Highness Seyyid Ali bin Said,† was in the course of last year (1890) dubbed Knight Grand Commander of the Star of India; but that distinction emanating from the British Crown was the price of, or the bribe for, the influence assumed by the Imperial British East India Company over Zanzibar in the course of the last year (1890). But the only African, the only African Ruler, who has ever had a distinction or an honour conferred upon him through motives of disinterestedness and genuine

* Thanks to the refined cruelty of perfidious Britishers, Opoban Ja Ja is no more, he having died in July, 1891, an exile and a homeless man.

† We are afraid, however, that the present Sultan of Zanzibar is an Asiatic—at least on his father's side.

brotherly friendship was His Excellency the late Liberian President Gardner, on whom, on February 11, 1882, His Majesty Alfonso XII., the late King of Spain, conferred the Knighthood of the Grand Cross of the Royal Order of Isabel the Catholic. While the only British subject of the Ethiopian Race who has ever been knighted is the Chief Justice of Barbadoes, Sir William Conrad Reeves—but he is only a Knight Bachelor.

Of course these honours and distinctions are of very little moment, particularly in a country like Republican Liberia. Yet as Europeans confer these favours on one another, and even on semi-barbarous Asiatics, the unenlightened and retrograding half-savage Sultans of Turkey and the Khedives of Egypt, why not, in Heaven's name, extend these courtesies to the cultured Sovereigns and other Chiefs of the African or Ethiopian Race in a similar manner?

With all these evidences of the attitude of the ruling white towards the subject black before him, any man will, we shall say any man *must*, infer and maintain that for the Americo-Africans to live on in continual and paradise-like dream, and for Laird Clowes to imagine that a white Government—the Yankee Government supported by the white Governments of Europe—will some day, spontaneously, and grateful for unrequited services rendered during slavery, as an atonement and a penance for wrongs heaped upon them in the course of the slave-trade and during slavery, and in a philanthropic spirit, hurry to the rescue of the African freedmen in America, and arrange to send them to their Fatherland, our Africa, and to her worthy daughter Liberia, is foolish indeed. If the African particularly wishes to leave the United States for Africa, he must, as we pointed out before, organize and marshal his ranks, and bring pressure to bear on the Yankee Government, by first of all petitioning them, and if unsuccessful, then by agitating as energetically for Repatriation and Liberia as Irishmen did towards the disestablishment of the Irish Church (which was finally disestablished on January 1, 1871); and as they (Irishmen) are now doing to obtain a grant of Home Rule.

The American Colonization Society, unaided by the Yankee Government, is, however, carrying on the work of Liberian Colonization with a pure and praiseworthy philanthropy. All honour, then, be to the American Colonization Society!

We have said, and we have shown, in the earlier part of this chapter and elsewhere in this work, that it would be to the interest of, and that it was of the greatest importance to, the British, as well as the Americo-African, that he should help to complete the Colonization and hasten the progress and prosperity of the Liberian Republic by joining the 'Lone-Star' of Liberia, and becoming her free and independent citizen.

But if someone were to say, It is all very well for us to advise migration by the British and Americo-African into Liberia: does the Liberian Government offer any material incentive to Liberian Immigration by non-Liberian Africans? we should promptly answer that Liberian President Johnson's Government is too enlightened and patriotic, and the Liberian Constitution is too liberal towards the descendants of Ham, not to make suitable provisions for the African Immigrant into Liberia. President Johnson[*] is himself a man of no ordinary ability, talents and culture. His Government guarantees a free grant of ten acres of fertile land to every single grown-up person, and twenty-five acres

[*] The present Chief Magistrate of Liberia is President J. J. Cheeseman, Mr. Johnson not seeking re-election at the end of his term.

of land to every family of Hamitic, or African, descent who elects to not only reside in the West African Republic, but to become a Liberian citizen with liberty to purchase more from the Government at a reasonable and moderate price.

We cannot conclude our work without venturing to submit some counsel to the gracious consideration of the present or any future Liberian Government. Members, both individual and aggregate, of white Governments of enlightenment and leading, in the olden times as in modern times, have not thought it beneath them to accept and follow good counsel at the hands of their inferiors—we mean, of those lower in rank or station than themselves, when asked for or voluntarily offered. We do not think that a black Government, like that of the Liberian Republic, progressive, enlightened and patriotic as it is, can remain indifferent to the advice which we venture to voluntarily offer it. For we should like to impress upon it the fact that greater exertions must be made by the Liberian Government if they wish the non-Liberian Africans to flock into Liberia and accelerate her progress and prosperity. Immigration it was that hastened the greatness of the United States of North America and the Dominion of Canada.

Canadian Immigration is encouraged by the Government. The British daily papers for February 23 of this year (1891) report that: 'In addition to the free grant of 160 acres of fertile land, offered by the Canadian Government to any male adult of the age of eighteen years and over in Manitoba and the North-West Territories, and to the land that may also be obtained at a moderate price in British Columbia, the Minister of Agriculture is now authorized to offer, until further notice, the following bonuses to settlers from the United Kingdom taking up land within six months of their arrival in the country: Fifteen dollars (£3 1s. 8d.) to the head of a family, 7 dols. 50 c. (£1 10s. 10d.) for the wife and each adult member of the family (over twelve years of age), and a further sum of 7 dols. 50 c. (£1 10s. 10d.) to any adult member of the family over eighteen years taking up land. Forms of application for the bonuses, without which no payments will be made, may be obtained when the passenger tickets are issued from any authorized agent of the Canadian steamship lines in Great Britain and Ireland, etc.'

We are of opinion that the example set by the Canadian Government should not be lost sight of, but should more or less be followed by the Liberian Government. Liberia is much smaller and less rich than the Dominion of Canada, we must admit. Still, we believe that the example set by the Canadian may be followed by the Liberian Government to some extent and with some modifications.

The following may be taken as our counsel to the Liberian Government: Does Liberia need non-Liberian Africans, her kinsmen, who are learned in the 'wisdom of the Egyptians,' and who are subject to and living beneath the sway of the 'Egyptians'? She does. Then she must make greater exertions than she has ever yet made. She must find the men and the wisdom she needs. She offers a free grant of 10 acres of fertile land to every Liberian Immigrant, and also 25 acres of the same to every family who migrates into the Liberian Republic, as an encouragement or incentive to Immigration by the non-Liberian of Hamitic descent. But we say, How many millions of Africans are there who may not know that there is such a Country, such a Fatherland, in existence as Liberia? Apart from that, we are convinced that there are millions of Africans who know Liberia only by name, and nothing more. These, then, cannot know that the Liberian Government pledges itself to give a grant of 10 acres of freehold land to the African adult, and 25 acres of the same to the African family who migrates into Liberia. What, may we be permitted to ask, is the cure for that disease of ignorance, what is the remedy, what the panacea? We believe we know the remedy; and we believe that a better state of things can be brought about in this way: In the first place let the Liberian Government appoint Liberian Immigration Agents* in all the English-speaking countries where the Africans abound—say, in British Africa, in the United States of North America, British America (including the British West Indies) and Australasia—with orders and powers to set up in the post-offices or otherwise, and put into circulation, Liberian Immigration Notices for the benefit and information of the Africans.

The above is to be construed as one of the chief points of advice we should like to give the Liberian Government. This will enable the Immigrant to know something of Liberia, if he should happen not to know anything of her. There are two other points of advice we should also like to give to the Liberian Government. In the second place, as Liberia cannot afford to follow the example of Canada and give 160 acres of land and bonuses besides to Immigrants, because she is neither as large nor so rich, artificially rich, as Canada, in order that all possible inducements for leaving the land where the white man rules and joining the Liberian Republic by non-Liberians of African descent may be made the greater and keener and the more effective, let the Liberian Government pledge themselves to give a free grant of twenty instead of ten acres of fertile land to every grown-up person of the age of eighteen years and over, and let them engage to give a free grant of fifty instead of twenty-five acres of fertile land, as is the case at present, to every family of African descent.

In the third place, let the Liberian Government charter a

* Liberian Consuls might efficiently discharge the duties of Agents.

line of Liberian Immigration Steamships, to be placed at the disposal of the Liberian Immigration Agents, and under their supervision, with the view of conveying to Liberia those of the Africans who wish to emigrate at a moderate or, if possible, very low rate, or even free of charge, with the proviso that the Liberian Immigrant who is conveyed free of charge should be given not more than two years within which to make up for expenses to which the Liberian Government has gone on his behalf. When the Government does these things, we feel confident that the desired results will be achieved and brought about in Liberia.

The three points in our advice to the Liberian Government are, we must admit, not easy things for the powers that be to undertake. But the points embodied in the advice indicate a broad and liberal, and certainly a *wise*, policy. Have the Liberian Government no money to carry out the broad and liberal scheme we suggest? If so, let them find the money somehow to carry out that policy, for Liberia has wonderful natural resources, as both her friends and enemies testify. Of course they must proceed gradually, and they should proceed cautiously. But we are of opinion that it is better for the Liberians to proceed gradually than for them to make no attempt at all in carrying out such a feasible policy as is indicated in the counsel which we make bold to submit to their consideration. For we fail to see how, save it be by the Immigration of the English-speaking Africans, the greatness, the progress and the prosperity of Liberia—the Land of the Free—the ' Lone-Star' of Liberia, can be accelerated, as it certainly should be, and as every true friend of the African wishes it to be.

THE END.

Elliot Stock, Paternoster Row, London.

www.ingramcontent.com/pod-product-compliance
Lightning Source LLC
Chambersburg PA
CBHW032352230426
43672CB00007B/670